RISK
AND
REWARD

How Small Colleges Get Better Against the Odds

Daniel W. Barwick, PhD

Copyright © 2020 by Daniel Barwick

All rights reserved. No part of this book may be reproduced or used in any manner without written permission of the copyright owner except for the use of quotations in a book review. For more information, address: barwickriskandreward@gmail.com.

Limit of Liability/Disclaimer of Warranty: This publication is designed to provide accurate and authoritative information in regard to the subject matter covered. It is sold with the understanding that neither the author nor the publisher is engaged in rendering legal, investment, accounting or other professional services. While the publisher and author have used their best efforts in preparing this book, they make no representations or warranties with respect to the accuracy or completeness of the contents of this book and specifically disclaim any implied warranties of merchantability or fitness for a particular purpose. No warranty may be created or extended by sales representatives or written sales materials. The advice and strategies contained herein may not be suitable for your situation. You should consult with a professional when appropriate. Neither the publisher nor the author shall be liable for any loss of profit or any other commercial damages, including but not limited to special, incidental, consequential, personal, or other damages.

First edition May 2020

Published by ABJames, LLC
8 The Green, Suite A
Dover, DE 19901

For Carin, Laura, and Leah

Table of Contents

Introduction 1

Section 1 - Fundamental Challenges 21

Introduction 22
Chapter 1: Competing for Students 25
Chapter 2: The Facilities Arms Race 55
Chapter 3: Competing with Other Colleges for Faculty 87
Chapter 4: Public Relations 102

Section 2 - Innovation and Experimentation 129

Chapter 1: The Mindset to Create Opportunities 130
Chapter 2: Entrepreneurship and Maker Spaces 141
Chapter 3: Re-imagining: Conversations with Academics Creating Change 147
Chapter 4: Three Immediate Opportunities for Your Institution 170
Chapter 5: Entrepreneurial Mindset Case Study: Last Chance U 183
Chapter 6: What Limits the President's Ability to Innovate? 209

Section 3 - Responding to a Crisis 229

Introduction 230
Chapter 1: Case Study: The Turf Field Controversy 239
Chapter 2: Termination and Due Process 247
Chapter 3: Case Study: Accreditation Opportunities 280

Conclusion 294

Summary 299

About the Author 300

Introduction

This book came about because I am an avid reader, and there are relatively few sources of advice on the operation of small community and technical colleges. As an administrator of such schools, I would frequently yearn for what I thought of as a "playbook" or manual, or at the very least, some examples of issues similar to what I was facing and how they had been approached. I found myself calling my colleagues often to get their take on specific situations because my reading had not addressed the circumstances I was facing, and I would field many calls from colleagues in the same position. We were all doing the same thing – leveraging each other's experience to reduce risk and increase reward.

As it turns out, there is a good reason such a playbook does not exist – the variables are too many, at least in the role of president. Unlike individual units within the school, the presidency requires an interplay of all of the units in varying proportions, combined with external forces. The many variables prevent a true playbook, but in the preparation of this book, I did discover a number of themes and even rules which apply very well to small and/or rural colleges. I have roughly classified those themes into categories in this book: challenges that all schools face, the beneficial effect of using an entrepreneurial mindset to re-frame specific issues, and crisis management. In each section, I include case studies that are introduced to show how specific strategies discussed in the book have been applied in unusual, extreme, or risky situations.

Although I have worked with dozens of organizations, both as a consultant and as a volunteer, as of the writing of this book, I have actually had just two full-time employers over the course of my career in

Risk and Reward

higher education – the State University of New York College of Technology at Alfred (more commonly referred to as Alfred State) and Independence Community College in Kansas. In both cases, because of the roles I held, I was privy to a great deal of confidential information. For those reading this book in the hopes some of that information will be revealed, you will be disappointed. All of the factual information contained in this book about these two organizations is either not of a confidential nature and thus available through public record requests, or, in the case of more sensitive matters, I have confined myself only to information that is already contained in the public record.

I think I always knew I would end up at a teaching college. While large research institutions have their purpose, I enjoy the thrill and immediacy of teaching. In graduate school, my roommate was two years older than me, and so he entered the job market earlier. Our field was philosophy, which was at the time insanely competitive. (Just for perspective, in my final year of graduate school, my department had a job opening for which we got 315 qualified applicants. Of the three finalists, all had more than one PhD.) My roommate got a job at a private school in the Northeast, and of course, I was thrilled for him. However, he was less thrilled when he met his department chair for the first time. The department chair told him that a chair's job was to support his faculties' efforts to achieve tenure and stated that tenure required "an average of two articles per year in peer-reviewed journals." My roommate, who certainly understood there would be a scholarly expectation in the job, asked, "and how is teaching effectiveness measured during the tenure process?" The department chair looked at him, paused, and replied with emphasis, "an average of two articles per year in peer-reviewed journals." He came home from that meeting a bit depressed, and his account certainly depressed me.

I was recruited straight out of graduate school to work at Alfred State by the Academic Vice President, an amazing woman named Carol Lucey. She had conceived of a combined teaching/administrative position, and as a result, I was given a succession of long-term projects in fulfillment of my administrative duties. These projects ranged all over the board: first the honors program, then assessment, then grants administration, then corporate fundraising. I also took on some shorter-term projects in public relations, as well as all of the typical project and committee work as a faculty member. As a result, I developed a relatively wide range of experience at an early stage in my career, experience that encompassed nearly every area of the College, aided by fantastic colleagues who cared deeply about their work and students, particularly the chair of my academic department, Rick Mitchell. He was a gifted poet and a sensitive administrator.

I had never given any thought to becoming a college president; it certainly was not an ambition of mine. I liked fundraising and teaching. I was good friends with the late Bill Rezak, the president of Alfred State, and frankly, his job looked awful: endless money issues, the hazards of being a very public figure, perennially dissatisfied employees, and the meanness that is often directed at the boss (sometimes, simply because that person is the boss and for no other discernable reason). Bill loved his job, although I could not see why.

At a certain point, a wonderful mentor of mine, the late Dick Miller, who had previously been the Vice-Chancellor of the SUNY system and the president of Hartwick College in Oneonta, NY, told me that the next logical step for me in my career was a presidency. I pooh-poohed him, laughingly explaining that I thought there was a difference between being underqualified for a job and being dangerously underqualified. He responded, "What is it you think you don't have? You've punched every ticket – teaching, fundraising, supervising, grants, administration, board relations, and so on." I said that what I really wanted to do was to go back and lead the fundraising effort for my undergraduate alma mater, SUNY Geneseo. He replied, "Well, guess what? That job's not available. So why not be a president?"

Just two weeks later, a headhunter friend called me to say that Independence Community College was looking for a president. He said that the job would be a good fit; the College was facing many of the same

Risk and Reward

issues on which I had experience working. I applied and went through the process and was offered the job. I asked three people if I should take it: my wife, who was all for it (she knew that I was starting to get bored at Alfred State), my best friend Chris (he loved the idea of me moving back to the Midwest), and Dick Miller (he said, "Well, if you don't take that job, I'll kick you in the ass").

My time at Independence Community College was a gift. The foundation for my early positive experiences was a strong Board of Trustees. Led by an energetic and honest board chair, Jay Jones, I felt like I was part of a team that truly wanted to improve the College. Time and time again, I recognized that I was having unique, often wonderful experiences, in whole or in part, because of the job. This book will describe some of those experiences, so at this point, I will just say that many mornings I would have to get up early to get in the car and head to another part of the state and initially, the feeling of the cold darkness was one of isolation and loneliness. However, as the dawn would break over the austere prairie in one of Kansas' incredible sunrises, I always felt the same thing: a sense of peace and joy, surrounded by beauty and the feeling that I was on a worthy mission working together with great people.

I had co-workers that I loved dearly, but more importantly, I worked with people that I respected. I respected their expertise, work ethic, and wisdom. Not all was smooth sailing – no leadership job worth doing ever is, I suppose, but if there is any indication of the totality of the time I spent at Independence Community College, it is that I look back with feelings of gratitude, joy, and love.

After finishing eight years as president at Independence Community College, a couple of friends pushed me to write a book. They laid out a fairly comprehensive case: they felt that the variety of experiences (both successes and failures) I have had so far in my career would be of interest to college leaders, and if written correctly, would prove instructive. As I considered their advice, I began to think that I could contribute something useful. My experience is lengthy, and my achievements in academics, management, and resource development are considerable, and include:

- Raising a total of $81.3 million in external funds over the last ten years;
- Overseeing ICC during a period of positive academic and programmatic progress that saw it:
    - Named Number Thirty-Two on CNN Money's 2013 list of Best Community Colleges in the US,
    - Ranked Number One in 2017 in Kansas for Success of Transfer Students,
    - Named Top Five Most Affordable in the United States in 2015
    - Named in Top One Percent for Student Educational Goal Attainment in 2016;
- Leading a team that increased philanthropic support by four hundred percent in FY 08-09;
- Working in partnership with a successful marketing team to design an award-winning approach that increased enrollment by nineteen percent in two years;
- Designing and implementing Alfred State's first capital campaign, which exceeded its goal by over one hundred percent;
- Leading the creation of a successful campus outcomes assessment program;
- Being awarded the first system-wide SUNY Provost Fellowship;
- Receiving multiple nominations for SUNY Chancellor's Award for Teaching Excellence; and
- Leading the 2018 statewide president's advocacy team that resulted in the first general funding increase to Kansas community colleges in five years.

Let me tell you a little about myself professionally, both specifically in terms of the experience I have gained and also the way I approach my work both psychologically and ethically:

Risk and Reward

I have a bachelor's degree from SUNY Geneseo, a master's degree from the University of Iowa, and a Ph.D. from SUNY Buffalo. For ten years, I was a Certified Fund Raising Executive (CFRE), the most demanding independent certification, possessed by only six percent of fundraising professionals. I have attended the Asheville Institute for General Education, and the CASE Institute for Educational Fundraising.

As I write this, I have just resigned following my eighth year as President of Independence Community College, which is part of a loose system of 23 community and technical colleges in Kansas. I was successful there, with strong success in resource development, workforce and entrepreneurship development, niche program development, and developing partnerships with other schools and K-12 school districts. Prior to my role there as president, I worked at Alfred State College of Technology, which is one of the sixty-four campuses of the State University of New York. At Alfred State, I worked in various capacities as part of the administration and faculty for fourteen years. For six of those years, I held the highest administrative offices in my areas, reporting to the president of the College. From the standpoint of teaching, I am an experienced, successful teacher with a background teaching in primarily associate degree-granting institutions. I taught for twenty-one years (and continue to teach occasionally), teaching thousands of students a variety of courses in a number of different formats. I was highly recommended for promotion to Associate Professor in 2002 and awarded tenure in 2003.

Those who know me say that I have an ability to assess current and future educational needs and to establish programs to meet those needs. When a campus needs to implement a new initiative, it turns to me to figure out how to do that. From the Honors program to outcomes assessment to the integration of entrepreneurship, my pattern has been to take on difficult projects and complete them. I could give dozens of examples, but I will focus on a recent one that I am particularly pleased with: when Independence Community College's engineering program faced enrollment shortfalls, a building was underutilized, and local school districts needed an additional way to bring STEM to K-12 students, I helped create the first solar-powered Fab Lab in the world without a dime of tax dollars. Good ideas attract resources – we were funded by the Kauffman Foundation, local industries, and individual donors. The result is that engineering students have a new facility where they can have life-changing experiences (like workshops where they 3-D print and assemble prosthetic limbs for children in poverty), a previously underutilized building is now the second most-visited site on the College campus, and elementary students are actually creating things using technology that they previously would not have even known existed. I firmly believe that funding follows good ideas – a federal grant and matching donor dollars have just allowed the college to double the size of that facility, and the College received a grant from Verizon to offer two years of a STEM summer camp for middle-school girls, making the remarkable success already achieved by members of the Fab Lab ICC team just the start. (You will get to meet two members of that remarkable team later in this book.) A good president can see solutions, energize the people around them and make things happen.

I am a passionate and energetic leader who is an effective fund and "friend" raiser. Unlike many people, I truly enjoy fundraising. At Alfred State, at Independence Community College, in the Independence Community, and for other organizations I support, I have raised millions of dollars in private funding from individuals and corporations, as well as grants from private foundations and government agencies. In my work in Alfred State's advancement division, I helped secure tens of millions of dollars in private gifts, corporate sponsorships, grants, state line items, and federal allocations. As a result, at Alfred State I led the team that generated more resources in less time ($63.8M in just five years) than ever before in the College's history, and I did it in the midst of what had been the most challenging fundraising environment in modern philanthropy – a lengthy recession that required us to be relentless and innovative (although the economic environment caused by the coronavirus may surpass that in severity).

Risk and Reward

"Friendraising" takes many forms. I am committed to working with faculty and staff, and other stakeholders in collaborative decision-making processes, building trust within a college and its greater community. I will mention two examples: First, when I was at SUNY Alfred, even though I became management and thus was no longer part of the faculty union, the faculty selected me three years in a row to represent them by speaking on behalf of the faculty at our New Student Convocation, an event with over two thousand attendees. Although there were hundreds of faculty members that could have fulfilled this honor, the faculty repeatedly requested that I speak for them even though technically I was no longer one of them. Second, when I arrived at Independence Community College, I found that there was no faculty role on the President's Cabinet, and immediately placed a senior, respected faculty member on the Cabinet. This inclusion of faculty in the weekly decision-making processes of the campus yielded rich rewards both in terms of transparency and the quality of decision-making.

I am committed to shared leadership and a participatory management style. I have a strong tradition of service in the leadership of the faculty senate at Alfred State, and I have supervised members of our professional union at both Alfred State and Independence Community College for years. Shared governance is essential for the creation of the collaborative atmosphere that characterizes high-functioning colleges. As you can see from the example of the New Student Convocation speech given earlier, I was typically liked, trusted, and respected by the faculty (although there are always bumps in that road!). All of the colleges at which I have worked have been collective bargaining environments.

I have a strong record of leadership and political representation at the state level. I recently finished serving as the President of the statewide system of community college presidents in Kansas, having previously served as Secretary and Vice President. In this role, I was the point person to the state system, to the legislature, and to the governor. During my term, I was part of the team that successfully lobbied for the first increase in state funding to the community college system in five years. I understand the legislative process and have worked effectively with the state government and our legislators for years.

I enjoy public relations and communication in general. I will give three examples that come to mind:

1. I have participated in four capital campaigns, and the second I designed at SUNY Alfred, a campaign that surpassed the majority of its individual goals as well as its overall goal by over one hundred percent. Notably, I managed to achieve these goals despite having no permanent President for the majority of the campaign period! I had to shoulder much of the role of communication with donors regarding why the College was worthy of support even without a permanent leader.

2. When I began my work in Institutional Advancement, our enrollment was languishing, alumni support was stagnant, and College marketing strategies were inconsistent. I volunteered to work with the excellent people in the Public Relations area to improve both our core messages and the ways those messages were disseminated. Four years later, our enrollment was booming, alumni participation was up, costs had fallen, and College publications won awards for their design and clarity.

3. I host the most popular podcast on higher education administration in the world – *The Mortarboard*, available on iTunes and all other major podcast outlets. That level of listenership only comes about when the host is able to effectively communicate with his/her audience about subjects that interest them.

I am an experienced financial planner and budget manager, with extensive financial management experience both in the public and private sectors. At Independence Community College, I bore ultimate responsibility for the development and maintenance of the College all-funds budget, which included the main college budget and coordination with three auxiliary units and multiple revenue streams. At Alfred State, I served on the senior leadership team of the College, helping to oversee the operation of the institution, including both our operating budget and gift budgets. I served as the Executive Director of the Alfred State Development Fund, which carried oversight responsibility for the monies expended annually in unrestricted funds as well as oversight of the investment policies and expenditures of the College's endowment. My CFRE designation was an objective certification that I met a high level of philanthropic regulatory ability. In my leadership role in Sponsored Programs at Alfred State, I oversaw both the pre-award grants process (including budget creation) and coordinated the staff who participated in the post-award process (primarily accounting and personnel). My Sponsored Programs responsibilities included oversight of the funds expended annually related to grant activities and the Sponsored Programs OTPS budget. From a regulatory standpoint, my experience is about as well-rounded as it gets: from the myriad of regulations associated with grant funding and reporting, to the financial and ethical regulations involved in fundraising processes and reporting, to my work in Middle States and Higher Learning Commission accreditation, to my work in outcomes assessment, I am familiar with all regulatory aspects of higher education.

At my core, however, are a few specific principles that have governed my professional life:

Absolute integrity – this point is not negotiable. I do not do anything that I am not prepared to see in the next day's newspaper headline. The truth is that the mere fact that a person is in a leadership role means that a vast trove of public information will be created about them, accessible by anyone. Some of that information is complete bunk. Some of it is accurate. My philosophy – strive to make the accurate information reflect well on you.

Team outlook fostered by compelling communication and consensus-building – I have worked for excellent team leaders and I have worked for people who had no use for the excellent talent around them. My goal is always to grow my team through trust, recognition, and an appreciation of (and ability to articulate) the virtues and cultures of the individual units under my direction and the overall value of what we provide to our students – a college education. I believe that administrators tend to think too much in terms of "leadership" and not enough in terms of "team member." How you see your colleagues and how you see your relationship to them is crucial to how they see you. I see myself as primarily someone who encourages, enables, and supports the good work of those in my area. I have been entrusted with our unrestricted funds as a foundation director and have been a successful ethics teacher because I understand that with trust comes responsibility. For a president, this includes a responsibility to the taxpayer, the students, the employees, the donor, and the community. A public institution of higher education requires a collaborative environment where the president uses the influence of his or her position to bring other people's projects to fruition. We have all seen presidencies that degenerate into an exercise in glorification of the position or into a cult of personality – those presidencies are short-lived, and ultimately the institution suffers from it. To genuinely serve others and the institution requires that the president work with everyone to achieve common goals and create an environment where people see those goals as worthwhile. Finally, such servant leadership requires honesty. You cannot ask for what you are not prepared to give yourself – if you are not honest with others, you cannot expect the trust of any constituency.

Passion – I have stayed in educational administration because I believe that the highest calling of a state institution is to prepare students to lead productive lives, which requires both workforce preparation and the skill of lifelong learning. Why are people willing to contribute money to what we do over and above their tax dollars? It is because education is noble. My philosophy – preserve that nobility.

Visibility and accessibility – Successful leadership is about forging productive relationships with a wide range of constituencies. People enter into strong relationships when both parties are available, personally accessible, and mindful of the needs of each other. My success in my professional life has come about because I work hard to create good relationships with all of the constituencies I deal with, be they board members, students, faculty, staff, individual donors, or corporate partners. (I do not have a perfect batting record in this area, though!)

No micromanagement – I hire the best people that I can find and then I treat them like the professionals that they are and let them do their jobs. This does not mean that people are not held accountable for performance, but it does mean that I do not substitute my judgment for theirs. In my opinion, the core of many people's dissatisfaction with the workplace is the tension between adults' desire for autonomy and the control exerted over those same adults in the workplace. We spend the first couple of decades of our lives craving the freedom that we believe adulthood will bring. Then we become adults and encounter the workplace: for the most part, we are told when to arrive, when to leave, what to wear, what kind of speech is permissible, what tasks to perform, how to perform those tasks, and we are punished when we fail in some way. What a disappointment – how is that substantially different from childhood? It is no wonder that people resent the workplace and, in many cases, resent their supervisors. This resentment is only partially because we chafe at the restrictions of the workplace – I am convinced that a big part of that resentment is because the restrictions exist at all, and that is not what we feel we were promised when we were younger.

The workplace needs rules, of course, and employees certainly need guidance as to what is expected of them. But there is no question that the rules have multiplied fast, primarily in response to outside pressures, and I believe this is producing a more negative experience for employees who treasure independence or autonomy or just plain want to be treated like a reasonable adult. I would suggest that this creates an opportunity to improve the working lives of employees, by remaining vigilant as a supervisor in avoiding unnecessary rules, unwanted feedback, and general edicts or directives that replace the judgment of paid employees. I use the word vigilance deliberately, because the opportunities for micromanagement are many. Those opportunities are increased by an interesting and paradoxical phenomenon: the desire of people to be micromanaged to avoid consequences or responsibility. If, for example, the vice president of the academic division makes an academic decision, but then seeks the president's permission before implementing it, what is really going on there? The moment the president substitutes his or her judgment for that of the vice president, I feel strongly that the vice president can no longer be held fully responsible for the consequences of that decision (and I am not sure he or she can receive full credit for it either). That is not to say that the president cannot provide input – but that input should come with a sincere and clear message that ultimately the decision is entirely up to the vice president. This is much harder than it seems – you may occasionally disagree with what that vice president plans to do. Yet, in all but the most difficult, consequential cases, I believe that it is better for you to adhere to the principle of non-interference. There is no reason why you cannot describe why you would do it differently if you were in that person's job, while at the same time reassuring them that the call is theirs to make.

It may seem as if under this approach, nothing really changes, because the employee will still get the message about what you want them to do. That will certainly happen if you sound ominous, or you do not use language that validates the person's training and professional judgment, or if their chief takeaway is that you would have done it differently. I do not do any of those things. I sandwich my opinion in between the same point expressed twice: "This is your job, it is your decision, and I will abide by your decision. I think that if I were in your shoes, I would take a different approach, but I am not in your shoes, and it is not my call to make. We have discussed the issue, so you understand my reasoning, and I understand yours. Make the decision, and I will support it."

This style of management has its downsides. Those who are used to interventionist supervisors find it disconcerting. Those who are looking for less responsibility by shifting the decision to a supervisor will of course be disappointed, and occasionally, employees will make bad decisions. But for me, the issue is a moral one. I do not think it is right to substitute my decisions for the decisions of a professional adult who is capable of making those decisions, was hired to make them, and is being paid to make them. There are also other downsides to this approach. It relies on finding good people to fill positions – people who are sufficiently skilled and competent to perform their jobs with little direct supervision. In any workplace, but especially a rural, sparsely populated area far from urban centers, this can be a real challenge. I am a bit philosophical (or perhaps jaded) about this – it has often appeared to me that a leader will always receive criticism, so perhaps that leader chooses not whether he or she will be criticized, but simply which criticism will be received. In this case I think a leader must choose between criticism that they are intervening or criticism that they are not intervening. For moral reasons – my desire to treat people as autonomous beings – I choose to err on the side of non-intervention.

Focus on systems, not goals – The level of autonomy I afford my direct reports is not nearly as freewheeling as it sounds. First, I hope it is clear that the decisions people are making fall within their sphere of responsibility. People have job descriptions and various assignments, and the decisions they are making live within those parameters. Second, there is an additional constraint on what people are doing in their jobs. I have subscribed my entire professional life to the idea that creating good ongoing *systems* should be the true objects of institutions, and that large, singular goals are not the best way to operate. In my experience, large goals lead to underachievement for three reasons: First, most large goals take time to achieve, and there is no way to know if a large goal developed in the present will still be an appropriate goal in the future. Second, focusing on a specific goal causes a sort of blindness to alternate, better goals. Third, truly large goals require the creation of a system to meet those goals, and it is better to think of a system that will not be obsolete when the goal is achieved, a system that remains behind and continues to serve the institution well regardless of the goals it adopts for itself.

Small goals, identifying the next thing to do, are useful and appropriate. Medium goals are fine too, but I tend to confine those to the building blocks of the system I want to build. Large goals are something that I think people focus on because either: 1) they have a boss that tells them to do so, or 2) they have never done it any other way.

Creating great systems that produce good results requires focusing on the system much of the time, and this is not an easy sell to people who do not think about systems. In academia, every strategic plan I have ever seen can be divided into two types: those built around achieving goals (99.99% of strategic plans) and those built around the development of systems. By the way, among successful companies, the ratio is not nearly so unbalanced, which should give one pause about the wisdom of the academic approach.

It is my belief that the reason so many academic strategic plans are about creating goals instead of systems is that, by and large, people in academia do not have private industry experience, and as a result they simply continue the strategic planning process using the same approach the institution has always used and following the procedures the institution's board of directors expects.

For example, consider enrollment. At every single initial meeting about strategic plan creation I have ever attended, one or more people take the following position: the correct strategic structure for increasing enrollment (and in fact increasing anything beneficial to the institution) is to identify a goal (e.g., 2,300 FTE) and then develop strategies to achieve that goal. However, I would argue that increasing enrollment is not even properly thought of as a goal at all. Instead, it should be thought of as a desirable symptom that occurs as a result of optimizing some system of variables (marketing, admissions, retention efforts, etc.), and optimization of the system around enrollment should be the real goal. After all, there is no reason why enrollment cannot be a measure of progress in the development of effective marketing, admissions, and retention systems.

A final thought about this: I am convinced that a key component of the appeal of goals and the aversion to systems is the reality that setting goals is simple, easy, and cheap (it costs nothing to write down a number) while creating effective systems is often difficult, complex, and expensive.

Creation of a safe, supportive, diverse environment – This is essential for student learning and creating successful academic and employee retention. Diversity is a goal for me, first, because I am an educator, and the data is clear that a more diverse educational environment is a better educational environment. Diversity is a goal for me because I believe in equality of opportunity, and part of creating that equality requires making an active, conscious effort to recruit, welcome, and foster diverse students and employees. Diversity is a goal for me because I am a team leader in the workplace, and the best teams are those which can generate a diversity of ideas that spring from diverse backgrounds and perspectives. Finally, diversity is a goal for me because I believe in institutional compliance, and in many cases a demonstrated commitment to diversity is a matter of institutional policy or law.

Despite the successes that adhering to these core principles has helped me to achieve, I am the first to admit that I have also had many, many failures. In fact, I would say that at least half of the examples from my career in this book are either outright failures or include episodes with major failure components. To paraphrase an old saying: Everything I know about being a successful president I learned from being an unsuccessful president. I am flawed as a leader in a number of ways. First, I often spend far more time examining an issue before I make a decision than those around me would like. Second, I am not good at recognizing when I am willing to take on more risk or change than the institution can psychologically handle. Third, I am probably too loyal – my evaluations often point out that I remain committed to a person beyond what is reasonable. Occasionally, this has led to employees remaining in a role even after it became clear that a change was needed. Finally, the role of a president is chock-full of rather soul-crushing conflict, and I think this has led to a tendency to avoid conflict or at least to avoid additional conflict beyond what naturally exists in the position (but then again maybe that happens to everyone?). After all, are there really leaders who never shy away from needed conflict in ways that at some point result in a failure to meet the needs of every situation? Based on my experience, I do not think so. I think that many of us have had a common experience: You work for a leader who deals beautifully with situations involving conflict (I will certainly admit that there are people who fall very high on that spectrum and I have worked for/with such people) and yet the more you work with that person, the more time you spend with them, the more you are with them during difficult times and in private moments, the more you see that even the best leaders falter at times. You eventually see the weariness, the slumped shoulders, and the expression of "Dear Lord, not this again." Leaders pick their battles for various reasons – sometimes the reason is deeply strategic, but sometimes even the most psychologically resilient leaders admit privately that they just do not want to deal with a particular person or problem again that day.

I point this out because I think many leaders labor under the impression that they come up short in this regard when compared to others. Like nearly everyone, they have built up in their heads an ideal of the mythological boss who always strikes just the right notes and because it is impossible to measure up to such a standard, we believe we have failed. A more realistic standard to strive toward is to be a supervisor who is able to rise to the occasion in the critical moments, and who is also able to differentiate between moments that are critical and those that are not.

I have noticed in my career that I see failure differently than many do. Anyone who is trying to do new and worthwhile things is going to fail periodically; to believe differently is a delusion. I am far more interested in a person's response to failure then I am in the failure itself. Generally, we all grew up in an environment that did not tolerate failure. After all, the grading systems and athletic scoring systems that most of us experienced in school are based on that mindset. I began to think differently about failure when I went into business with my father-in-law, the late Jack Weaver. Together, we owned a real estate holding company, and property acquisitions were essentially carefully considered bets we were placing on whether a property would be profitable. Sometimes those bets were correct, and sometimes they were not. As long as the bad bets became the basis for a better decision later, Jack was satisfied. I once questioned him about this. He replied by telling me about an experience in his own past: he was working at a Fortune 500 company in the late 1970s and he made a mistake that cost the company $73,000 (I shudder to think what that would be in today's dollars). Jack went to his boss, admitted the error, and said that he would understand if he needed to be fired. The boss looked at him and said, "Why would I fire you when I just spent $73,000 to train you never to make that mistake again? I can tell from the fact that you are here that you do not want to make that mistake again, and I can tell from your explanation of the mistake that you understand what went wrong. So, let's just think of it as some very expensive training for you, and now go put that training to work."

One brief commentary on my commitment to honesty in this book: Perhaps one of the most frustrating aspects of the job of president is the loss of one's First Amendment rights. Of course, I do not mean this literally; the president cannot lose his or her First Amendment rights any more than anyone else can. However, the reality is that like any CEO, as president of a college you represent many, and like all CEOs, your voice has a disproportionate impact. The result is a near constant self-censorship of what you might like to say. A previous president under whom I served told me he planned to write a book (I do not know if he ever did), entitled "Emails I Never Sent." I certainly sympathize with that urge! I certainly do not think I have gotten my First Amendment rights back – there is much that a president is privy to which cannot be discussed, because it would be improper to do so or because the information is legally protected. But I will always write as frankly as I can, and when something cannot be said I will indicate that.

Having said that, let me give you a preview of what lies ahead. I have tried to address the most fundamental, important, or pressing issues early in this book, in a section that deals with some, but not all, of the fundamental issues that I think confront nearly every institution, from enrollment, to competition between schools for good teachers, to the retention of first-time donors, to strategic planning. Not all are applicable to every school – an online school has fewer facilities issues to deal with than an on-ground school, for example – but they are the issues that have confronted me in my career and from which I have learned some hard lessons.

In the second section of this book, I focus on a fundamental issue that has preoccupied me for years – mindset. I discuss a specific entrepreneurial mindset that has served me well for years and offer a number of ways it has surfaced positively in my work.

Finally, I discuss crisis management, as presidents have no shortage of crises they must deal with, and in my own career I have found each crisis, whether self-created or thrust upon the institution, to be a genuine opportunity for personal, professional, and institutional growth. I offer a series of case studies of different crisis types from my career (some large, some small), and describe the lessons each has to offer.

Few books are a solo effort, and this one is no exception. I have tried to include descriptions of incidents in which I have personally been involved and from which I think lessons can be learned. We are unreliable narrators of our own careers; I do not see myself as an objective observer, especially when I was directly affected by these incidents (sometimes negatively), and so I am indebted to colleagues who helped review those sections for accuracy. I owe a significant debt to the colleagues who reached out to me after listening to one of my podcasts, reading one of my blog entries or other articles, hearing a speech or interview, or seeing me on *Last Chance U*. They offered their opinions freely and persuasively, and many of the passages in this book are informed and improved by their comments.

I am specifically grateful to Jessica Morgan-Tate, who reviewed and commented on this book and was kind enough to have some substantial conversations with me about how to approach some difficult parts. She improved the book significantly.

Any errors that remain are mine. If you have opinions about anything in this book that you would like to share with me, please feel free to e-mail me your comments at barwickriskandreward@gmail.com. I look forward to your thoughts!

Section 1

Fundamental Challenges

Introduction

Certain recurring themes run throughout higher education – challenges that nearly all colleges face. Not all colleges aggressively seek grant money; some do not rely on public funding; others do not have long histories and traditions. However, some challenges face nearly all colleges, and in some cases, bigger risks can mean bigger rewards. That is not always the case – in some areas, like fundraising, best practices are well-established, and a college loses to its competition by failing to follow those practices. As I described earlier, the variables are many. While these variables prevent the creation of a true playbook, in considering these issues, I did discover some themes and even rules which apply very well to small and/or rural colleges. Higher education administrators can apply these principles to move forward in most situations.

All colleges face a need to recruit students. The enrollment of traditional students is eroding, and this erosion is projected to increase. Enrollment decline will have the single most significant impact on the higher education landscape in the next ten years, with growth in online course offerings being a close second. The decline has its origins in a combination of a reduction in the national birthrate, the decreased unemployment rate, and increasing college costs. This combination is already driving colleges to close or merge, and the pace will accelerate. In addition, virtually all students take on debt of one kind or another in order to attend college. As of this writing, the total United States student loan debt is now about $1.6 trillion, with millions of Americans in default on their student loan debt. Many students graduate from college or from graduate school facing payments that restrict them very significantly financially and limit their ability to buy homes or even to start families. The average debt load is about $30,000 per graduate. There is debate about the severity and impact of this debt – this situation is described along a spectrum that ranges from "crisis" to "ordinary market forces." However, for the foreseeable future, there will be calls for the elimination of student debt, and I discuss that concept in this section.

All colleges have some kind of infrastructure, typically a combination of brick and mortar and technological resources. The competition for student enrollment has led to a specific phenomenon: a kind of "arms race" of college facilities. Facilities are expensive to start with, and because students select their colleges partly, or in some cases entirely, based on facilities, colleges repeatedly try to out-do each other in their facilities. In many cases, this is a fool's errand. I will focus on dorms, which present unique challenges and opportunities, and small college libraries, which typically have a significant physical footprint and whose purpose is shifting rapidly, by addressing how libraries can be re-conceived to address modern needs while fulfilling their traditional mission.

All colleges hire teachers, and better teachers have increased employment options. Ensuring that the good teachers choose your institution, even if it means relocating or teaching repetitive introductory courses, can be a difficult challenge that, in my opinion, few colleges take seriously enough during either the search process or in the creation of the work environment. This neglect creates risk by creating a competitive disadvantage, especially since there is a snowball effect – good teachers act as a recruitment tool for other good teachers, and the quality difference between colleges grows as a result.

All colleges are ranked by various organizations. (If your college is not being frequently ranked, I would say that by itself constitutes an implicit ranking!) Some of those rankings are accurate, and some are not. Some have a clear basis, and some do not. Some are well-publicized, and some are not. What is clear is that colleges that do well in the rankings should use them to their advantage – how should colleges regard rankings, and how should colleges respond to them?

As part of their public relations efforts, nearly all colleges seek donor support. As colleges compete for donor dollars, one of the greatest struggles receives little attention outside of the fundraising division – donor retention. Fundraisers know that one of the most reliable indicators of future gifts is evidence of past gifts, but this is relative – as they also know that donor retention following a first gift is very low – and so I discuss techniques and strategies that institutions can employ to create on-going relationships with first-time donors. Finally, I will offer a case study on how a college can leverage strategic planning, a process in which all colleges engage at some point, to create better public relations. Even if a college is not inclined to plan comprehensively, other constituencies, like regional accreditors, boards of regents, state governments, and taxpayers expect it (and in some cases demand it). Much has been written about strategic planning, but as I describe in the introduction to this book, I believe educators poorly conceive of strategic planning as the meeting of goals rather than the creation of effective systems. However, strategic planning can be very effective when done well, and in this section of the book, I discuss the method used at Independence Community College to create widespread participation in the process and buy-in of the results.

CHAPTER 1

Competing for Students

There is no gentle way to put this: for the foreseeable future, traditional college enrollment is going to decline, so much so that it will drive a significant number of colleges out of existence. (Although this book was written during the coronavirus pandemic, the conditions that prompted this prediction existed prior to the pandemic and the pandemic does not change the conclusions of this chapter.)

Total college enrollment is determined primarily by the total pool of traditional college-age students, and the national annual birthrate determines that pool. The birthrate since 1940 has looked like this:

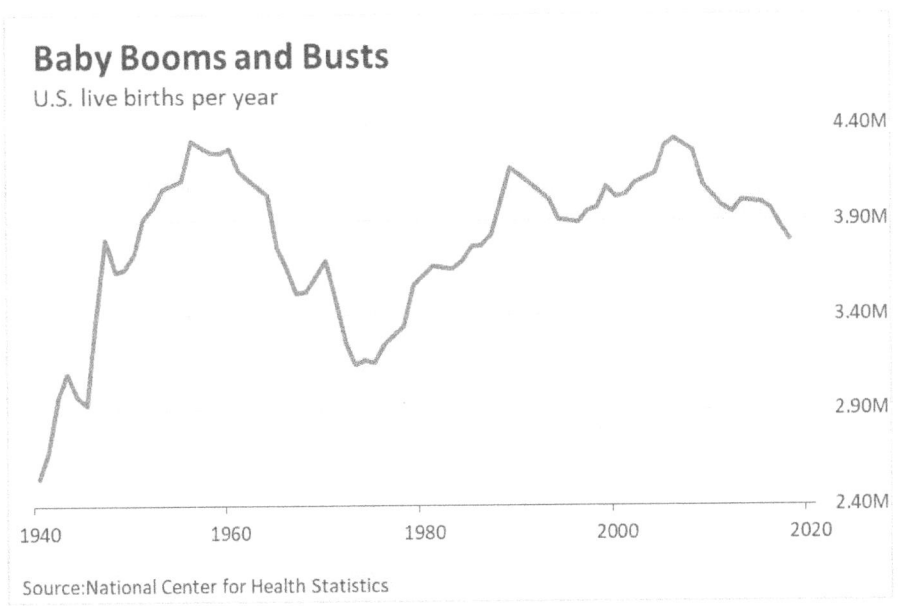

Between 2007 and 2013, hundreds of thousands fewer babies were born in the United States, and by 2025, the shortfall in population will begin to surface in college enrollment. Even worse, this decline will not be felt evenly throughout the United States. The projected decline in college enrollment for each region in the United States look like this:

Declines to Come - South Region
Actual and projected number of high school graduates

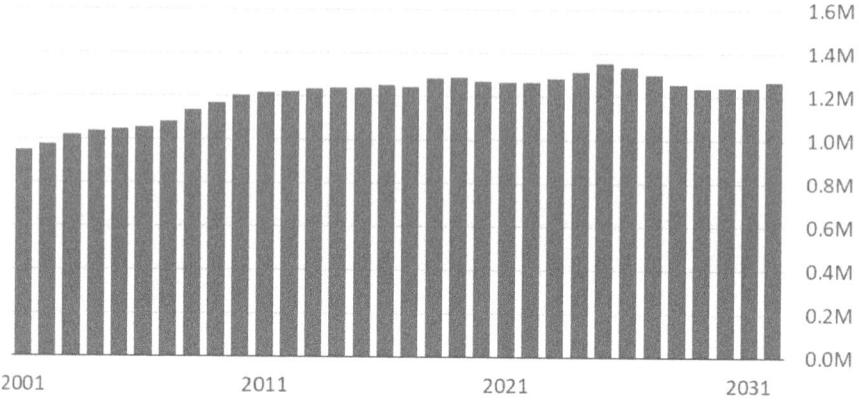

Data is by academic year, with 2001 = 2000/2001.

Declines to Come - West Region
Actual and projected number of high school graduates

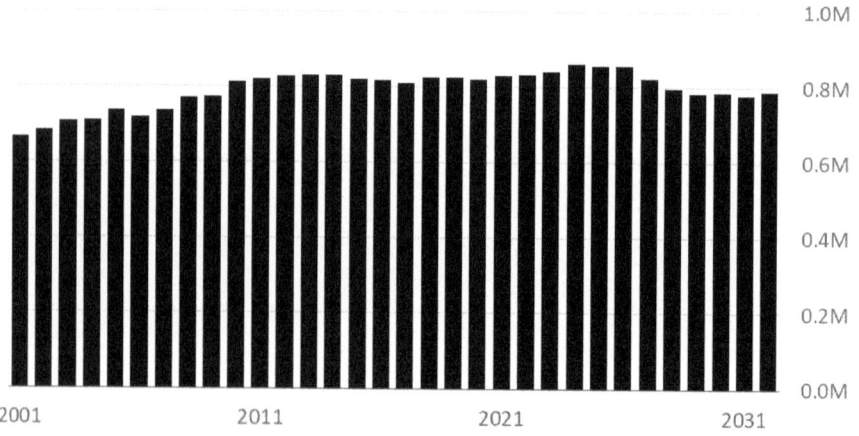

Data is by academic year, with 2001 = 2000/2001.

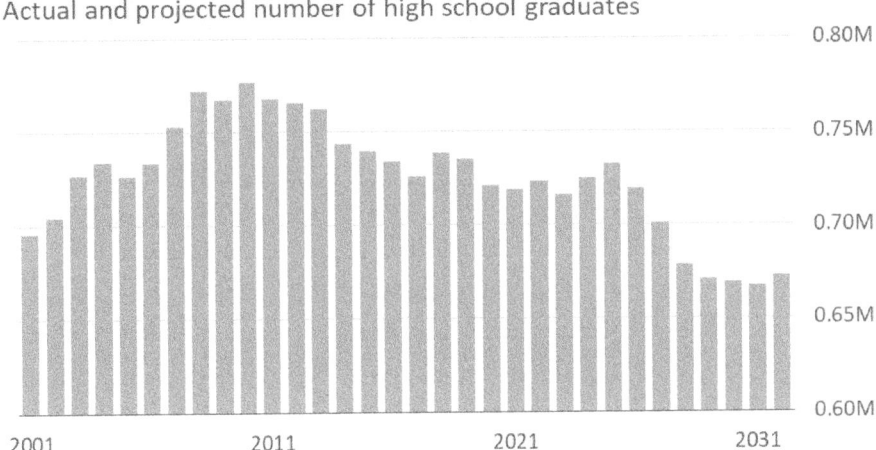

Data is by academic year, with 2001 = 2000/2001.

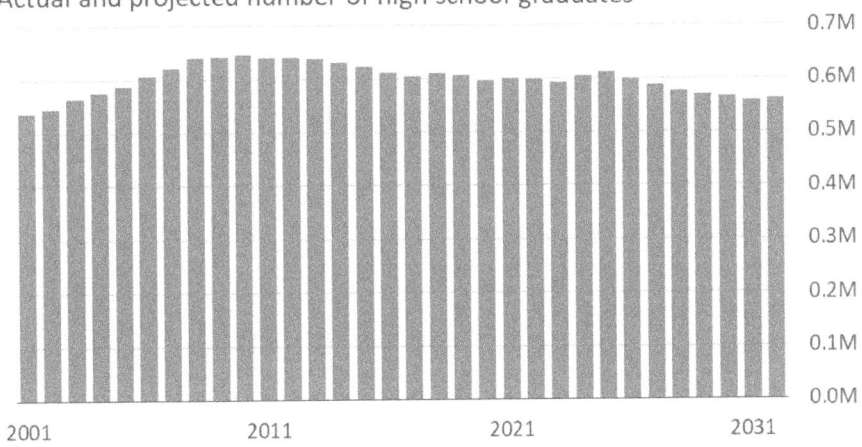

Data is by academic year, with 2001 = 2000/2001.

The South will see the smallest decline, but the drop will be felt everywhere. Unfortunately, it gets even worse because birthrate is not the only factor that will negatively impact enrollment as one must also consider the relationship between the employment rate and college enrollment in the United States over the last decade.

Higher education is complex, with affordability often playing an extended role in enrollment decision making. Decisions are made regarding the cost of future opportunities and are weighted against an inventory of factors relevant to a student's present situation. Allocation of time and money are typically at the top of the inventory of factors considered, and both are greatly affected by things like recession or current economic times. With a high unemployment rate of 9.6% in post-recession 2010, many job seekers were interested in garnering new skills to assist them in standing out as employable candidates in a tough job market. American college enrollment in both two- and four-year institutions increased dramatically from 17.2 million students in 2006 to 20.4 million students in 2011, with the greatest increase seen within 2-year institutions (community and technical colleges). While there was an initial increase in college enrollment from 2010-2011, college enrollment eventually began a downward decline as the number of students dropped slightly to 19.1 million students by 2015. (College enrollment is expected to drop further as a result of the coronavirus pandemic, although it is too early as of this writing to know the extent.)

Furthermore, many private for-profit four-year institutions saw a sharp drop in enrollment during this period due to high costs as the country was repairing its post-recession economy. While there is certainly a relationship between the unemployment rate and college enrollment rates, there is not enough to prove causation between the two. It appears likely the costs in terms of time and money for an education at a four-year institution affect the rate of return that job seekers require for educational investment during economic times of high unemployment. A closer relationship is seen with unemployment rates and enrollment at community colleges, where costs are typically lower, and skills are obtained more expeditiously.

It is instructive to look at enrollment trends up to this point because the last decade (which began on a high note from an enrollment standpoint) has not been kind to college enrollment and has left many institutions in a weakened and vulnerable position. For instance, consider the relationship between the unemployment rate and community college enrollment in the United States from 2010-2018. Community colleges saw a much more rapid rise and subsequent drop than four-year institutions. Following the 2007-2009 recession in the United States, there was a large increase in community college enrollment. In 2010, the unemployment rate was 9.6%, providing an incentive and an opportunity for many job seekers to return to college in an attempt to obtain new skills. Peak enrollment at community colleges occurred between 2010 and 2011, with thirty-three percent higher enrollment than in 2006. From 2011 onward, however, the overall trend has been downward.

Like many rural states, my home state of Kansas saw dismal enrollment rates over the last decade. Enrollment in Kansas community colleges, measured by both headcount and FTE, has shrunk dramatically over the past six years (Source: KBOR 2020 Data Book):

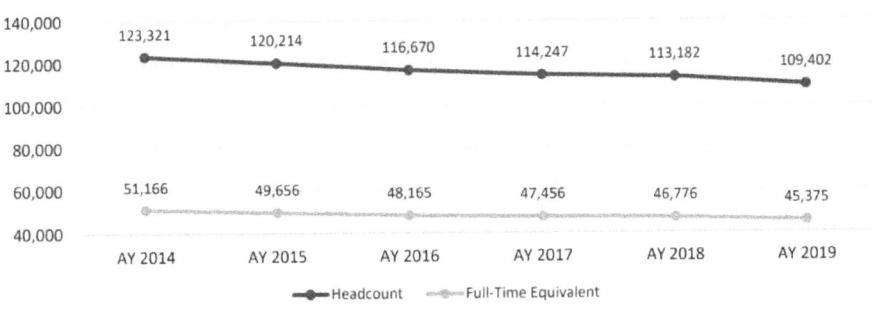

This chart represents an 11.3% decline in both headcount and FTE. The decline was remarkably consistent across campuses – during the six years represented above, sixteen of the nineteen community colleges experienced an enrollment decrease. Independence Community College's FTE decrease for that period (9.8%) actually beat the state average, but not by much.

What caused this statewide decline in enrollment? There were two factors, a low unemployment rate and overall shrinkage in the state population. What is the relationship between the employment rate and community college enrollment in the state of Kansas from 2010-2018? During the recession, Kansas saw a sharp increase in unemployment (from 4% to 7.3%). By 2010, Kansas unemployment hovered around seven percent, with a decrease in the unemployment rate to 5.7% by 2012. Unemployment continued to decrease through 2018, lowering all the way to 3.3%. Community college enrollment in Kansas throughout this period greatly mirrored the rest of the country in that increases and steady holds were seen initially in the 2010-2011 and 2011-2012 school years. However, once the 2014-2015 school year arrived, Kansas community colleges began to see a decline in community college enrollment that coincided with the continuing decline of unemployment rates. (Because higher unemployment rates tend to favor community college enrollment, the community college sector may be the only one which either sees an increase from the coronavirus pandemic, or remains flat. It is too early in the pandemic to know, however.)

During the 2010-2011 school year, the enrollment at community colleges was listed at 131,203, which fell to 123,331 by the 2014-2015 academic year. Kansas continued to see a drop-off of enrollees, with the 2018-2019 student count at 109,402, a total drop of 21,801 students from 2011. Once again, as with much of the United States, as the economy and job market saw improvements, job seekers felt less incentive for additional schooling as they were able to retain employment and/or gain additional skills through their employment.

Likewise, this enrollment decline did not reflect migration to four-year colleges. For example, in Fall 2018, when thirteen of the nineteen community colleges in Kansas lost enrollment (down by one thousand FTE students from the previous year across the community college system) these students did not migrate to the combined technical colleges or the universities, since the combined Kansas higher education system was down by 808 net students. Even so, the combined technical colleges did see an enrollment increase, while the combined universities were responsible for the bulk of the decline in enrollment numbers.

Where does this leave us? I began this section of the book by saying that enrollment pressures will have the single greatest impact on American higher education in the next two decades. Small colleges face the greatest jeopardy, but nearly all colleges will suffer. In my travels across the United States in preparation for writing this book, I have watched a gradual awakening among college employees to this fact. The earliest alarms were sounded by admissions officers, but those responsible for financial planning at higher education institutions are clearly beginning to catch on that tough times are ahead. A review of higher education related literature published over the last three years shows a dramatic sevenfold increase in the number of publications related to enrollment pressures. Some colleges, particularly less selective, smaller, liberal arts colleges, are feeling accelerated effects from changes in enrollment, and there has been a rash of closures and mergers of those types of colleges in the areas of the country where they are most concentrated geographically, primarily in New England. This will no doubt spread more widely and quickly as a result of the coronavirus pandemic, but it is too early to know the extent.

But the snowball is at the top of the hill and has just begun to roll downwards. The pool of available traditional students is beginning to shrink, and it will shrink for the foreseeable future. More importantly, it will shrink by enough students, and for a long enough time period, that few colleges will be able to "ride out" the problem without, at a minimum, painful priority choices, and at a maximum, closure.

The strategies available to colleges are, sadly, few. The vast majority of colleges are designed to be fairly static. This has always been a strength; if a prospective student is going to commit to four years or more of an expensive, full-time relationship with an organization, that student expects that what he or she signs up for on day one will look the same when he or she completes the program. Colleges are built on the notion of permanence and solidity, that the degree awarded will still be meaningful decades later. It is no accident that the basic form of higher education has persisted for centuries. Colleges do not change willy-nilly,

Risk and Reward

and in fact, there are many gatekeepers both within and external to institutions that act as a substantial check on any meaningful change. Hoping to change a curriculum? The process is typically lengthy and deliberatively and requires input and buy-in from multiple parties within a college. Looking to create a new curriculum? In that case, the hurdles are even more substantial, requiring many layers of review and approval both inside and outside the organization. Thinking of canceling a curriculum? That is often the toughest one of all – a lawmaker once said to me, "If you think it is hard to get a law passed, just try to get one repealed." I am reminded of this in the case of curricula that clearly deserve to be canceled. Often, a program has low enrollment, no prospects for future enrollment growth, no demonstrated need for graduates in that area, and little support on campus. But even in those circumstances, academia has a strong distaste for the idea that anything it offers is no longer needed. I have worked at colleges where no objective rationale for the continued existence of a program was possible, and yet the program continued. Decision-makers, lacking any quantitative basis for continued investment, drag out the same tired, old arguments: they participated in the program themselves and it was very valuable; they have a friend who participated in the program twenty years ago and that person's life was changed; the college has had the program for so long that the school's identity would be intolerably indistinct if the program were lost ("this program is a part of our heritage"); alumni would be distressed to see the program end; and on and on and on. No one ever speaks to the opportunity cost, where the decision to continue a failed program is, in essence, also a decision not to fund a possibly successful program.

Many forces conspire to maintain the status quo at colleges. Colleges are big ships that are slow to turn, and academics are not salespeople and often find marketing tactics and activities distasteful. Public institutions do not like to have public discussions about their problems, partly out of pride and partly out of a legitimate concern that a free-for-all discussion might make the problem seem worse than it is or might actually make it worse. It is a safe bet that if a college cannot have a genuine discussion about a problem, it is very unlikely to be able to solve that problem.

For the foreseeable future, there will be only four distinct routes to higher enrollment or the maintenance of existing levels in particularly tough or shrinking markets. These recommendations are unaffected by the current pandemic, and are made even more urgent by it: a more sophisticated online presence for colleges, increased workforce development, cost control, student return on investment, and the development of new student markets.

Online. Many colleges have pinned their hopes on increased online enrollment, and with good reason. As much as some of us do not like to think about it, there is no rational reason to believe that higher education will escape the virtual evolution that is affecting the rest of our lives, and shaping everything we do from shopping to entertainment to the filing of our tax returns. The online space in higher education will grow for all of the same reasons that the online space has grown elsewhere: it is cheap, convenient, and familiar to the next generation of consumers. In the short term, enrollment gains in the online space will be quick and easy, but in the longer-term, the situation is much murkier. We take for granted that traditional colleges are far more than just the classroom instruction they offer, how then, is that gestalt being preserved as more and more students seek only the online coursework that a college has to offer, and participate in no other way in the intellectual or social life of the campus? American higher education is successful because it has created a culture in which people want to immerse; as that culture changes, how will we ensure that whatever replaces what we have now is not only attractive to students, but is a sustainable economic, intellectual, and cultural model that supports the continued existence of a college? On an episode of my podcast, my guests Matt Reed, the chief academic officer at Brookdale Community College, offered a description of the online evolution that was haunting and on-point:

> Our faculty by contract expect to have four days a week on campus… When you walk the hallways where the faculty offices are, there's usually a certain amount of buzzing going on. What's starting to happen, though, as

more faculty are teaching more of their courses online, they may not come in all four days. It may only be three, or sometimes two… So we're starting to see an effect where more folks are coming in fewer days a week, which means there are more empty offices, there are more days when corridors are kind of empty or nearly empty… And it creates issues in several ways. One is with the environment for students walking through. We are still primarily an onsite institution, but students take unintended messages from first impressions that they encounter and if they walk through areas where faculty are supposed to be and they see a whole lot of closed doors and empty offices, that's not a very welcoming impression. The other piece is in terms of shared governance and doing the business of the college, it becomes harder to schedule meetings. You'll get a lot of, "I don't want to come to campus just for one meeting" … But what starts to happen, you start to lose the informal interactions, the sort of hallway rapport when people just aren't around very much. If they compress their schedules to two or three days… I don't mean every single person; I'm talking in the aggregate… when you compress schedules to two or three days, people tend to pack those two or three days pretty solidly. And so even when they're here, they're distracted. And so you lose some of that informal interaction… and I think people start to lose touch with each other. You lose some of the common culture. And we're in that awkward phase right now where the old culture is, is increasingly strained. But whatever's going to come after it hasn't quite arrived yet. So we're in that in-between space, and it's a very awkward space to be in.

A college that can find a substitute for what it currently offers may be able to continue, but a college that does not find a way to replace what is being lost will find that it has transformed itself from a college to a place that simply offers college courses in exchange for money. There are certainly plenty of potential students who would be willing to engage in such an exchange, but it is impossible to ignore that what has made American higher education a success for centuries has been that this exchange is only a fraction of what a college has to offer. After all, traditional college insists, with some justification, that substantial learning occurs outside of the classroom. This does not mean that such an exchange is completely undesirable (in fact, I would argue the opposite if it brings higher education to a greater number of people), but my concern is that the implementation of online instruction (most of which lies in the future, not the present) will gradually short-change other areas of colleges that also have legitimate, substantial enrollment markets.

Workforce development. It is a fact that over time, more and more colleges have offered more and more degrees to more and more students in ways that do not lead directly to employment. As such, it was only a matter of time before colleges developed a reputation for doing just that. (Google "degrees least likely to lead to employment" and settle in.) Higher education deserves some skepticism about the value that it adds, and that skepticism is growing. It has long been argued and demonstrated that a college degree leads to increased earnings. But what if those earnings are no longer translating into financial security and long-term prosperity? For example, a study by researchers at the Federal Reserve Bank of St. Louis concludes that while college still boosts graduates' earnings, it no longer increases their long-term wealth. In the 1930s, white college graduates were worth 247% more than their non-college-educated peers, but by 1985 the wealth difference was just forty-two percent. The decline was even greater among black graduates: for graduates born in the 1970s and 1980s, the wealth difference between them and their non-graduating peers is zero.

Risk and Reward

Annie Lowry of the <u>Atlantic</u> describes several reasons for this:

> The first has to do with asset prices. Older generations were able to buy houses and stocks when prices were low, then saw the value of those assets rise. Recent generations have faced high housing prices, and have found themselves unable to buy their way into the stock market. Therefore, they have not been able to take advantage of the recent run-up in asset values…. The second potential factor involves Wall Street's financial engineering. Younger folks have come of age during an era of consumer debt, with banks more than happy to load customers up with credit cards, car loans, and so on. Those debts then get subtracted from the value of families' assets when determining their net worth, helping to explain the Millennials' crummy wealth accumulation…. Finally – most obvious, and perhaps most important – is the cost of college and graduate school itself. The price of consumer goods has increased by a factor of four since the late 1970s. College costs have increased by a factor of 14… More and more students have taken out heavy debt burdens to be able to go to college, burdens that then eat away at their earnings, month after month, for years on end.

The pendulum must now swing in the other direction; to gain back students and trust, colleges must offer credentials that lead efficiently to employment for those who want it, and more importantly, colleges must conquer the bias that led to the de-emphasizing of workforce development in the first place. The problem with that bias is not so much that colleges have moved away from being hotbeds of workforce training, it is that they never were. Traditionally, tradespeople learned their trade from other tradespeople, and college was seen as a higher-level endeavor. College was accurately described as a marketplace of ideas, not a place to get your hands dirty. However, a shift has occurred in modern industry, causing the majority of skilled trades to become far more sophisticated, far more technical, and to change far more quickly, thus requiring continuous professional development. From cars to veterinary care to human health care to surveying to forensics, many fields have grown so complex and sophisticated that a dedicated educational environment is a far more appropriate place to develop the skills necessary to handle those complexities than traditional apprenticeships. Even in cases where an apprenticeship is appropriate, it should generally only be seen as a part of students' formal education. For colleges to fully embrace their appropriate role in workforce development, they must overcome the cultural bias present in American higher education, and they need to do something else as well: A college can offer an English degree with relatively little input from the outside, but it cannot offer technical degrees without meaningful dialogue and information sharing between the college and the industries that hire its graduates. To do this, colleges must learn to talk with those same industry leaders that they have excluded from higher education for years. Although colleges are finally coming to this realization, and are, by necessity, beginning to rapidly grow "industry partnerships," they are also exposing the limitations on colleges' ability to satisfy the needs of these same industry partners. Those limitations can be considerable – for instance, the industry partner may need a time frame or a specific location that is not permitted within the faculty labor agreement. But a college that has the right mindset can overcome these issues.

Reduced student cost. The widely used practice of discounting tuition through the application of scholarships exists because colleges learned long ago that they could create the appearance of value by offering a net price lower than the published tuition rate to the students that they were targeting for recruitment, such as students with better academic records, groups that enhanced diversity, etc. However, the effectiveness of this strategy is diminishing for two reasons:

First, student consumers are becoming savvier – as a result of a wider understanding of the use of discounts and greater access to comparative information among colleges. Some colleges are abandoning the discounted tuition model altogether, in part due to concerns about equity, transparency, and fairness, but also because the practice of discounting tuition is so widespread that some colleges hope to achieve a marketing distinction by no longer engaging in the practice.

Second, as I discussed earlier, there is growing concern about the return on investment for a college education. If the price of a degree remains the same or increases, while the perceived value of that degree declines, the consequence is fewer people who will invest in that degree. There are many ways to increase the value of what is received in return for the cost of a college education – the experience of the education itself can be improved in a myriad of ways, and the impact of degree attainment on income or quality of life following graduation can also be improved, all of which I will discuss at various points in this book. But for now, I will point out only that the investment/return on investment equation has two variables, and one way to improve the outcome is to adjust the investment (i.e., the cost that the student pays for his or her education). Although the methods used to market these lowered costs to the student is beyond the scope of this book, acquiring the resources that are a prerequisite for either applying a discount or lowering tuition uniformly is something on which presidents and other administrative leaders spend a great deal of time, and I will be talking about some of those efforts in this book. Suffice it to say at this point that one way to increase enrollment is to lower student costs by transferring those costs somewhere else, such as to state or local taxpayers, donors, or through other methods or even increased institutional efficiencies.

The opportunities for greater efficiencies in higher education are everywhere. In my opinion, one of the dirty little secrets of higher education is its relative inefficiency, especially in the case of small colleges. That is not to say that small colleges should not exist but rather that small colleges everywhere seem to shy away from efficiencies that run counter to their established culture. For instance, why do community colleges just a short distance apart and within the same state use different information systems to run their campuses, when the costs of those systems are based on FTE and become lower when FTE rises? The most common response I have heard to this question is: "We want to be able to choose our own system." That sounds reasonable (if a bit indulgent) but colleges rarely quantify the extra money they are spending simply because they refuse to partner with other institutions, and as a result rarely have to answer for costs incurred as a result of those types of inefficiencies.

Lowering overall cost is difficult but not impossible. The major reason why lowering costs is difficult, although not widely discussed, is what is known as the Baumol effect (sometimes called Baumol's Disease). The Baumol Effect is the rise of salaries in jobs that have experienced no or low increase in labor productivity, in response to rising salaries in other jobs that have experienced higher labor productivity growth. The costs of education rise faster than the costs in other parts of the economy simply because productivity growth in education is slower. Class sizes are largely the same as they were ten years ago and time to graduation is the same (take your pick of whatever productivity measure you want to use – it will largely be stagnant), and yet salaries, utilities, and other costs continue to rise. This means that those costs must be passed along to students and taxpayers. (We see the opposite phenomena in industries like consumer electronics, where tremendous efficiency and productivity gains have occurred, causing prices to drop.)

However, some colleges have beaten the Baumol effect. A good example is Purdue University, which, as of this writing, has not raised tuition since 2013. The University has also reduced the price of food services and textbooks. Inflation has also reduced the real cost to students, since the $9,932 in annual tuition is worth less today than it was in 2013, but still buys just as much at Purdue as it did in 2013. An undergraduate degree from Purdue, in other words, is less expensive today than it was in 2013. How is this happening? Is it because services have been cut, or the University successfully lobbied for more state support? Did Purdue increase the number of adjunct instructors? No, instead, the University has focused not on cost-cutting, but on efficiency – lowering costs while preserving production. Specifically, here is how the _Atlantic_ describes the financial situation at Purdue:

> Increased enrollment since the [tuition] freeze has brought in an extra $100 million, reckons Chris Ruhl, the university's treasurer and chief financial officer. The benefits of the improved balance sheet can be seen across campus. According to the university's figures, Purdue's full-time faculty at all levels has increased, resulting in a student-teacher ratio of 13 to 1, compared with the Big Ten average of more than 15 to 1. Faculty pay is up too. The salary of a full-time professor at Purdue has increased by 12 percent over the past five years, against a conference-average increase of 7 percent... Meanwhile, a visitor can't help but notice that large stretches of Purdue's campus are construction sites: for new research facilities; new residence halls; a learning center the size of a power plant, which is what stood in its place until six years ago. Applications for admission are up 37 percent... And so a virtuous circle was established, according to Purdue and its president. The predictably flat tuition attracted more students, creating a larger student body that brought in increased revenue, which allowed for the hiring of more and higher-quality faculty, whose research the university could profitably license to the private sector, where alumni, delighted at the celebrated achievements of their alma mater, helped increase donations by 136 percent over six years, which in turn has helped keep the freeze in place.

Another widely discussed option for reducing cost, and thereby improving the educational return on investment for the general population is through the cancellation of student debt. While I wrote this book in late 2019 and early 2020, various democratic candidates were making their case to the American people in their individual bids for candidacy in the 2020 presidential election, and student loan debt has figured heavily in that conversation. Now, in May of 2020, the coronavirus pandemic has increased the calls from some people and groups for the cancellation of student debt. As such, I am going to talk a little bit about the various proposals that are before the American public for forgiveness of student loans, both because I am intensely interested in the subject and because most people do not fully understand the connection between student loan debt and other aspects of education, including how student loan debt affects other aspects of the American education system.

First, it is worth taking a moment to talk about the sheer size of America's student loan "problem" or "debt," depending on how you look at it. I will not disguise for a moment that I think the problem is real. The total debt is now about $1.6 trillion and millions of people are in default. Many graduates from college or from graduate school face payments that restrict them financially, hindering their ability to buy homes and even to start families. In fact, the situation is so widespread that it has actually resulted in an "upside," in that some employers now compete for employees by offering the perk of potential loan repayment benefits.

Some data suggests that the total amount of the average student's debt load is not necessarily increasing and may actually be declining slightly when adjusted for inflation, but even so, it is already significant. Regardless of whether it continues at the same rate or modifies slightly, the underlying problem remains – people are graduating from college with a category of significant debt that the vast majority of people did not have several decades ago.

So, what is the current average debt load? Well, for students who are just receiving bachelor's degrees, the average debt load at graduation was about $30,000 in 2015 and 2016, which actually is not all that different from previous years. Although it does adjust very slightly, there is a reason that this amount is not changing significantly. It is not clear that

Risk and Reward

people can borrow any more money than they are currently borrowing because it is believed that most students are actually currently borrowing the maximum they are permitted to borrow under federal student loan program limits. Further, it is important to remember that not just students go into debt to go to college – their parents often go into debt too. So much so that in 2015 and 2016, the average debt load for parents at graduation for federal plus loans was $33,000. This is very significant, as students and their parents are simultaneously taking on large debts to pay for students to go to college.

Even so, it is important to understand that those numbers only reflect the economic reality for students attending undergraduate school. Graduate school actually accounts for more debt per student than undergraduate school, with about forty percent of all student loans taken out to attend graduate or professional school (e.g., master's/Ph.D. programs, law school, business school, medical school). Graduate students take on more debt for several reasons. Graduate school is often more expensive, and graduate students do not have the same strictly enforced, federally imposed borrowing limits that undergraduate students do, which allows graduate students to borrow far more money. This is especially relevant when, for example, students go to a graduate school in another state where they often do not receive any kind of in-state tuition break or where the tuition is high in addition to the cost of living expenses, fees for books, etc. I did this myself when I relocated to Iowa from New York to obtain my master's degree at the University of Iowa. Because I was not a resident of the state of Iowa, my tuition was higher than it would have been if I had been a resident and so I borrowed more because I was attending graduate school as a non-resident.

Second, it is worth noting that there are problems inherent in all of the proposals that have been raised by the Democratic candidates. That said, I should make clear two things upfront: First, this is not a political book and I am not arguing for a particular political position or advocating for a particular candidate. Second, I commend anyone who is trying to think seriously about the problem of the high cost of education and the correlating high rates of borrowing because the high-cost part of the equation is important. The cost of education in the last four decades has exceeded the core rate of inflation every single year, which also means that the cost of borrowing to purchase that education has gone up each year as well. In the following chapters, I discuss several contributing factors, ranging from regulations that are expensive to comply with to the perceived need to create ever-improved facilities that students want but which are of dubious educational value.

Senator Bernie Sanders has proposed canceling all $1.6 trillion of outstanding student loan debt in the United States while Senator Elizabeth Warren has previously proposed canceling $140 billion of the debt. There are serious problems with any plan that is being proposed that would eliminate debt. Let me offer a general overview of the kinds of problems that arise when the nation tries to simply cancel debt for the specific purposes and the targeted expenses that these candidates have proposed.

It is important to remember that these proposals are typically coupled with proposals for making all undergraduate programs at public colleges and universities free, which it is argued reduces the need for borrowing. Equally important to remember is that providing free tuition does not actually eliminate student debt. After all, most student loan debt is not taken out to attend undergraduate programs at public colleges. If you look at the data, you will find that the majority of borrowing originates from people attending for-profit colleges, private colleges, and graduate school. You certainly do not need me to tell you how expensive private colleges can be to attend and, even though private colleges often have a discount rate, that is, they rarely charge everyone the published tuition rate by offering students some type of scholarship, the fact is the net amount that students pay can still be considerable. Of course, it is not just that private colleges are expensive, it is also that because public colleges are cheaper, students need to borrow less to attend them, which means that if students choose to go to a public college, they are going to borrow less to cover less overall cost, resulting in a reduced debt load. So

Risk and Reward

the first problem with the proposals to forgive student loan debt is that they are targeted not at the *worst* examples of student loan borrowing, but at the *lowest* examples of student loan borrowing because those who attend a public college are typically borrowing less than people who chose different avenues for their education. In the words of Kevin Carey, in his *New York Times* article "Canceling Student Loan Debt Doesn't Make Problems Disappear" because most student loan debt is actually used to attend private colleges or graduate schools,

> the day after Senator Sanders hits the reset button as he put it in the news conference, the national student debt odometer would rapidly begin spinning again. Will those later debts be forgiven too? If not, his plan would create a generation of student loan lottery winners with losers on either side. People who had already paid back their loans would get nothing. People with future loans would get nothing. People with debt on the day the legislation was enacted would be rewarded.

One must also consider the political resistance against student loan debt cancellation by those people who have paid back their loans and would not benefit from a cancellation of student loan debt. In fact, during the course of my research on this topic for this book, I posed this very question about these proposals, and consistently one of the very first responses I received from people was "well, you know, I worked hard, I paid back my student loans. Why should somebody else just get a free ride?" I too am an example of that. When I left graduate school, I did have student loan debt, which I paid back over a period of years. It was burdensome to do that, and nobody helped me with it. So, I think now people who have paid back their student loan debts are asking, well, if this is possible to do, why is it only happening now? While I do not think this is a good argument, I do believe that it is a natural human response, and it carries with it a polarizing political reality.

In addition, there is a second issue, namely that once the government begins to forgive student loan debt, there will be some people, some considerable number of people, who believe that that the loan forgiveness will happen again, and that will borrow on that assumption. For example, if you are considering a car loan and you know that every five years or so the federal government forgives all car loans, it would be reasonable to think, "well, we are due for another round of car loan forgiveness," which might actually lead you to take out a larger car loan than you might have otherwise. Not only that, but the automobile manufacturer would also have an incentive to charge more, under the expectation that at some point the loan will be forgiven. In the same way, student loan forgiveness provides educational institutions with an incentive to charge more for education, believing that at some point the loans used to pay for that higher cost education will be forgiven again. Also, because the institution itself generally does not loan the money, and does, in fact, get paid immediately after students borrow money from financial institutions, and because the institution knows that students will likely be willing to borrow more money believing that the loans they take out will eventually be forgiven, the institution has an incentive to pass along increased costs to students in the form of additional tuition increases.

Thus, it is important to recognize that these proposals do not actually make college less expensive; they just reduce the cost to the student. Transferring the cost of higher education from the individual to a large group of taxpayers, increases the odds that the final total cost will increase. Under the plans being proposed, none of the banks are simply being told to take a hike. Under every proposal, the banks are paid back with taxpayer money, resulting in a move away from an educational system at least partially self-funded by students toward a system totally paid for by everyone. This is important because this "solution" fails to address a genuine underlying issue, high educational *costs*, not just the high borrowing. Without tackling the issue of why higher education costs so much in the United States, the system creates the need for someone to continue to pay a premium for the education that students obtain here. The presence of large amounts of student loan debt is not just an indication of people's willingness to borrow money, it is also an indication of the ease with which people can borrow student loan money because, of course, people can borrow student loan money without collateral because the loan is guaranteed in many cases by the United States government.

Finally, the most important thing is that high levels of student loan borrowing is an indication, and symptom, of the underlying cost of the education itself. After all, high borrowing for anything, whether it be cars, houses, or education, necessarily means that the original purchase underlying the debt was expensive to begin with, and that is ultimately the conversation that we as a country need to engage in with regards to education finance. Unfortunately, candidates are instead focusing on the immediate problem of the voter, which is having to write a check for student loan payments every month. While I do understand the desire to solve people's immediate problems, the proposals being put forth for solving these problems would, in my opinion, simply continue the problem into the future for other students, in a way that would actually accelerate the central problems surrounding education finance by driving education costs ever higher.

So, what is the solution? Well, I would suggest that the accreditors of colleges, which have a sort of ultimate authority for whether colleges continue to exist in most cases, should have stricter standards for the value that a college must provide to its students and other constituencies. Although accreditors do currently consider institutions' default rates, examine the success of graduates and consider other indicators of value, the truth is those standards could stand to be much more stringent. Likewise, in my opinion, colleges are not being held to task about the value they are providing. While accreditors are starting to attempt to do this more and more rigorously, there is still a long, long way to go. Ultimately, I hate to use words like "efficiency" because the ideals of efficiency and education do not always go together perfectly, but the fact is that what this country needs is an educational system that provides greater value for the money spent. While it is certainly true that many institutions provide excellent value and an excellent education to students, I would also argue that in many cases, the cost for that educational value is simply too high. So, the real challenge is to figure out how to provide the quality education that the United States is known for, at a cost that does not require people to mortgage their futures.

Increased return on investment. We can also work to improve the other side of the equation – the return on investment. I conceive of this quite broadly, in large part because students do. When my daughter decided to attend her university instead of the local community college, she did so not only because she believed that her degree would be more valuable but also because she was willing to spend money for the experience that she believed she would get by moving away and having a residential student experience at a large university. For her, this experience was part of what she was getting in exchange for what she paid, and indeed the data is overwhelming that the majority of residential, baccalaureate students, are seeking, and willing to pay for, "the college experience."

This means that we can change the equation by improving the student's college experience because that experience is part of what the student regards as a return on his or her investment. This is no secret – colleges caught on long ago that recruiting would be more successful if, for example, campus amenities were provided. I discuss this issue a bit later in this book, but for now, I will simply point out that finding effective ways to improve a student's experience provides a good medium-term recruiting advantage. Providing additional value to the student by providing more valuable degrees is a very separate issue. The effect is not as immediate: it takes time, resources, and cultural change to develop more impactful degrees, and even then, those degrees must be effectively marketed to students. There is a reason why colleges have historically offered new amenities, new extracurricular programs, and improved facilities at a faster rate than they have developed new academic programs – the former are considered to be the better (and faster) bang for the buck. This short-term thinking has created the situation in which higher education finds itself: students are paying at least as much for the experience they have while *in* college as they are for the degree they will carry with them *after* college.

Developing new student markets. The number of new student markets seems almost infinite. As new fields emerge, new technologies are created, new population demographics enlarge, and new delivery methods develop, there will always be people who want to learn, either by choice or by necessity. The primary impediment to exploiting new markets is cultural; as I described earlier, colleges have done things a certain way for a long time, and resistance to change is baked into the system in a myriad of ways. In addition, colleges do not always recognize opportunities in a specific instructional space if they are not already in that space. For example, a vocational school that lacks a culinary program might not recognize a state-wide need for more bakers, because the lack of a culinary program means that the school has no culinary-related curriculum advisory group to alert the school to the baking credentialing opportunity.

An excellent example of unique student market, and one that is of particular interest because both educators and the public have increasingly focused on it, involves the education of prisoners. Currently, there are about 2.5 million people incarcerated in the United States, but only a fraction of these inmates are eligible for college-level education funding (and an even smaller number actually receive it). Of course, because prisoners have little or no income, the most pressing issue becomes how their education should be funded and whether prisoners should receive access to a free, taxpayer-funded college education.

I understand that this is can be an emotional issue for taxpayers – in fact, I am not sure that I have ever met a taxpayer who did not almost automatically have an opinion on this subject. Although the topic of prisoner education has traditionally been somewhat of a niche subject in higher education, it has recently come to the fore for two very different reasons: 1) the continued accumulation of data supporting the overwhelmingly positive effect of education on recidivism rates among prisoners and 2) the continuing tightening in enrollment for colleges, which is projected to get worse over the next ten years, and which provides colleges with a strong incentive to leave no stone unturned in their quest to maintain enrollment levels. While this second reason obviously gives colleges generally, and administrators and admissions departments specifically, a reason to discuss the issue, the mounting data that we have about the benefits to prisoners and their families creates the opportunity and incentive to discuss the issue in an intelligent way outside of the arena of education administration.

When discussing the subject of providing college education for prisoners, invariably, one of the very first things that people ask is: Why should I pay for a college education for someone in jail? I would say that the simplest answer to those people is *because you are going to pay more if you do not provide a college education to that prisoner.* If you are concerned about the cost of the incarceration of prisoners and you are concerned about adding to that cost through education, the first thing you need to understand is that education reduces the total lifetime cost for incarceration of prisoners; it does not increase it.

Why is that? It is because the likelihood of a person re-offending is lower when they receive a college education while incarcerated and because re-offending is a major contributor to the total cost of a prisoner's incarceration over his or her lifetime. According to a 2018 Rand meta-analysis of the literature, inmates participating in correctional education programs are twenty-eight percent less likely to recidivate when compared with inmates who do not participate in correctional education programs. The United States Sentencing Commission found that inmates with less than a high school diploma had recidivism rates at a depressing sixty-or-greater percent while those inmates with a college degree had an overall recidivism rate of just nineteen percent – consider that – nineteen percent versus over sixty percent! In addition, there are tremendous economic benefits to providing prisoners with access to education programs. For every dollar invested in correctional education, governments save nearly five dollars in reincarceration costs over three years.

Risk and Reward

Of course, the economic benefits go beyond just not re-offending. People who receive a college education while incarcerated are going to be better able to become productive members of society. One study performed by researchers at the Vera Institute of Justice and the Georgetown Center on Poverty and Inequality in 2019 showed that providing prisoners with access to Pell grant funding would increase post-incarceration employment rates by ten percent and collective earnings by former inmates by $45 million in their first year after release. Imagine the ripple effect this could have on the lives of inmates, their families, and their communities.

Finally, the benefits of educating prisoners go well beyond the economic benefits that society would enjoy. Remember that recidivism means that a person is returning to prison because they have re-offended. If inmates do not re-offend that means, by definition, there is less overall crime. Offering incarcerated inmates educational opportunity means living in a society where there are fewer crimes, where people make more money and where society spends less to incarcerate offenders. Also, do not think for a minute that an educator is not going to point out that we would also be living in a society with a greater number of educated people, which is always a benefit to any society!

There are several ways to provide a college education to prisoners. While the most basic way would be to create education programs specifically for those prisoners, that is, to build the cost of educating prisoners into the cost of incarceration, I am not advocating for that. Actually, I do not know anyone who does advocate for that, because there are other, better ways to offer educational opportunities to inmates. The best way to offer education to inmates is to simply make the existing aid currently available to everyone else available to prisoners as well, making this less a proposal for some freebie for prisoners that the rest of the population cannot access, and more of a situation where society simply extends what is available to the general population to those who are incarcerated. Thus, in practice, the simplest option is to use federally available Pell grant funding along with any available state funding that is typically designed to replicate or supplement the Pell grant money which is generally available in most states. However, currently prisoners cannot receive Pell grant money and are generally ineligible for state grants, either because state law makes prisoners outright ineligible for grant money from the state government, or because states have enacted rules forbidding state assistance for education go to anyone who is ineligible for federal Pell grants.

Prisoners used to be generally eligible for federal Pell grants. The Pell Grant program was initiated in 1965 and offered undergraduates from low-income families financial assistance for various types of undergraduate study. In the beginning, there was no prohibition against prisoners receiving Pell grant money. In 1994, due primarily to a rise in the use of crack cocaine, there was a general political trend supporting a tougher stance on crime throughout the country. Both Republicans and Democrats were very keen to appear tough on crime, with Democrats (who were sensitive to the portrayal by Republicans as being soft on crime) in particular joining in support of legislation that appeared tough on crime. The 1994 Crime Act, which banned Pell grant eligibility for prisoners, was one such piece of legislation.

I can understand the desire to react to a high crime rate and, truth be told, in 1994 there was far, far less data available (to say nothing of the ability to analyze that data) regarding whether or not college programs were effective in reducing recidivism, or regarding the impact of education on the total cost of incarceration. However, that is not true today. Amid mounting data about the effectiveness of education among prisoners, advocacy groups have begun to push for restoring Pell grant funding eligibility at the federal level. In 2015, when the Obama administration created a pilot program called the Second Chance Pell Pilot Program, Pell grant funding for inmates was revived on a limited basis. Sixty-seven colleges and universities across the country were selected to receive funds in exchange for very careful tracking of data to measure the effectiveness of that program. Both the data, some of which I discussed earlier, and the narratives that came out of the program (both by the people who administered that program and the prisoners who were its beneficiaries) offer incredibly compelling evidence that this program should continue to be expanded.

In June 2016, the pilot program was expanded and as data began to accumulate and societal beliefs about those who are incarcerated primarily for drug-related offenses began to change, there has been a clear shift in public sentiment on this issue, including at the state level. For example, in 2014, New York Governor Andrew Cuomo experienced tremendous resistance to his proposal to offer free college education to prisoners. However, over a period of years that opposition diminished to the point that, in 2017, he was easily able to get approval to spend about seven million dollars to provide educational opportunity to inmates in correctional institutions throughout the state. The increased support for this program came about at least partly because of the existence of reliable data from the federal Second Chance Pell Pilot Program.

Things also continue to change relatively quickly at the federal level. In 2018, the Senate created the First Step Act, which promotes prison rehabilitation, which was endorsed by President Donald Trump. A group of bipartisan senators also introduced the Restoring Education and Learning Act (the REAL Act), a bill that would restore Pell Grant eligibility for prisoners throughout the country and restore eligibility for any state grants whose requirements are tied to federal grants. The REAL Act is winding its way through Congress, and although as of this writing in 2020 it still has not passed, I continue to remain very hopeful that ultimately it will pass.

In the meantime, there are some specific things that states and colleges can do even in the absence of federal regulation. I gave the example of New York, but other states have taken similar steps. North Carolina lawmakers introduced a bill that would make state-based scholarships available to incarcerated students. Michigan, which participated in the Second Chance Pell pilot program, is now considering similar legislation using language that would allow incarcerated students to access state scholarships. Other states are considering similar measures as well.

However, even in the absence of legislation, there are specific steps that colleges can take to acquire funding for incarcerated students. While Pell grants and some other forms of grants are unavailable to prison inmates, many jail inmates do qualify for these programs. In addition, funding programs are also available for other inmates who are on a GED pathway. Colleges can also create policies around institutional funding to allow access to educational funding while also creating policies that, for example, restrict funding to nonviolent offenders or use some other kind of criteria to address the specific concerns of local taxpayers.

The good news is that these programs can also be created in such a way to appear to be budget neutral. I say *appear to be* because I am going to give some cautions at the end, but essentially if an incarcerated student is (and I am going to oversimplify here) Pell-eligible, an institution can create a program that matches every hundred dollar increase in cost with a hundred dollar increase in Pell grant eligibility. The same approach could be used for almost anything that is a legitimate educational cost.

However, the downside to this is that it is not going to cover all the costs. After all, if Pell grant funding provided sufficient money to cover all of the costs of providing a college education, then there would be colleges that could operate solely with the support of Pell grants by simply charging eligible students the amount of their Pell grant award and using those funds to create balanced budgets. Unfortunately, students are nearly always shouldering only a portion of the total cost of their education, which ultimately means that even if, for example, an institution devises a program that applies Pell grants to students incarcerated in jails but not prisons, the institution will not be able to provide this educational opportunity to the student inmates without at least some local taxpayer money. As a result, an institution interested in providing educational opportunities to incarcerated students will eventually need to make the case for local or statewide taxpayer buy-in (depending on how the state finances higher education).

I hope that I have given you some reasons to think seriously about education for inmates not as a cost, but as an investment that reliably yields a positive return. But beyond the financial consequences, education for me is about human empowerment and human dignity. Providing educational opportunity allows prisoners to visualize possibilities for themselves that go beyond the possibilities that they may otherwise see for themselves especially when they are confined in prison. Likewise, providing educational opportunities allows inmates something constructive to do and this is actually one of the reasons why prisons that offer educational programs have been shown to have safer facilities for both the prisoners and the staff than those who do not emphasize educational programs. This country once recognized the value of education, even for those who were incarcerated, and provided federal funds to support that. I hope that the federal government and all fifty states will once again recognize that truth, and will return to the practice of funding education for anyone who would derive a benefit from it, not just because they derive a benefit, but also because society as a whole derives a series of very real, very measurable benefits as well.

Conclusion

My opinion is that for the foreseeable future, these four routes to higher enrollment (or the maintenance of existing levels shrinking markets) are the only effective tools that higher education has at its disposal. These recommendations – a more sophisticated online presence for colleges, increased workforce development, cost control, student return on investment, and the development of new student markets – are unaffected by the current pandemic we face in 2020, and in fact are made even more relevant.

CHAPTER 2

The Facilities Arms Race

Nowhere in higher education is the risk/reward relationship more evident, or more pervasive, than in the creation of new facilities. The competition for student enrollment has led to a specific phenomenon, a kind of "arms race" of college facilities. Facilities are expensive to start with, and because students select their colleges partly, or in some cases entirely, based on facilities, colleges repeatedly try to out-do each other in their facilities. Some of these facilities are academic, and so colleges can at least attempt to justify their existence and expense with the claim that they are directly supporting the educational enterprise (although this claim is highly suspect since it is not at all clear that educational outcomes have improved at the rate at which instructional facilities are improved). Other facilities, the ones that draw the most criticism but also draw the most students, are non-instructional and include everything from small, simple "safe spaces" to billion-dollar athletic complexes.

The institutions I have worked for have certainly not been immune to this issue. In my fourteen years at Alfred State College, we built over sixty million dollars in facilities, including new residential facilities, a new student union, a culinary facility that mimicked a fine dining restaurant, a football stadium, and lots of other smaller projects. In my eight years at Independence Community College, we built a veterinary technician center, a culinary lab, an adult basic education facility, a fabrication laboratory building, a weight room building, a new multi-use turf athletic field, a black box theater, and an additional residential facility. We also remodeled our student union, relocated and built a new bookstore, expanded our dining hall, converted all of our classrooms to smart classrooms, replaced one hundred percent of the physical IT network infrastructure, and completed dozens of other smaller facilities improvements. Some of these were required (like ADA improvements), but most were discretionary. Even some of the mundane maintenance items can be mind-blowingly expensive – wait until you see the bill to resurface an entire parking lot!

The explosion in facilities is not a fringe topic, nor is it one that has been ignored in most higher education circles as it is a concern familiar to almost all educators. As each college tries to outdo its neighbor, the cost for students to attend institutions of higher education continues to increase (because someone has to pay for all these improvements). Of course, higher institutional prices create higher expectations, leading students to compare the amenities offered by their institution to the amenities available at others, which prompts institutions to improve facilities, and the cycle continues. The trap is that as expectations increase, no individual institution has the option to throw up its figurative hands and say, "sorry, we just cannot afford to continue this vicious cycle of competition." After all, students at small community colleges expect to have the same essential services as those at a much larger institution – for instance, they expect that their wireless internet will be just as fast, just as reliable, and just as widely distributed as the wireless internet at any other institution.

One of the real ironies about the facilities arms race is that there will be ever fewer students to enjoy the facilities that we as an industry are continuously improving. In addition, many institutions have a substantial number of students who take online courses, and many have entire programs available entirely online. Of course, the students in those courses may live anywhere, and if they are not on campus, it is doubtful they are going to see, much less use, many of the facilities for which they are probably indirectly paying. (For some institutions, the coronavirus pandemic may accelerate the shift away from physical campuses, but it is too early to know the impact.)

The facilities arms race trap is frustrating on many levels: first, it clearly increases costs for students. Students currently pay for at least some portion of their education, including those costs incurred to build and run campus facilities. Loan payments for new facilities, as well as increased operating expenses when a facility is substantially expanded or a new facility is built, increases those costs. Moreover, the one type of building that tends to do the "best" with regards to covering its costs (sometimes actually generating a positive return) – the shiny new residence hall – usually does the best both because the ratio of paying students to paid employees is the lowest, and because living in a new residence hall nearly always costs students more than living in an older one.

Second, it requires expenditures on non-instructional spaces of dubious value. The questionable value of the facilities arms race becomes most apparent when an institution decides to improve or even build a facility without any data to indicate that the facility will be used in any meaningful way, and instead chooses to upgrade or build a facility simply because not doing so would be noticed and negatively commented upon. There are some kinds of facilities that are considered the markers of certain types of institutions, and if an institution wants to be seen as having a certain level of service or quality, it needs to have that marker. For example, some institutions build fitness centers even when other fitness options are nearby, or health centers even when health options abound in an urban setting. Higher education is not alone in facing this particular problem – a city manager once told me that it was critical for his city to have a golf course even if almost no one used it because the people considering relocation to the community from outside areas would evaluate the city differently if it was known as the "type" of community with golf courses. Likewise, a very similar argument was recently raised in my town to support the creation of a dog park. While I am actually quite sympathetic to these arguments (I am not criticizing them), it is important to understand that the facilities arms race surfaces outside of the context of education as well.

The addition of new facilities always results in additional costs to the institution, the students, or both. Although there may be a hypothetical situation in which an institution simultaneously has a way to pay for construction costs and set aside funds for deferred maintenance, while also setting aside funds for future operating expenses or generating enough revenue from the facility to cover its operating costs, I have never personally seen such a case, except perhaps in the case of residential facilities. Even in that case, I have not been able to find an example that did not at least increase costs for students. Rather, in the cases that I am familiar with, the financial consequences of new construction ranged from considerable to very considerable, with the best-case scenario being a situation where a donor or a state agency pays for the full cost of the building, and the activities in the new building create enough revenue to offset *most* of the new facility's operating expenses. Of course, that is the best-case scenario, and something I have only personally seen a few times. For example, at Alfred State College, we completely re-built and expanded our student union at a cost of tens of millions of dollars, a project we were able to persuade the state to fund. Yet, even in that case, there was no provision for the payment of the costs of true deferred maintenance, and there is certainly no plan for what to do when the building is at the point of replacement.

For those that might not know, deferred maintenance refers to the problem that arises when colleges and universities do not have adequate resources for building upkeep, including the costs for recommended servicing or upgrades to building systems, such as HVAC or electrical, or replacing components that have outlived their useful life, such as roofing or flooring. Deferred maintenance is one of those things that the business officers of colleges often worry about, but almost nobody in the public does. Yet, it is the largest unfunded liability of colleges, with the possible exception of pension debt (and since most state systems carry higher education pension liability on the state books instead of on the books of individual institutions, one could argue that deferred maintenance is actually the largest unfunded liability of individual campuses). Some individual schools have hundreds of millions of dollars in deferred maintenance, and some state higher education systems have tens of billions of dollars in deferred maintenance. Estimates vary, but in 2016 the total estimate of deferred maintenance for higher education institutions nationwide was thirty billion dollars, according to a poll of university facilities officers. However, I believe that the real number is actually much higher than this, probably about twice this amount at around sixty billion dollars. In my comparisons between published materials provided by various colleges and off-the-record conversations with maintenance directors, I have found that schools consistently underestimate or understate the amount of their deferred maintenance. In addition, if institutional deferred maintenance calculations also included the collective cost of replacing facilities at the end of their designed lifespan (they do not), the nationwide bill for the collective maintenance and replacement of its higher education faculties would come to nearly $180 billion.

Even knowing all of that, one of the arguments in defense of building new facilities is that donor funds are often paying for at least some portion of the costs associated with the building of these facilities. While true, there are many reasons why donor funding alone does not provide a sufficient response to the facilities arms race problem.

First, statistically, donors are only paying for a minority of the costs associated with building new facilities. Most states contribute far more to capital construction for their public colleges and universities than donors do. Second, even when donors contribute funds to build a new facility, they rarely contribute in any significant way to the continued operating and maintenance expenses for those facilities. Further, while colleges usually claim that a new facility generates some kind of additional revenue, either through increased enrollment or through fees or something else, that pays for the operating expenses, that is simply not the case – there is absolutely no way that institutions are correct in that

Risk and Reward

estimation even half the time! In fact, new facilities that can cover their own costs, including overhead, are so rare that institutions invariably brag about them when they do exist. I have encountered precisely two such facilities in my entire career (one was a bookstore, and the other was a dining facility that rented all of its space to various fast-food franchises). Finally, when considered from a thirty-thousand-foot institutional standpoint, the final, and most financially significant, issue is that even donor-funded facilities add to the deferred maintenance burden of campuses in the long term (and recall that deferred maintenance does not even include the most significant cost of all – the eventual replacement cost for the facility).

Significant to the issue of replacement cost is an understanding that the current lifespan of a commercial building is only fifty years – and colleges typically exist much longer than that, requiring that deferred maintenance considerations take into account the eventual necessity to fund facility replacement costs. Of course, one might object to the idea that the replacement cost of a college facility should be considered when building a new facility. After all, when a commercial building such as a McDonald's is built, the franchisee does not include the cost of the eventual replacement of the building in the calculation of the cost of the new enterprise. The reason for this in the case of a business enterprise is that it is assumed that the cost of new construction will be paid for by future sales after the new facility is constructed. Construction is not typically paid for through savings – it is paid for through a loan that is paid back after the facility is constructed, with income that exists because the facility was constructed and therefore generates revenue. However, public construction projects, including the building of college facilities, differ significantly from commercial projects in that educational institutions and public institutions do not typically turn a profit in the way that commercial enterprises do. (Residential facilities are a notable exception, but institutions often make the math work by simply charging students more money to occupy them.)

While this does not necessarily mean that the cost of a replacement building needs to be calculated at the time the original building is constructed, it does mean that colleges need to be aware that buildings have a finite life. Unlike the local McDonald's, which can be replaced often and easily, and where new construction may, in fact, be desirable, as things like the design of the restaurant changes to meet customer tastes or efficiency needs, higher education facilities have a much longer intended lifespan. Even more importantly, higher education institutions themselves have a much longer lifespan than the average business, and often there is a sense that an institution (although not its facilities) will exist indefinitely. My previous college in Kansas (a state which is neither particularly old nor particularly young relative to the age of our country) is nearly one hundred years old. Can the same be said about a private business? Rarely, as the average age of an S&P 500 company is less than twenty years old.

That said, one reason that the replacement cost of a building might not be as relevant to the initial equation regarding the financial wisdom of building a new facility is that having to sweat the replacement cost at the time of replacement is healthy. It is a rare construction project that is just a vanity project for a well-heeled donor – most donors want to create something of real educational, cultural, or social value, and as public dollars become scarcer, institutions are also becoming choosier in terms of the projects they support – and that process of choosing is healthy. On the other hand, it is beneficial for college leadership to remember that every new facility that a college builds using the excuse that a donor paid for it is really just a building that will have to be re-built in the future. Plus, the more expensive a facility was to build the first time around, the more expensive it will be to refurbish, rehab, or rebuild the second time around. The simple fact is that the more complex facilities an institution builds and the more maintenance it defers on those facilities, the bigger the day of financial reckoning will eventually be.

Risk and Reward

Residential Facilities

One of the most visible, expensive, and frequently constructed facilities built by institutions of higher education are residential. College residential facilities are common, expensive, experience high wear, and must be refurbished regularly. As a result, it is not always clear why a community college, which supposedly exists to serve the needs of its community, specifically its local community, would choose to build residential facilities so that students can live on-campus, especially when most of the student population at the college already live in the community. At every college for which I have worked, we have built new residential facilities, usually for very specific reasons and under very specific circumstances. I am generally quite skeptical about the need to build these facilities under many circumstances. As such, I am going to speak to the circumstances under which building new residential facilities is a huge mistake both financially and from a community relations standpoint, and the limited circumstances under which building these facilities is both appropriate and beneficial to the college and its community.

There are some very, very bad reasons to build new residential facilities. One of the worst possible justifications is as a means to boost enrollment – especially if a college is in a small community and thus has insufficient local students to support its general enrollment needs. When an institution is in a small community and does not have a lot of long-distance commuter students, it may seem like a good idea to relieve enrollment pressures by building residential facilities to attract new non-local students. However, this is generally a terrible idea. Residential facilities are expensive to build and almost certainly require that an institution take on debt (granted there are some very specific circumstances in which an institution does not have to take on debt, but those are pretty isolated circumstances and will not be discussed here). In most cases, financing these facilities means having to make debt payments regardless of whether or not the gamble for increased enrollment comes to fruition.

For example, if a college builds a facility with two hundred beds and it takes four years to get to full occupancy (not uncommon for a small school), it is a safe bet that during the majority of that time the college will lose money paying for the new facility. Even if the college manages to reach full occupancy, the truth is there is never any guarantee that it will maintain that occupancy. After all, enrollment waxes and wanes, both due to internal and external factors, which means that some years a college may suffer from low enrollment, particularly in its residential population, and every bed in its residential facility that is not occupied by a student is a bed that will ultimately have to be paid for by the college.

While obviously sometimes colleges need to make investments, the fact is a college needs to weigh the cost of each proposed investment against other potential projects that it could spend that same money on – the opportunity cost – and against the negative public perception that it will likely face when taxpayers learn what it has decided to spend taxpayer dollars to build student housing. Nevertheless, my research suggests that the majority of small rural colleges that build new residential facilities are doing so to boost enrollment. This is particularly egregious in a demographically small state like Kansas with a stagnant population, because it really just means that for the most part, the institution is spending a relatively large sum of money to compete against neighboring colleges for a finite number of students who live primarily within the same state. The only possible exception to this might be if the additional students are athletes coming from outside of the state, or non-local students who are drawn to enroll at the college specifically to participate in some well-known or unique program that it offers. This compound strategy can be used by colleges to increase enrollment – by creating additional sports teams or offering unique programs that allow for the recruitment of out-of-state or non-local students – while also simultaneously requiring the college to increase its residential options to meet the housing needs of those students. However, the problem with the decision to build residential facilities to attract students in general is that although the college may successfully compete for enough students to fill its new residential facility, the truth is most of those additional students were likely to get educated anyway. In effect, these students will receive an education, but at a higher cost because the institution had to build facilities to attract those particular students to its campus.

Another terrible justification for building residential facilities is to provide what is often referred to as the "college experience." Although there is a lot of research to support the idea that traditional college-age students truly crave a traditional college experience, I think this phrase is probably a misnomer for what is really just parental or hometown escapism. If you talk to students and drill down on what they are looking for in that "college experience," you will very often find that they are really looking for the opportunity to live on their own (i.e., not to live with their parents anymore). For example, my oldest daughter could have gone to community college locally, but she wanted to feel grown-up and independent, and did not associate living at home with her parents with being an independent adult and so she decided to go to a university that would allow her more parental independence.

As a result, I am very skeptical about the wisdom of building facilities simply because your research shows that students want that college experience because doing so often unnecessarily and negatively impacts the student's long-term return on investment. Living on campus, especially when compared to a more traditional community college enrollment structure in which students live at home and commute to college, dramatically increases the cost of education for students. While there are some circumstances in which paying this additional cost does make sense, for the most part living at home is much cheaper than paying for campus housing or rent. In addition, living on campus often comes with a variety of other fees, including the need to purchase food, which is in most cases prepared by someone else through a dining hall service, which is essentially the most expensive type of food students can purchase. Even those students who attempt to cook their own meals often struggle to meet all of their dietary needs on their own or may not even be allowed to cook for themselves at all due to various rules imposed by their institution.

Philosophically, spending millions of dollars to build residential facilities as a means of providing potential students with a traditional college experience is rarely going to be consistent with the overall mission of most community colleges, which are typically driven by other considerations. While it generally is the responsibility of a college to provide an education to any students who want it, it is not the responsibility of the local taxpayers to provide a traditional college experience for anyone who wants it no matter where they live if doing so means spending millions of dollars to build unnecessary college housing. In the end, a college living experience is something that students that want it badly enough, and can afford to pay for it, should seek out at institutions that already provide that service because ultimately the college experience is a luxury, not a necessity.

However, that is not to say that there are not some very good reasons for a college to decide to build student housing. Building residential facilities can provide student housing in areas that have no other affordable housing available to students. In some cases, non-traditional students, or even traditional students that for one reason or another cannot continue to live at home while attending college, may wish to continue to live in the area where the community college is located but there simply is no affordable housing. Although this situation is particularly prevalent on the coasts and in urban areas, it can also occur in small towns if the supply of available residential housing is generally inadequate to accommodate any significant increase in the number of students. In those cases, if a college is actively experiencing (or expecting) growth in its enrollment, and there is no affordable off-campus housing for students, the college might reasonably decide to engage in a project to provide affordable housing. After all, in terms of serving the local constituency, providing affordable housing, especially when it also provides increased stability for students seeking an education at the college, is probably going to be much closer to the mission of the college than many other potential facilities projects the college could choose to undertake.

Risk and Reward

By providing affordable housing, a college may also provide a secondary benefit to its students through a significant reduction in students' commuting time. Although those of us who do not live in communities with long commutes may not always fully appreciate this (as a college president in a small community, I lived close enough to walk to the college when so inclined), significant commuting times can dramatically reduce productivity. For instance, in the more densely-populated areas of California, some people commute an hour and a half or even two hours each way, which can clearly add up to a significant amount of "wasted" time (for example, more than 150,000 people in Los Angeles County alone spend over three hours commuting to and from work). While it is true that modern conveniences may allow commuters to be somewhat productive during that kind of downtime, perhaps especially when using public transportation (driving necessarily reduces one's options for worthwhile productivity), an especially long commute can significantly reduce a student's options by lessening the amount of time available to the student to work to earn an income, attend class and engage in educational activities like studying or doing homework. Thus, to whatever extent an institution can increase student productivity by reducing commuting time, it can also potentially improve its students' likelihood for success by assisting students to maintain employment to help fund their education or to spend time on their schoolwork so that they can be better students. While I fully understand that people in middle America may not be overly sympathetic to the argument for building housing to reduce commuting time, I can tell you that in urban areas, particularly on the coasts, the commuting time can make or break a career opportunity or educational experience.

Finally, another good reason to build campus housing is that it provides a social network for people that might not otherwise have one. At first glance, this might not sound like much of a reason to invest in college housing (and might sound like a vague, even irrational or touchy-feely rationale) but there is no question that a robust peer social network boosts student retention in colleges. On my podcast _The Mortarboard_, I have frequently discussed the abysmal student retention rates that are the reality for many colleges. The average American does not understand just how few students actually finish their college education – and anything that the higher education system as a whole can do to improve that statistic, in an affordable and sustainable way, and help students complete their education is a positive. By the way, improving student retention does not just help the students – it also makes financial sense for the institution because it is ultimately less expensive to retain a student than it is to recruit a new one.

As is probably apparent, there is a clear pattern emerging here. New residential construction at the community college level often makes more sense in growing urban areas than it does in more stagnant rural areas. Although building housing may make sense in growing urban areas, there are generally very few circumstances that justify building new residential facilities in small community colleges in stagnant rural areas. That is at least in part because the needs of a stagnant rural area, including whatever underlying reasons the area is economically or demographically stagnant, are very unlikely to be effectively addressed through the building of an expensive residential facility at the local college. Residential facilities are expensive to build and the decision to build new facilities should be approached very, very cautiously with full consideration of the opportunity costs of any other local opportunities for growth that may be lost. As such, an institution should carefully consider whether there might be more effective long-term projects into which the college might invest for the benefit of its students and the local community.

That said, there are definitely individual institutional circumstances that make building new residential facilities a sound financial investment for an institution, so long as the decision to invest in new campus housing is motivated by more than a simple desire to compete against other community colleges for the same students. In fact, the public, taxpayers, and even sometimes college employees often fail to completely understand the benefits that a strategic decision to build residential facilities can bring to a college and its local community, especially when doing so serves to benefit the college while also fulfilling a local, and sometimes even regional, educational or workforce need. For instance, when an institution is in a position to leverage the interests of people and industry outside of the service area of the college in a way that produces local graduates, and creates the opportunity for local students to enroll in a program that would not otherwise exist but for the opportunity to also recruit students from outside the local community to participate in that same program, there may be sufficiently adequate demonstrable growth in non-local student recruitment to justify adding to a college's existing residential facilities. So much the better when an institution finds a way to extend this model to multiple new programs, allowing it to spread the collective financial risk for both the building of new residential facilities and the creation of new programs across multiple industries and constituencies, while also encouraging a greater diversity of students, and additional opportunity for increased occupancy in its residential facilities.

As an example, at Independence Community College, one of the programs that the College was able to develop, both as a means of enhancing its program offerings for the local community and justifying its decision to build additional college housing, was its veterinary technician program. The conversation about adding the program originally arose because several local veterinarians were having trouble finding veterinary technicians. For those who may not know, veterinary technicians are essentially to the veterinary field what physician's assistants are to the medical field – they fulfill many of the roles and perform many of the procedures that veterinarians do not necessarily have to perform themselves. Because local veterinarians simply could not find people to fill these positions locally, and because there was only one other public veterinary technician program in the entire state of Kansas (a geographically large state with a robust agricultural industry), the argument was made that the College could create a program that would enable it to recruit students from outside the College's service area, in a way that would justify offering a program that would also supply veterinarian technicians to the local veterinary industry. However, given the size of the Independence community, and the relatively small demand regionally for veterinary technicians (maybe a combined need for five new veterinary technicians annually) it was absolutely crucial that the program be able to attract non-local students to remain viable.

The creation of the veterinary technician program at the College was successful because of a very specific set of circumstances. The program itself was well-conceived as a technical program for the College as there was both a clear need for the program and an obvious market for it. Because of the cost to support technical programs, there typically needs to be donors willing to step up and in the case of veterinary technician program, the College had a very small focused capital campaign that allowed it to adequately equip a new veterinary technician facility. As a result, the College was able to begin the new program without having to finance much of the program's initial capital outlay from the College's budget, limiting its initial investment in the program to personnel costs, and allowing the College to serve a very limited number of local students and attract numerous non-local students all while remaining a viable program at the College – even in its infancy. Significantly, the College was able to convince its local taxpayers to subsidize a program that would primarily educate non-local students by providing both an educational and financial benefit to local industry and tapping into the benefits that non-local students can bring to a local economy – the payment of increased tuition rates and the opportunity for non-local dollars to increase local economic activity.

The veterinary technician program at the College was a great example of one of the ways enrollment strategies can work together to satisfy a clear educational need, while also supporting an institution's investment in residential facilities. At the same time, it is important to understand that the veterinary technician program at the College was successful in large part because it was not introduced simply to boost enrollment or justify the building of additional housing. The program was developed in direct response to a verifiable local workforce need and as an attempt to satisfy a demonstrated workforce need for a specific skill across the state of Kansas. As an aside, in this particular case, the College went one step further to reduce its financial risk with regards to the building of new student housing (because it was unwilling to absorb the construction costs to build a new residence hall) by contracting with an outside organization to build and operate the new residential facility, limiting the College's financial exposure to the payment of an operating fee calculated as a percentage of the facility's occupancy.

How do these considerations apply to institutions that do not currently have residential facilities? This is often a far more difficult issue to address than those previously discussed as it is obviously much more challenging to transition from being a completely non-residential commuter institution to offering residential options, than it is for a residential college to decide to increase its already existing residential footprint.

Several justifications are offered for moving to a residential-style school. Some of these justifications involve some very real benefits while other justifications are generally overstated. The first and most significant reason is always the anticipated – and often overestimated – increase in enrollment. Most institutions overestimate how quickly a new residential facility will yield an increase in enrollment. Typically, the only case in which additional enrollment from college housing facilities can be clearly justified is when the college is already over capacity – which necessarily requires that they already have a residential program. As an example, for several years, Independence Community College actually placed students in local hotels at the start of each semester, allowing a certain statistically expected number of students to drop out, before transitioning those students from hotels into available on-campus housing. Obviously, in that kind of situation, an institution can calculate fairly precisely its expected capacity for a new facility, even if enrollment remains unchanged. Even so, in my experience, most institutions tend to understate by about fifty percent the amount of time it will take to fill a new residential facility. For an institution moving from having no residential facilities to becoming a residential institution, it is even more difficult to make accurate projections about enrollment and potential occupancy in new campus housing facilities. After all, an institution without an established reputation for offering residential options will not be a natural destination for many students interested in a residential experience. As a result, the institution will need to be careful to make very conservative projections about how long it might take for a residential facility to reach, not just full capacity, but even just a capacity in which the new residential facility is not a drain on the institution financially.

Another justification that is often offered as a benefit of moving to a residential platform is that it will enable the college to offer new programs. For example, in the case of rural community colleges, there may not be enough local commuter students to develop a particular program, but with enough residential students, there might be sufficient critical mass to offer that program. While that can be a good argument, the institution will need to determine how to accurately calculate the cost of the program, which will necessarily include both the costs to develop the new program AND the costs to convert to a residential platform in order to make that program work. Somehow, the institution must factor the cost of becoming a residential college into its cost-benefit calculation for the new program and its decision about whether to move toward becoming a residential college. Likewise, an institution must understand that moving toward becoming a residential college involves expenses outside just the cost of building new facilities as there are many other costs associated with being a residential institution.

A final and truly excellent benefit of becoming a residential campus is that doing so provides increased opportunity for diversity within the student body, especially for a small rural community college. It is certainly true that small rural community colleges that predominately serve commuter students from its surrounding service area, are often going to attract a fairly uniform group of students. Whereas institutions with housing facilities can recruit students from a much wider area – even internationally – which provides a college with the opportunity to create as diverse a student body as it would like, depending on the financial and other resources it decides to invest in that effort. Thus, student housing can provide the necessary capacity for an institution to reshape its student body into one that is more diverse, and the research is pretty clear that a diverse student body produces a better educational experience for all students. Finally, a related, but somewhat different justification often given for moving away from a non-residential format towards a residential platform involves a desire to provide students with a traditional college experience. The assumption is that there are students, perhaps even local commuter students, who would prefer to live on campus. For all the reasons previously discussed, I am suspicious of this justification because while it certainly may provide something that students want, it is not necessarily an educational improvement. It is more of a lifestyle experience, and I am not sure, especially for a taxpayer-supported institution, that it should be used to justify additional costs for the local taxpayer.

In addition to potential benefits, there are also some very real potential drawbacks to moving a college to a residential platform, including some very real financial costs. In many cases, the full extent of the financial cost that an institution will incur is relatively unknown, and in my experience, is almost always understated. Some of these costs are completely obvious, including the construction of the residential facility itself and calculations about whether the college will reach an occupancy sufficient to cover the costs of that construction within a given timeframe. However, other potential costs are much less obvious. For instance, does the college have campus security? I am going to suggest that if an institution is strictly a small commuter campus in a rural area, it is very likely that it will not have a traditional security department. As a residential campus, it will absolutely need to have security of some type. Depending on the size of the residential housing facilities and the college's precise circumstances, that security need could range from hiring private security that minimally patrols the institution all the way up to creating a police force. There is obviously a wide range of costs associated with these different options, and every one of them is significant. Likewise, does the institution have dining facilities capable of handling the increased capacity? For instance, at Independence

Community College, hundreds of students live on campus, and those students are accommodated in a dining hall that was originally designed to serve only ninety students. Obviously, the College has had to enlarge its dining facilities (and absorb the costs of increased dining hours) to accommodate feeding all of the students housed in its residential facilities.

Not only are there significant financial implications for an institution to consider, but there are also some cultural considerations that an institution must consider. When a college elects to become a residential campus, it takes on the responsibility of caring for students on an all-day, everyday basis throughout the academic year. Residential institutions require additional staff – especially in the areas of student and residential life personnel and counseling and even medical services. In addition to caring for students' health and safety needs, the institution will also be responsible for ensuring that the emotional (and entertainment) needs of its students are met. For instance, rural community colleges with residential students need to provide student life activities for those students, as rural colleges will often find that entertainment opportunities and student life activities do not just present themselves organically. Beyond providing a wide variety of activities to satisfy the needs of a diverse residential population, the college will also need to provide access to things like transportation (such as to and from airports), shopping and even medical care.

Thinking about student needs in this way requires a shift in culture, but a culture shift will also occur in other ways – including community relations. Although nobody likes to think about this, one has to consider the potential that a college's local community may react to an influx of non-local students in an unexpectedly xenophobic manner. If an institution imports hundreds of students from other states and even from other countries, the local population may have something to say about that (the reaction may be positive or it may be negative), and college leaders must consider what that reaction might be in advance and prepare for it. Likewise, although nobody likes to think about racism within their own community, it is also important to consider to what extent the local community is racially tolerant. In a community that is not naturally racially diverse, it may be very difficult or even impossible to avoid race issues if the college begins recruiting from racially diverse locations, and college leaders will need to be prepared to address those issues both in the community and even within the institution itself. Finally, the institution will need to assist its community in coming to terms with using their tax dollars to support an institution that is educating a greater number of non-local students. Although people may initially believe that non-local students will "pay their own way," the truth is at public institutions that is very, very rarely the case. Although it may be the case that international students pay all of the costs associated with their education, typically the education of domestic students requires a direct or indirect taxpayer subsidy to help cover the costs of that education. But even *if* those students are paying their own way, there will be a percentage of the population that does not know that, and who will assert incorrectly that they are paying for the education of a group of people who have come into the community, taken advantage of a taxpayer-subsidized educational opportunity and then left without ever contributing anything beneficial to the local community or its economy.

Ultimately, an institution that decides to move from being a commuter institution to a residential campus is going to have to educate its community regarding the costs and benefits of recruiting residential students. Because unfortunately if the institution does not make the effort to educate its community, incorrect information will flow in to fill that vacuum (after all, nature abhors a vacuum). In a short section of a single chapter of this book, I can only hope to offer the most general of warnings about the cultural changes that will take place by emphasizing that those changes will be profound. The very nature of the institution itself will be changed, as will the perception of the institution by the very people who are funding it. Finally, if the institution fails to adequately maneuver that cultural transformation, the actual financial cost of a housing project for the institution, and the taxpayer, will increase. After all, if the residential experience for students suffers, the institution's ability to retain its current students and recruit new students will also suffer, leading to a reduction in the occupancy within student housing, and creating increased costs for the institution.

In summary, I will just say that while there are certainly circumstances that justify the building of new residential facilities on a college campus as a sound financial investment, college leadership should be quite skeptical of claims that it can increase institutional enrollment by simply building housing facilities that are so gorgeous that no one can resist living at the college. The fact is that many institutions build beautiful residential facilities and using that strategy as a means of increasing enrollment simply leads institutions into a facilities arms race that results in a vicious cycle of competition that cannot be won. For the same reason, it is a mistake to build housing facilities merely to provide students with a traditional college experience. Both of those rationales for building facilities – an increase in enrollment and providing a traditional college experience – tend not to correlate very well with the missions of most colleges and (although college missions vary widely), I have rarely seen a mission statement that would directly support building facilities for either of these specific reasons.

Academic Libraries

Libraries represent both a serious challenge and a source of opportunity for colleges. Although all academic libraries face *some* of the same challenges and opportunities, my focus here is specifically on the experience of small college libraries, and not necessarily libraries at large research universities.

Because some of my comments about the current state of college libraries might come across as pessimistic or even outright negative, it would probably be a good idea for me to take a moment to establish my personal credentials to avoid any suggestion that I am some kind of library-hater. Most importantly, my wife is a librarian, and in the interest of marital harmony, she read (and approved!) the draft of this chapter long before its publication (as you can imagine, I dare not overstate or say anything unfair to the profession because I will suffer terribly for that). In addition, I live in a community that cares deeply about its libraries. The town where I live, Independence, Kansas, is home to a library that just a few years ago was named the *Best Small Library in America*. Our community has excellent school libraries, community libraries, and there is very strong financial, cultural, and volunteer support for the library in the community. My wife and I personally donate to our local library, the college library here, and to the library of our alma mater. The main library in Independence is just about a block and a half from my house. My family and I use the library all the time and I often volunteer at the local library. As a frequent patron of the library, I have a deep appreciation for librarians and the hard work that they do (and I am not just saying that because I am married to one). Librarians work very hard and a lot of people do not really understand what it is that they do.

That said, one of the problems libraries currently face relates to the fact that people generally do not have a very good understanding of the work of libraries do and the role that librarians play. Of course, it is very difficult for people to be supportive of something they do not understand. Most people have a traditional conception of a library as a book repository, which no longer has wide appeal, especially as the vast majority of books (at least in the college library in the town where I live) are never taken off the shelves. Library collections are weeded all the time, getting smaller and smaller and smaller, primarily due to disuse. I was recently at another community college library and asked the librarian (this was on a Thursday), how many books had been checked out over the past week and she told me that not a single book had been taken out that week. While I understand that the plural of anecdote is not data, I do think that it is pretty interesting when you could have a college library with thousands and thousands of books and there is not even one person who has taken advantage of borrowing even one of those books from the library. If then, libraries are not merely or even primarily book repositories, what core purposes do libraries serve?

Virtually every library provides a source for internet access, especially in the case of community access libraries, but also for college libraries. Many students may not have their own computers and may need to access the internet in ways that are very cumbersome on a smartphone. Yet, although this allows the college library to serve a very useful purpose, providing internet access is not inherently a function of the library, as the college could provide internet access in many other ways that do not require the use of a vast physical space with thousands of books and trained librarians and so forth. Thus, while libraries clearly do provide internet access, they are not the sole method by which a college must provide that access. In addition to providing internet access, college libraries also provide a quiet place for students to study. Unfortunately, a library is a very expensive way to provide a quiet place to study and ultimately the argument against the conception of libraries as study spaces is the same as it is for internet access. If you think about all that is going on in a library, simply to provide a quiet place to study, it suddenly seems as if it is a very elaborate setting. I will point out that in the case of both internet access and a quiet place to study, this rationale is typically used as an argument for preserving libraries, but never to build them. People will say that the library is very important because it provides internet access or provides a quiet place for students to study (both are true), but no one ever says, "we need a place for internet access, and we also need a quiet room for people to study – let's build a library."

Libraries clearly provide services such as entertainment, meeting spaces, instructional space, and although these things obviously have real value, none of them are, once again, inherent to the mission of the library – they are services provided by the library because the library is already there, and its presence within the college or community is conducive to the provision of those services. For example, because the library already loans out books, it seems reasonable to extend that to other forms of entertainment, such as DVDs, and to allow people to borrow DVDs in the same way they borrow books. Likewise, because the library has tables and quiet spaces, it naturally seems like the kind of place for a meeting and because it has a place where you can interact with students without disturbing others in the library, it seems to be an ideal instructional space. But again, just because all of these things are what people use the library for (because the library is available and serves those purposes well), does not mean that people would necessarily build a library for those same purposes.

It is this struggle for relevance that libraries (and librarians) are struggling with and that libraries and colleges recognize as a central problem – and one that they discuss all the time. If you go to a library conference, you can pretty much assume there will be workshops on techniques and ideas for making the library relevant (note that if you went to an IT conference, you would not see such workshops). Another symptom of this concern and evidence that libraries and colleges know there is a problem is that typically the metrics that libraries use to justify their existence are based on inputs like traffic, and not necessarily on value-added metrics. For example, a library reports that X number of people came through the library over a period of time to show that a lot of people use and benefit from the library. However, further research suggests that the library has worked very hard to encourage people to use it as an instructional space or a group or quiet study space, by bringing people in to use the computers for internet access or encouraging students to visit the library by creating assignments that specifically require library access, so that it is not entirely clear how much of the use of library space is something that is occurring organically versus something that is being artificially generated and measured. Furthermore, even if the increase in usage is occurring organically and shows an increasing interest in using the library, accounting for the number of people that merely access the library space certainly does not necessarily measure whether, and to what extent, the library is providing any value-added services to the college community. You can see evidence of other ways that libraries, librarians and even colleges are responding to concerns around the current and future relevance of the library. For instance, pick up any trade publications from higher education to read stories about librarians unionizing or go online to read about librarians fretting about or even writing articles about whether or not the libraries they work with are taking adequate measures to remain relevant. Likewise, it is clear that colleges are not building new libraries, unless perhaps there is a very specific donor project involved, as colleges are certainly not willing to invest their own funds into building new libraries.

Finally, the libraries that exist are shrinking. Hard data is tough to come by on this, but a survey of twenty small colleges across the United States regarding the amount of physical space devoted to the library found that out of twenty college libraries, sixteen have reduced the total amount of space devoted to traditional library services. The shrinking of library space can occur in a couple of different ways. Sometimes a part of the library is absorbed into another function of the college. For example, a community college relatively near Independence in southeast Kansas moved their bookstore into the library itself. The design of the bookstore is such that in the middle of the library, with no walls separating the bookstore from the library functions, the college sells textbooks along with sweatshirts and t-shirts and other merchandise. By coincidence, even my previous institution, Independence Community College, removed about twenty percent of the physical space devoted to the provision of library services, in order to move the bookstore into the same building as the library. As a result of this transition, the library became smaller. We were comfortable with the space reduction for the library because we had done some studies to determine the appropriate square footage of library space per student, and the college's library space was still above the average. Although we were comfortable taking away that space to provide the benefit of increasing the accessibility of the bookstore to students and the community, the library did get smaller. Similarly, my research unearthed no examples of a college choosing to enlarge its library except in cases where the size of the institution itself was growing.

Given all of these dismal statistics, one might begin to wonder why academic libraries continue to exist, and yet, there are actually some very important purposes served by academic libraries, some of which are very well known and others which are much less widely known:

Risk and Reward

The most obvious reason academic libraries continue to exist is that academic libraries *do* serve all the purposes previously discussed. Academic libraries are a repository for various types of books and other materials, both scholarly and otherwise, that people might not otherwise be able to access. Libraries also provide internet access to students and others who might not otherwise have reliable or adequate access (especially in the case of a small, rural college with a large number of low-income students). The college library also allows for a quiet place to study and other services like entertainment opportunities and meeting and instructional spaces. Regardless of your general opinion about libraries, there is really no question that most of these functions of the college library have value, and that an institution would need to find another way to provide those services even in the absence of a library. Likewise, most academic libraries also serve the public, which is something that is certainly not emphasized by institutions and by academic libraries themselves, but it is a fact that most academic libraries and certainly the academic libraries that are at public institutions are typically available or open to the public. While that does not mean that all of the services that are available at an academic library are available to the general public, it does typically means that the public can enter and use the facilities and avail themselves of some of the general services the library has to offer. In the same way, the library also serves to promote the access mission that drives most public institutions (i.e., the mission of most public institutions to provide educational access to members of the public regardless of the ability of the public to pay for that access). The provision of these traditional library services is one of the most effective ways to go about fulfilling that mission because the fact is if someone is of modest means financially, he or she may not be able to afford access to certain services (e.g., a subscription to the local newspaper or reliable internet access) but may be able to access those services at an academic library, which in turn allows libraries to provide a kind of leveling effect through the provision of general access to certain services that might otherwise be unavailable to certain people.

A second function of academic librarians, and one which is very much unappreciated by the public, is professional curation. A hundred years ago, information itself was difficult to come by, whereas nowadays the exact opposite is true – information is very, very easy to come by – and so librarians are called upon to make library resources more accessible to the general population, in order to enhance our understanding of the information provided and create more efficient and time-effective means of accessing information. Librarians curate the information in their library by selecting and organizing and generally caring for items both in specific collections housed by their library and more generally in the entire collection of books and resources owned by their respective library. Through their knowledge of the use of the library, librarians both acquire new and remove old materials from their libraries' collections based on that expertise and their unique knowledge of various trends and/or the unique tastes of their patrons. The curating of materials most often surfaces in the handling of special collections that a library is responsible for, such as a donated collection of papers and writings or other works by a famous or otherwise important person. However, librarians also curate the entire collection of materials held by a library, including collections that people may be very fond of, and may even use regularly. For example, during my time there, the most popular collection of materials at the Independence Community College library was the DVD collection. Thus, librarians spend a great deal of their time thinking about what materials should be included in a particular collection based on the wants and needs of the patrons that frequent their library. Curation is just one of many of the valuable tasks that librarians perform, but I find it is one of the roles of the librarian that is least understood or appreciated by the general public.

Finally, a much less widely known reason for the continued existence of the academic library (even though it is probably actually one of the most important factors in the preservation of academic libraries as they exist today, especially at the community college level) involves regional accreditation. Without accreditation, an institution cannot receive federal financial aid, which means for most colleges (and certainly all public colleges), accreditation is essential as the institution absolutely cannot afford to operate without federal financial aid for its students. There are also several other reasons that an institution wants accreditation (accreditation is an important part of a peer-review process and thus is a valuable learning experience for any school), but it is important to understand that no matter how important accreditation is, it is also the financial lifeblood of most institutions.

In the United States, there are seven main regional higher education accrediting bodies, each of which provides accreditation to institutions in different parts of the country. Each of these accrediting bodies have different standards, which vary considerably both in their general standards and in the way their standards apply to libraries. For example, the Higher Learning Commission, which accredits a large number of colleges throughout the northern central states, including my previous institution in Kansas, has no specific section on the regulation of libraries although it does mention libraries in its general section on "Teaching and Learning" standards. Likewise, both the Middle States Commission on Higher Education and the New England Association of Schools and Colleges have no specific section in their standards for the regulation of libraries, although libraries are specifically mentioned in four different standards in Middle States' criteria and two different standards in New England's criteria. In addition, while the Western Association of Schools and Colleges, which covers the Pacific States of California and Hawaii, has no specific section on libraries, it does mention both libraries and information literacy. In contrast, the Northwest Commission on Colleges and Universities specifically dedicates the second section of its criteria to the regulation of library and information resources in addition to mentioning the regulation of libraries in another standard. The Southern Association of Colleges and Schools Commission on Colleges dedicates a section and a subsection of their standards to the library and other learning resources in addition to mentioning libraries elsewhere in its standards. Finally, the Accrediting Commission for Community and Junior Colleges dedicates an entire section of its standards to the library and learning support services. As you can see, each accreditor includes some level of guidance related to the regulation of academic libraries.

However, the role of accreditation in the regulation of academic libraries goes beyond even that because, at least at most colleges, libraries provide a wide range of academic and other services. If an institution were to tamper with its provision of those services, it could be sanctioned if its accreditor were to conclude that doing away with the library services resulted in a reduction of some crucial academic or student service. In practice, the reduction of library programs or services, which one would assume would have passionate supporters who are unhappy to see the role of the library reduced, deactivated, or changed, would likely result in complaints to the accreditors that the institution had lost its commitment to academics and the student services provided by the library. Once notified of the change, the accreditors would begin to review that decision, and if the institution could not justify its actions to a skeptical regulatory audience, its accreditors would very likely sanction the institution for the change.

Ultimately then there are some accrediting bodies that out-and-out require an institution's library to meet certain standards. However, even more common are the academic or student life standards that make tampering with or altering your institution's library services risky because it subjects the institution to criticism, based not on whether you have an adequate library, but whether or not you are providing adequate services to students. These services can range from providing a sufficient information literacy component to students' education to having adequate study space or providing sufficient types of entertainment outlets for students. In these ways, the library helps colleges meet accreditation standards and if those things are altered, a college may be found to have not met those accreditation standards.

Despite the clear benefits that academic libraries provide, there are also limitations that the higher education community needs to address immediately. First, accreditors need to think differently about libraries. One of the purposes of accreditation is to preserve the benefits of

Risk and Reward

American higher education, a system that is often the envy of the world. However, if you look carefully at the requirements for libraries contained in many accreditor's standards, you will find two very real issues: 1) accreditors' conception of the purpose of libraries is, for the most part, antiquated, and 2) accreditors assume an explicit need for libraries regardless of the outcomes they are producing, which paralyzes colleges that may want innovate or experiment with alternative ways to meet academic and student needs. Second, higher education as a community needs to have a conversation about the future of libraries. That conversation must be facilitated by librarians but must also be a collaborative effort that moves beyond librarians, as the lone voice in the wilderness, and creates real conversations between librarians and other campus partners and advocates.

Denise Troll, a distinguished fellow at the Digital Library Federation, and an assistant university librarian at Carnegie Mellon, spoke to the need for real conversation around this issue when she wrote in 2001: "If we're not diligent, the speed of change will inhibit, if not paralyze, attempts to make sense of what's happening in libraries and intervene for the good of our constituencies." What she described is exactly what has come to pass, as change has not slowed down but instead has sped up and has truly interfered with the ability of the constituencies of libraries to understand both the role of the library in our current society and the opportunity for innovative change and growth for libraries in the future.

We can make an analogy between small college libraries and shopping malls. Both are physical facilities that are prevalent throughout our infrastructure. Both serve distinct audiences and tend to be open to all. Both seek to serve people in a variety of ways and have a core service they have traditionally provided. Both require a great deal of space. Most significantly, both are experiencing a migration of consumers away from the services they traditionally provided, as the internet has increasingly found ways to approximate or replace those services in ways that people find more convenient, less restricted, or otherwise more desirable. As a result, both are attempting to find ways to reach new audiences as their traditional market shifts away, and a failure to adapt necessarily means a reduced role in our society.

With regard to libraries, that should be a national conversation. It may be that the single greatest obstacle the library faces is nostalgia. When my wife Carin and I gave a gift to the local public library, it allowed us to attach a message to the gift. We chose a quote from Carla Hayden, who was a librarian of Congress and a former president of the American Library Association: "Libraries are a cornerstone of democracy where information is free and equally available to everyone." That quote certainly resonates with me, but I wonder how much of that quote is describing libraries fifty years ago versus libraries today. I am not sure. But I do know that things have changed, and my emotional attachment is to the libraries that I grew up with. Many people who feel strongly about libraries that I have talked to seem to feel the same way. That nostalgia is something that we have to free ourselves from if we are to make academic libraries the vibrant intellectual places that they were fifty years ago.

Conclusion

Schools are creating facilities to compete for students, but it is not clear to me that what will successfully compete for students today will match the needs of students during the lifespan of those facilities. Specialized buildings like residence halls, academic labs, or athletic facilities are not like a student life program that can be activated and deactivated in a relatively short timeframe. These facilities represent a decades-long commitment of resources, for both the construction and maintenance of that facility, along with human resource costs for its operation. A facility is a bit like a financial bet regarding the physical needs of the campus thirty years from now. In my opinion, bets based on future student headcount are wild guesses at best (and usually wildly optimistic in light of the long-term data), and bets made purely for competitive reasons are based on immediate competitive needs rather than the likely long-term needs of the campus. Colleges are trapped, competing for students now using methods that will tie the institution's hands later. Colleges should approach the creation of new facilities with a healthy skepticism – no doubt, future leaders will appreciate the foresight and restraint shown by the leaders of today.

CHAPTER 3

Competing with Other Colleges for Faculty

The vast majority of teachers with whom I have worked in my career were dedicated, hardworking professionals who truly cared about their students. Often, people migrate toward teaching because they rightfully see teaching as a noble profession and want to share in the experience of creating a greater good. Teaching is a noble profession, but the nobility of teaching alone does not create excellent teaching performance, nor does it necessarily reward excellence. Teachers know that high-quality teaching is the result of training, passion, and time devoted to preparation. Not all teachers have adequate training. Not all teachers are provided sufficient time by their employer to prepare adequately for class, and not all teachers have the mentorship, tools, or desire to be top performers. Caring about students is not the same as being a skilled teacher.

Because the nobility of teaching does not automatically lead to high performance, this also means that the nobility of teaching does not automatically lead to a performance distribution that is anything other than a standard bell curve. There are millions of teachers in the United States, and those teachers come from a variety of backgrounds, have vastly differing levels of ability, and teach in diverse types of working conditions that may actively encourage or discourage high-performance. As a result, teaching performance has a distribution that one would expect: a relatively small number of truly excellent teachers, a large number of teachers somewhere near the middle of the performance spectrum, and a relatively small number of low-performing teachers. That said, when drilling down into teaching performance metrics for specific states, municipalities, and school districts, the bell curve does get distorted. For example, a school district may have a poor record of documenting poor performance or acting on that documentation, which allows poor performing teachers to persist in their jobs, and encourages high performing teachers to leave because they do not want to work in that environment. Anecdotally, it seems that this type of situation is becoming less common as 1) better evaluation and record-keeping tools are available, 2) information about poor performance becomes more accessible to the public, and 3) schools begin to grasp that with poor employee practices comes increased liability.

At the college level, recruiting the best teachers is especially challenging because teachers lead double lives in the workplace: they need to teach, and they need (or at the very least want) to conduct research in their fields. Sometimes, this research is a requirement of their position, whereas in other situations, it is merely recognized or rewarded during the evaluation process. Regardless, college faculty as a group tend to be more focused on their disciplines than K-12 teachers. That is not to say that K-12 teachers are unconcerned about subject matter currency, but it is less common and rarely required to be demonstrated through scholarship. Instead, K-12 teachers tend to be more focused on teaching pedagogy as it relates to their disciplines, whereas college faculty tend to be equally focused on pedagogy and scholarship or research. As a result, colleges need to demonstrate to teachers that professional development is supported, even when that development only indirectly benefits students or teaching ability.

At Alfred State, I routinely participated in faculty recruiting efforts, primarily for the department of English and Humanities, but also for other areas on occasion. At Independence Community College, my role in the faculty recruitment process was both far more involved and also less formal. Shortly after my arrival, I deliberately hired a far more aggressive recruiter as HR Director, and the College began a campaign to actively seek out the best new faculty it could find in two specific ways: First, the College dramatically increased the pay for its teachers. When I arrived at the College, the faculty salary schedule was in the bottom quartile for the entire community college sector in Kansas. Within four years, the salary schedule was in the top quartile, and the College had the highest base pay of any community college in southeast Kansas. Dramatically increasing faculty salaries allowed the College to make the case to outstanding teachers that it recognized the skills of its faculty and actively wanted to both reward and retain high-performing faculty. Second, the College rigorously screened new applicants, requiring outstanding teaching skills – as evidenced through multiple teaching demonstrations and other quantifiable measures of those skills, including proficiency in their field and demonstrable ability to adapt to the different learning styles and varying levels of student proficiency that are a hallmark of open-access institutions. The result was dramatic, and within five years of my arrival at the College, a state study found that students who transferred from the College to four-year institutions had better outcomes than students from any other community college in Kansas.

Following the dramatic change in faculty recruitment practices, the College discovered that the excellent faculty it hired were also more likely to remain at the institution. In addition, because student success is not merely a matter of good hiring, and continued faculty development is absolutely critical, both for improving learning outcomes and for the retention of good teachers, the College committed to doubling its funding for faculty professional development across campus, with the majority of a separate discretionary budget line dedicated to faculty support. Finally, I revived the practice of sabbaticals for faculty to allow them to pursue interests within their disciplines, a practice that had been discontinued nearly a decade before I arrived at the College.

In my experience, professions tend to reward top performers in one of two ways – monetarily (as in say, baseball), and in ways that are largely unrelated to pay (as in say, custodians). At the College, we did not have the option of paying top-performing faculty more than their peers because, lamentably, while our contract with the faculty included options for penalizing poor performance, it offered no incentives for superior performance. In New York, the statewide teaching contract did have a small bonus system, but it was poorly conceived – too small to make exceptional faculty feel appreciated or to make much real difference to them. As a result, it made everyone feel bad: those receiving a bonus felt it was inadequate, and those who did not receive a bonus felt slighted. I have gradually become convinced that while paying faculty for outstanding work is theoretically desirable, implementation would require a truly rigorous evaluation system that genuinely distinguishes among teachers, while also factoring out issues beyond individual faculty member's control. I have yet to see a system that contains all of these elements.

Competition for faculty is complicated by the rural nature of many small community colleges. The opportunity for a quality education is essential for the development of a rural community. Without such access, economic growth is stymied, employers have difficulty recruiting, and adult learners have no creative or educational outlet. Access to education and health care are the two biggest support challenges that rural communities face. Even so, the effect of college access on a rural community goes much deeper. Often, for example, the college is the chief provider of artistic activity and athletic entertainment in a rural community and provides a cultural diversity from which the entire community benefits.

Another vexing problem that a) receives little attention, b) is technically not very complicated, c) is nearly entirely within the control of the organization, and d) has turned out to be darned difficult to solve – is how best to reconcile the traditional interests of labor unions with the interests of young recruits. To be absolutely clear: *this is NOT about preferring younger employees or encouraging age discrimination.* Instead, it is about how organizations are inadvertently making themselves less appealing to younger workers. The majority of people entering the workforce are young people, and an organization that intends to compete for those employees needs to think carefully about how to satisfy their unique needs.

Although some states do not have teachers' unions (but, to be clear, most do), unions offer excellent insight into the dichotomy between what some types of teachers want and what teachers get. Union negotiating positions represent what the elected leadership of the union believes the union should seek on behalf of those it represents. In my opinion, there is a growing disconnect between what unions seek and what union membership wants, and this has led to less enthusiasm for union efforts from its membership. This, in turn, has led to a decline in the ability of educational institutions to meet the desires of workers, particularly in the case of smaller higher education institutions. I do not celebrate the overall decline in unions – in fact, I think that there is compelling evidence that unions contribute to overall economic and industrial strength, industrial and personal economic wealth, and economic equity.

Unfortunately, the long-term news about unions in America is mostly bad. The media is fascinated with the overall decline in unions, a decline that is well-documented. According to the Bureau of Labor Statistics, in 2016 only 10.7% of American workers (or 14.6 million employees) were union members compared to the 20.1% of American workers (or 17.7 million employees) that were union members in this country in 1983. Union membership within the private sector fell even more significantly from sixteen percent in 1983 to just under seven percent in 2016 – and is at levels not seen since 1932. The media has certainly noticed and commented on this in articles such as *Bloomberg's* "Weakened Unions Explain Stagnant Wages," *The New York Times'* "Writing the Unions' 'Fight or Die' Survival Chapter," and the *Pacific Standard's* "What Caused the Decline of Unions in America?"

Risk and Reward

Conventional wisdom generally attributes this decline to several factors, including the following as described in the *Economist* in late 2015:

> The decline [in unions] is largely due to structural changes in advanced economies. Total manufacturing employment in America has fallen from nearly 20 M in 1979 to 12 M today. The kind of workers who have lost out—in particular, unskilled men—were precisely those most likely to be in a union in the first place. And what has sprung up to replace them crimps unions further. If you went to a factory in the 1970s, you would have seen assembly lines of people. Such workers were much more amenable to the idea of "class consciousness." Go to a factory today and you might get a few people monitoring robots and other whizzy bits of machinery. Add to the mix globalisation, which makes it harder for unions to regulate work, the rise of a more flexible service sector, and government policies (such as those imposed by a Conservative-led government in Britain in the 1980s under Margaret Thatcher) and the loss of union clout seems inevitable. More recent reforms to minimum wages and workplace discrimination have also reduced the need to be in one.

This discussion overlooks a significant reason for the decline in unions over the past ten years, particularly in the service sector. Put very generally, the appeal of subscribing to a paid membership in an organization declines as the benefits that membership provides are seen as increasingly less valuable. The people managing and negotiating on behalf of unions view the processes and services provided by unions as being as valuable as they ever were. Yet, there are clearly entire groups of people within the population of union employees who view unions as being increasingly less valuable. Young people are increasingly disenchanted with the union process, in large part because the values of the union often do not align with the values of this category of employees. For example, on the podcast *The James Altucher Show*, LinkedIn CEO Daniel Roth stated that a review of LinkedIn user data shows that people twenty-four and under care far more about workplace culture and workplace relationships than workplace benefits.

Anyone who has participated in union negotiations knows that they typically stand or fall based on whether talks reach an agreement regarding compensation – typically salary and benefits. Given the recent significant increase in costs and the general complexity of benefits, increasingly these conversations center around benefits. However, if traditional benefits do not critically interest young people, then that means that the union is focusing an inordinate amount of time, energy and resources advocating for something that does not interest or motivate young employees, causing increasing numbers of young employees to become indifferent to the service unions provide.

This dichotomy between the desires of younger union members and older union members is, in many cases, codified. For example, state statutes that list mandatory negotiated items never mention the kinds of benefits in the workplace that younger workers are typically seeking, but they always mention the kind of benefits that older workers favor. Likewise, when unions survey members, the survey language they use often draws specific attention to the types of benefits that unions typically focus on and advocate for within negotiations. Union surveys will ask questions such as how much of a raise do you want? How much of a deductible are you willing to pay for your health insurance? How much of a 403b match should we seek? These are familiar topics. Yet, how often does a union ask its members whether it should hold firm on asking for Friday afternoons off? Or for the company to allocate a specific amount of money strictly to pay for social opportunities between employees? Or anything else that might fall into the general heading of negotiating for more "fun" in the workplace? Not because "young people just want to have fun" but because there is clear data that shows that the values of younger union members often differ from those of older union members.

But more importantly, the union position that focuses nearly entirely on salary and benefits may actually be driving young people away. Assuming that all benefits provided to employees require institutional resources, and assuming that an institution pours all available institutional resources for employee benefits into meeting the demands of union negotiations (which will often be requested by the union to be in the form of salary and traditional benefits), there will be very few resources available for the institution to devote to the kinds of cultural shifts that younger union members value. As a result, when younger union members attempt to advocate for workplace practices that fall outside of those types of benefits, such as to provide increased opportunities for social interaction, if those benefits require resources (either in the form of time or money), institutions will often truthfully respond that those resources are simply not available.

The result is that while everyone certainly intellectually appreciates a higher salary or good healthcare coverage, these are simply not what many are yearning for and find motivating, which leads to two negative results. The first is that these employees try working somewhere else, someplace where they hope that their yearning will be satisfied. The second and more important consequence is that these employees become less enthusiastic about (or perhaps indifferent to) the role of the union in the workplace. This is fundamentally different than what the media focuses on when they report on the general decline of unions. The media focuses on those people or groups that are hostile to unions. But I would suggest that in an era where there is genuine hostility toward unions, a bulwark against that hostility would be the enthusiasm of workers for their own unions; however, simply put, the workers who are enthusiastic about unions are largely aging out of the workforce. This process continues because the people who are typically negotiating on behalf of unions are either representing the interests of the older union members who are more active in those unions, or are actually drawn from the ranks of the older union members.

Further driving this destructive cycle is the culture that has been created, which perpetuates this belief that unions are primarily about workload and compensation. Unfortunately, this cultural understanding is embedded not only in the unions themselves but in the broader context, which includes the perception of the legislators who create the statutes that govern union negotiations. Compounding this issue is that once companies – including higher education institutions – buy into this definition of compensation as primarily focusing on the transfer of financial resources to the employee, rather than modification of the work experience itself, these organizations create an incentive to negotiate only on those items to which they are already devoting resources.

In Kansas, as the President of Independence Community College, I participated personally in negotiations nine times. In all cases, the team of faculty negotiators consisted of about two-thirds older faculty and one-third younger faculty, and the older faculty did nearly all the talking (because often the younger faculty were participating in negotiations for the first time). In the College negotiations in which I participated, the average age of the negotiators was approximately forty-five, but the average age of the union members they represented was about thirty-six.

The Atlantic noted in 2015 that among demographic groups, union membership is lowest by far among millennials, with only around four percent of workers aged sixteen to twenty-four and nine percent of workers aged twenty-five to thirty-four belonging to a union. In 1980, those figures were fifteen percent and twenty-eight percent respectively. While there has been an uptick in labor union membership generally and among young people specifically from 2017-2018, it is not clear that this is due to an enthusiasm for unions as those same years saw a significant increase in new positions in union shops due to strong economic growth during that period. In the year 2000, approximately 13.5% of the workforce were union members, with the average age of a union member being around forty-nine years old. Workers in the age range of forty-five to sixty-four were more likely to be union members than any other age group. The average age of a union member in the year 2015 was approximately fifty-nine years old, with the most common age range being fifty-five to sixty-four years old. In 2016, this changed slightly, with the average age range expanding to forty-five to sixty-four years old. The year 2017 retained the downward trend of the average age continuing to lower, likely because the ages sixteen to thirty-five started to see a substantial increase in union membership.

The evidence is strong that unions are not meeting the needs of all of their members and are losing popularity as a result. Other evidence appears to confirm this shift is occurring. One of the best places to look for evidence of this shift is within companies whose benefits do not come about through collective bargaining. For instance, consider some of the amazing benefits that Google provides its employees (here is a list of just *some* of the benefits afforded to the employees at Google, according to Inc.com):

1. Free Food

Google employees are extremely well fed, getting healthy and varied options for breakfast, lunch, and even dinner if they stay late – for free. Google even has coffee and juice bars scattered throughout its campuses. One Googler commented about loving the food perk because, "it saves me time and money, and helps me build relationships with my colleagues." (Obviously, I include that last quote for a reason!)

2. Exposure to Amazing People and Great Thinkers

Google employees have the opportunity to collaborate with amazing colleagues on fascinating projects. According to one Googler, the company is a great place to see, listen to, and meet with people he grew up reading about ("never in my life have I met so many people with a Wikipedia page than in the last year!" he writes). In the words of another Googler with only great things to say about his coworkers:

> We are surrounded by smart, driven people who provide the best environment for learning I've ever experienced. I don't mean through tech talks and formal training

programs; I mean through working with awesome colleagues — even the non-famous ones.

I've worked at several other .coms and have never been more challenged and energized professionally from my colleagues than at Google. People are generally happy to work there, they come from diverse backgrounds, and almost always have an interesting story to share. Besides being exposed to tech leaders, there are often talks with celebrities and other thought leaders.

3. Dogs are welcome!

Googlers are free to bring their pets to work. A former Googler describes why bringing his dog to work is so great. He says that it not only helped keep his energy up but also brought spontaneous joy to his coworkers and helped him meet people he probably would not have otherwise.

4. Free Transportation

Googlers at the Mountain View campus get a free ride to and from work. Even though Google's buses have become controversial, they are still an amazing resource for its employees. All the buses are equipped with Wi-Fi, so not only can employees live anywhere in San Francisco without needing a car to get to work, but they can relax, have fun, or get work done on the way to the office.

5. Free Massage Credits

Employees can give each other "massage credits" for a job well done on projects, and these massage credits can be redeemed for a free one-hour massage on campus.

6. Parental Leave Policies

At Google, new parents get the time they need to acclimate to parenthood and bond with their new child. While it is typical for mothers to get unpaid leave off from work for up to twelve weeks after having a child in the United States, Googlers get significantly more parental leave at the birth or adoption of a new child. New fathers receive six weeks of paid leave, and mothers can take up to eighteen weeks, *and* all employees' stock continues to vest (and they continue to receive bonuses) while they are on leave. When parents return to work, Google has free on-site daycare options.

7. Passion Projects

Google's application of the 80/20 rule to project development allows Googlers plenty of opportunity for creativity. The 80/20 rule permits Googlers to devote eighty percent of their time to their primary job and to dedicate twenty percent of their time to working on passion projects that they believe will help further the mission of the company.

8. Extended Time Off Policies

Google employees can get extended time off to follow their passions. In addition to vacations, Google's leave policies give employees additional opportunities to explore life outside of the workplace. Googlers can take a three-month leave of unpaid time off, under specific circumstances. (This is different from the way summer leave is typically conceived of for teachers, who usually receive an "annual" salary that includes summers off. In addition, teachers typically do not have the option of taking extended leave at any other point in the year.) Healthcare benefits continue during unpaid leaves of up to three months. Googlers can use their time off to work with nonprofit organizations, political campaigns, and other community-oriented projects that interest them.

There are many more benefits to working at Google – this is just a partial list. Did these appealing benefits come about through union negotiation? No. In fact, all of the top five companies on the list of the top companies to work for in the United States are either non-unionized or primarily non-unionized (i.e., are only small elements of the company that are unionized). So, the appeal of these companies is both a symptom of the problem and the cause. It is a symptom in the sense that these companies are largely free from the cultural and legislative context that governs our union environment and produces typical union-negotiated results, and it is a cause in the sense that young people migrate to these companies and away from union shops, weakening unions both by lessening their current ranks, and setting the stage for future decline by reducing the ranks of younger, mobile people in union shops who might advocate for what they value in the workplace.

Support for Teachers

Colleges have dorms, but there are not primarily hotels. They have dining halls but are not primarily restaurants. They have athletic teams, but athletics is rarely included their mission. Colleges exist to provide education, and the mission statements of colleges typically reflect that academics is the central function of the organization. The exercise of that function primarily involves faculty, and yet many colleges are not doing a good job supporting the work of their faculty. I have found that genuine support for faculty consists of five specific areas of focus:

- Teaching: Recruiting good teachers in the first place is the foundation of academic excellence. The head of academics and the president must be willing to aggressively recruit top performers – teachers who have excellent skills and the mindset to continue professional development, both in their disciplines and in their teaching pedagogy. Once those teachers are part of the organization, they must be supported both with resources and with recognition. These are each crucial: resources without recognition lacks accountability, and recognition without resources shows a lack of commitment to supporting teaching.

- Research, creative activity, and grant writing: These three are really just extensions of hiring and supporting excellent teachers. Teachers want to do research; they want to be creative; they want to seek funding sources. Support for each of those comes in different ways. For example, research and creative work is most often a function of making sure faculty have time to invest in those pursuits, while grant writing also requires specialized administrative support often in budgeting and compliance.

- Program development: One of the most exciting developments for an institution occurs when a faculty member or a department has a new program idea. Institutional leadership must listen and help to evaluate the feasibility of that program. Once an institution commits to building a new program, that commitment must be real and substantial. After all, no one enjoys working to develop programs that are underfunded from the beginning and which ultimately cause people to question why they do not live up to expectations that were initially projected. The institution must ensure that does not happen.

- Compensation: I will put this as plainly as I can – teachers should be paid more, in many cases, much more. Paying teachers more has a multitude of benefits for a higher education institution: 1) Most importantly, it puts into practice the educational priority of the institution, codifying into the budget what the institution supposedly values; 2) it justifies rigorous evaluation of teachers; 3) it improves internal morale by reducing the sense that teaching is not valued, and 4) it acts as a recruitment tool. As I described earlier, when I started at Independence Community College, our faculty were in the bottom quartile of instructor pay for the community college sector in Kansas. Within four years, they were in the top quartile, and had the highest base pay of any community college in southeast Kansas. This allowed the College to make the case to outstanding teachers that the College recognized their skills and wanted to reward and retain them and significantly altered the dynamic of conversations with potential new hires.

- Negotiations: An institution must adopt a position of good faith. Normally, "good faith" in negotiations simply means that each party will deal honestly and fairly with one another so that each party will receive the benefits of the negotiated contract. However, here I am alluding to something more specific, more psychological, and less transactional. In her excellent article, "<u>The Presumption of Good Faith in Campus Conversation</u>," Emily Chamlee-Wright describes this orientation as the expectation that our conversation partner is interested in learning from us and is seeking to understand our point of view. It means that without good evidence to the contrary, one should assume that the intent of the other party is not to deceive or to offend. She writes:

> A presumption of good faith demands a lot from us. It requires that we suspend judgment long enough to ask questions in a spirit of openness and curiosity. If a colleague and I disagree, I should focus first on figuring out why it is that he and I draw different conclusions even though we are looking at the same world. Perhaps there's something in his history, or mine, that led us to different places. The practice of good faith is not an obvious remedy. It' requires discipline. It offers none of the psychic rewards that moral outrage delivers. But it's a practice that keeps the conversation going. And it's a practice that allows everyone in the conversation to teach and to learn.

This is the negotiation-specific application of the adage that when you are a hammer, everything looks like a nail. If you see those negotiating with you as adversaries intent on deception or insult, this lens will distort their honest attempt to negotiate with you, and they will clearly see how you see them: as dishonest and duplicitous. Instead, one should strive to always start from the opposite viewpoint – one of trust and honesty.

CHAPTER 4

Public Relations

In this chapter, I will not discuss public relations in general, as that is a comprehensive subject that has received excellent treatment in other works. I also will not discuss crisis management, which I address elsewhere in this book. Instead, I focus on two areas in which small colleges consistently come up short: understanding college rankings and retention of first-time and small gift donors. Finally, I offer a case study of how better public relations can be created through a collaborative strategic planning process that creates both goodwill and buy-in from internal and external constituencies.

College Rankings

Independence Community College recently declared itself "the most academically-decorated community college in Kansas." It did so based on evaluations of the College by various outside organizations that rank community colleges against one another based on various criteria. Should colleges (or the public) pay attention to such rankings?

Education reporter David Tomar writes: "These publications – which academics take special pleasure in deriding and universities take particular pains to satisfy – are a major driver of endowment decisions, enrollment figures, and employment opportunities. Rankings play a direct role in how aspiring college students select schools, how researchers build reputations, and how colleges position themselves in the marketplace."

There is no question that such rankings have Public Relations value. Colleges newly ranked in the *U.S. News and World Report*'s "Top 25" will experience a six to ten percent increase in applications. Colleges that already appear on that list and move just one percentage point upward on the list will see a corresponding one percent increase in applications. Colleges that appear in *Princeton Review*'s "Top 20 Best Overall Academic Experience" will see a 3.2% increase in applications in the year after they appear. Rankings are of particular value in professional programs. For example, rankings are critical in the legal profession, where the precise value of any prospective employee is clearly ranked – both by the ranking of his or her law school and the rank the student individually achieved within his or her law school program. These rankings have a significant impact on employability, salary, and career trajectory for lawyers.

Using Independence Community College as an example, let's examine the way that rankings can impact a college's public perception. In 2018, this was my email signature line at the College:

Daniel W. Barwick, PhD
President
Independence Community College
Like me on Facebook here, Twitter here, or visit my blog here
2018 – Ranked #1 Community College in Kanas
2018 – Ranked in the Top 25 Community Colleges in the United States
2018 – Ranked "Lowest Net Price" College in Kansas
2017 – Ranked #1 in Kansas for Success of Transfer Students
2016 – Ranked in the top 1% of Community Colleges in the U.S. for Student Educational Goal Attainment
2015 – Ranked in the Top 5 Most Affordable Community Colleges in the United States
2013 – Ranked in the Top 50 Best Community Colleges in the United States

Risk and Reward

Let's consider some of the rankings on this list (by the way, the College has also received other impressive rankings which it has chosen not to publicize – more on the rationale for that later):

Schools.com, an online higher education resource, ranked the College first in its 2018 report "Best Community Colleges in Kansas." The company ranked twenty-one community colleges in Kansas based on multiple factors, including the percentage of students enrolled in distance education, cost of attendance, student-to-faculty ratio, graduation rate, transfer-out rate, and flexibility (this is defined as the ability to accommodate varying student needs). The report cited the College's intimate campus environment, the large number of degree and certificate programs for its size, and the unique opportunities the College's Fab Lab offers students. The full 2018 schools.com Kansas community college ranking is available at https://www.schools.com/community-colleges/top-community-colleges-in-kansas.

Previously, the College was also ranked in the Top 25 "Best Community Colleges in America" by the web-based financial advisory company SmartAsset. Also, in 2019, the College was named the "Lowest Net Price College in Kansas" by the U.S. Department of Education's College Affordability and Transparency Center, which studied ninety two-year public institutions in the United States.

Other significant College rankings in recent years include being ranked number one in Kansas for "success of transfer students," according to a study published by the Center of Science, Technology & Economic Policy at the Institute for Policy & Social Research at the University of Kansas in 2017 and ranking in the top one percent of Community Colleges in the U.S. for Student Educational Goal Attainment as ranked by the National Higher Education Benchmarking Institute in 2016.

About such rankings, only two things can be said for sure: institutions that appear in such rankings typically tout them, and those that do not appear in such rankings typically dismiss them.

Unfortunately, it is often unclear why a college falls precisely where it does in an organization's ranking system. The reason for this is that many of these ranking systems are proprietary – the organizations doing the rankings know that if they disclosed the actual process for ranking selection, colleges could technically perform the ranking process themselves and would not need the organization publishing the rankings (or might game the system by performing the technical requirements instead of meeting the underlying goals of the ranking). As a result, the exact reason for moving a couple of spots from year to year in any particular ranking is often a complete mystery. (An exception is the U.S. Department of Education's College Affordability and Transparency Center, which is, appropriately, very transparent.)

So, what helpful information do rankings actually provide? There are two situations in which college rankings are particularly noteworthy:

1. High rankings over time based on a fairly specific criterion: In most cases, when a ranking is measuring a specific criterion, and the outcome is pronounced and consistent over time, it is reasonable to infer that the institution's ranking is warranted. For example, a fairly common ranking is affordability. Although the actual affordability of a program at an institution for a specific student varies tremendously based on the student's specific circumstances, it is safe to say that if an institution consistently ranks among the most affordable institutions among dozens or perhaps even hundreds of peer institutions, that institution is in fact relatively affordable. Likewise, if an institution suddenly becomes one of the least expensive institutions in the state, without ever having been recognized as a good value and without having made any changes to leapfrog over competing institutions, there is good reason to be suspicious of the ranking methodology being used. (It is possible, of course, that these changes may cause legitimate concerns about the institution. If the institution has suddenly lowered tuition, by what could be a large percentage compared to other similarly priced colleges in the same area, it

would be legitimate to ask why and how the college found a way to lower costs and what impacts those lower costs may have on the quality of education being provided at that institution).

2. A consistently higher ranking across a range of ranking organizations: Since each organization performing various rankings of different higher education institutions uses slightly different criteria and also weighs those criteria slightly differently, it is reasonable to assume that the more ranking organizations have examined an institution, the more accurate is their cumulative judgment of the institution. Therefore, when an institution consistently receives higher rankings in a specific area, such as student educational outcomes, it probably does indeed have better outcomes than an institution whose evaluations are all over the map.

These considerations drove the decisions around which rankings my previous institution, Independence Community College, chose to emphasize/publicize. Nearly all of the rankings included in my signature line emphasized specific features, like affordability and academic outcomes, to emphasize the repeated recognition of the College in these areas.

Since these rankings have potential public relations value, institutions should consider these two points:

1. Institutions need to make a deliberate effort to determine whether they appear on such rankings lists as typically, ranking organizations do not notify institutions that they have been placed on its list (I have no idea why — surely, a ranking organization would want its list disseminated, and who better to do that than highly-ranked institutions?) There are many rankings — some put out by public organizations, some private, and some are the result of research studies, many of which do not reach the public unless institutions promote the result. Small institutions with correspondingly small public relations departments are

following ranking results vis a vis their own institutions – in fact, less than half of the highly ranked institutions named in the US Department of Education's affordability and transparency ranking promoted their ranking on their websites. When I contacted those institutions, over three-fourths of them were unaware of their ranking, and one-quarter of them were unaware that the list even exists!

2. Institutions should consider emphasizing positive rankings, especially those it receives over time. After all, institutions that genuinely meet a specific ranking criterion are likely to meet that criterion repeatedly over time, which presents a positive public relations opportunity for an institution. Consider, which makes for a better headline on an institution's website: "ICC Ranked #5 for Affordability" or "ICC Among Top 5 Most Affordable Colleges for Fourth Straight Year?" While there may be a tendency to believe an award given to an institution four years before has little value, if that award is part of a long-term pattern, it can have significant public relations value.

First-Time and Small Gift Donor Retention

All colleges compete for donor dollars, and one of the greatest struggles in that competition receives very little attention outside of the fundraising division – first-time and small gift donor retention. Fundraisers know that one of the strongest indicators of future gifts is evidence of past gifts, but this is relative – they also know that donor retention following a first-time gift is very low (about thirty percent), and that is a terrible figure. In this chapter, I am going to address what I regard as the biggest potential return on investment – retaining small gift and first-time donors. While fundraising departments pay a lot of attention to large gifts, and the section on innovation and entrepreneurship focuses on raising large gifts from entrepreneurs, the attention paid to donors of large gifts obscures how poorly institutions nurture first-time and small gift donors. After all, most large gift donors typically begin by donating small gifts.

Donors are often highly motivated to give. People who make a gift to a higher education institution, assuming it is legitimately a gift, are not receiving a tangible something in return. Instead, they give because they want to give and because the institution is providing something that they want to support. Donors that support an institution by giving a first-time gift are statistically likely to give a second gift to the same institution only thirty percent of the time, which strongly suggests that something about the experience of giving that first gift failed to meet the expectations of the donor. Obviously, that begs the question – what about the experience failed to meet the donor's expectation, and what can an institution do differently? Luckily, there are some best practices for gift acknowledgment that can help an institution improve donor relations by promoting donor retention.

People that decide to give a first-time gift at the college level, particularly the community college level, generally do because they are alumni who graduated from the institution (perhaps recently, perhaps not) and have engaged in sufficient contact with the institution and after receiving some sort of prompt from the institution have elected to make some sort of modest first-time gift. These first-time gifts tend to be small, and it is important to understand that the experience that the first-time donor has when they make that initial gift has a tremendous impact on whether they will be inclined to donate to the institution again. Unfortunately, there are several points within the fundraising process where the experience can go wrong, the simplest of which is the failure by most institutions to thank donors sufficiently.

The general rule of thumb in fundraising is that a donation needs to be acknowledged in some way by an institution about seven times before the average person truly internalizes that gratitude (i.e., the donor truly feels their gift has been acknowledged and that their gift was truly appreciated). Although that might sound like a lot of interaction, especially with a first-time donor of a small gift, in fact, it is often actually quite routine and, and some of it can even be automated. For example, when a person donates to the institution through an institution's website, the donor will receive some type of acknowledgment in the form of an automated receipt. An obvious tip – since after all the screen is going to display something – make sure that it displays a "thank you." Believe it or not, I have literally seen automated donation receipt screens that do not even say thank you! Another easy initial step – an automated email "thank you." Generally, this email contains the same basic information as the on-screen receipt, but it provides the institution another opportunity to say thank you.

Of course, there are many other opportunities to acknowledge a donation, including a hard copy, snail mail, thank you note. Generally, institutions have policies regarding the types of gifts that warrant a mailed acknowledgment. In most cases, it is going to be worth it for the institution to send first-time donors a personalized, mailed acknowledgment of their gift. An institution can also acknowledge a first-time donor on its foundation website by creating a list of first-time donors, a revolving ticker or an accumulating list of donors that have given to the institution within the past month or year. Likewise, an institution can create similar acknowledgments on individual websites dedicated to the purpose for which the gift was made (e.g., if a gift is given to the chess club, the chess club could acknowledge the donor and the gift on its own page on the college's site).

In addition, an institution can acknowledge its donors through social media. So long as a donor has not requested that the gift be anonymous (most people do not make that request), most people are fine with having their gift publicized on social media. An institution can acknowledge a gift and thank a first-time donor through targeted social media messages expressing appreciation. Ideally, an institution will find a way to tag the individual donor so he or she is aware that they have been thanked. Nothing is more gratifying to donors than being unaware that the general public (or even just their personal friends and acquaintances) are aware of their gift, walking into Walmart and meeting someone they know and having that person says, "Oh, I saw that you made a gift to the chess club, and that was really nice of you." Social media presents literally dozens of opportunities to thank donors – an institution can acknowledge a donor at the time a gift was initially made, as part of a weekly wrap-up of acknowledgments and perhaps even as part of a monthly acknowledgment of institutional supporters.

Finally, do not forget about telephone calls. Depending on the size and type of gift, a donation may warrant a phone call or even more than one phone call. At my previous institution, we had very specific policies about acknowledging first-time gifts of varying sizes and situations, including who would call the donor to thank them. It sounds burdensome, but it is not the slightest bit, primarily because most people do not even answer their cell phones, and so in most cases, the phone call involves just leaving a short, very appreciative message that anyone would enjoy receiving in their voicemail. Gifts of a certain size may warrant a phone call, especially if the donor is a first-time gift, from the annual giving director, and some gifts of an even larger size may also require a phone call from somebody at a different level or department of the institution.

In every case, the purpose is to thank the donor for their gift, especially if it is a first-time gift. My recommendation is that institutions explicitly acknowledge that a donation is a first-time gift, in part because doing so helps personalize the acknowledgment, which helps to create an impression that the institution, and specifically the person acknowledging the gift, clearly understands who an individual donor is, at least in terms of his or her history with the institution, and makes donors feel as though they have made a personal connection with the institution and vice versa.

There are easily two dozen different ways to thank new donors, including some less obvious ways. For example, an institution could include donor information in a monthly report created by either the fundraising office or the president and directed to the institution's board, which is in the public domain and so can be used to publicly thank all new donors or all donors in general. A department or program within an institution could acknowledge gifts made to it by sending separate correspondence to donors, providing information about relevant programs that the donors have elected to support or even inviting donors to participate in an event that involves the department or program within the institution that they have elected to support.

Honestly, there is almost no end to the number of ways an institution can acknowledge and engage its donors. Does this require a lot of work? No, it does not. It may sound like a lot of work, but in fact, there are a couple of things that successful institutions do that minimize the amount of work involved while also creating a culture of donor acknowledgement and engagement. First, institutions can employ automation, by ensuring that there are at least two or three points of contact with donors built into the process that provide acknowledgment of a donation in a manner that is automated and does not represent additional work for any employees at the institution. Second, an institution can build donor acknowledgment and deliberate engagement with donors into processes that already exist at the institution. For example, anytime an institution has an event, planning for that event exists anyway, as does some process for inviting attendees to the event. An institution can choose to deliberately improve donor relations by adding one additional step to its already existing process for hosting events, such as simply requiring that its events committee communicate with its fundraising office to ascertain whether there are any recent or large donors who have contributed to the program or department hosting the event that should receive an invitation to the event.

So, why is all of this acknowledgment and engagement with first-time and small gift donors so important? The truth is, even though the rate of donor retention is generally low, the fact is, if that problem is corrected, the outcome (and benefits) for the organization can be very significant – if for no other reason than because it is simply easier to keep a donor than it is to recruit a new one. As an example, in the early nineties, Harvard performed a study involving their major donors that was designed to identify predictors that a donor will make a major gift to Harvard. In the end, the study showed that major donors who were alumni ultimately had two things in common: 1) high net worth, which of course is not surprising, and 2) annual gifts to the institution beginning within three years of graduating. The lesson this study provides is simple: the opportunity to develop major donors exists because annual donors with money become major donors if stewarded correctly.

So, let me be more specific about the kinds of things that truly convey appreciation. To impress first-time and small gift donors and keep them coming back, an institution needs to make the donation process a truly memorable experience for them. Ultimately, there are really three kinds of donor experiences: One in which the receiving institution was very appreciative, one in which the receiving institution produced some kind of negative experience for the donor, and one in which the receiving institution appeared to be indifferent to the donor and his or her gift. This should really give institutions pause – there are only three types of donor experiences, and two of those lead to non-renewal of donations. It is probably no accident that the retention rate for first-time and small gift donors is about thirty percent since two of the three possible outcomes lead to poor donor retention. So, how then can an institution differentiate itself and retain donors by taking steps that really make a donor think, "that was pretty amazing – I feel really good right now?"

Institutional decisions around when to personalize acknowledgements to first-time and small gift donors, and the level and size of gift that triggers an individualized, personal response should be based on the size and workforce availability of an institution. That said, I would urge organizations to keep that gift level as low as possible because first-time and small annual gifts now can become large annual gifts later. In effect, this is really about investing institutional time and resources in a future outcome. I strongly recommend the first-time donor be explicitly welcomed into the donor family through some kind of welcome packet that basically conveys that the institution is aware that the donor made his or her first gift, provides some information about the exclusive group that the donor has joined and the organization the donor is supporting and provides the first-time donor with information about institutional activities and events that he or she has already demonstrated an interest in becoming involved with at the institution. Likewise, the packet of information that the donor receives cannot appear to be something the institution sends to just anybody – it has to be significantly personalized. There should be some handwriting on it; ideally, it should include a handwritten note to the donor. There needs to be a way for donors to respond to the institution after receiving the packet that is not very forward but allows them to be so impressed that they follow up with some kind of reply. It needs to include the business contact information of somebody at the institution so that if the donor wants to follow up in that way, they can do that as well. Ultimately, the packet needs to be carefully drafted to demonstrate that the donor's gift has made an impact on the institution, in the way that the donor envisioned, and that the organization recognizes that and appreciates it.

I did mention earlier that institutions should utilize some kind of newsletter, and I want to stress the need to produce two kinds of newsletters, one electronic and one print. Obviously, electronic newsletters are less expensive in many ways to produce and to disseminate and they tend to target a younger demographic, which from a certain standpoint is very desirable because as the previously referenced Harvard study shows, institutions need to get people in a pattern of annual giving as early as possible after graduation. However, the fact is the print newsletter can often have a much greater impact because there is clearly something that resonates with people when they receive a physical object that they can hold and because some people simply prefer to receive something in print. Any readers interested in obtaining additional information around creating effective newsletters, are encouraged to contact me personally for some excellent source material around creating newsletters that have a real impact (my email address can be found at the end of the introduction to this book.)

Risk and Reward

Ultimately, all of these techniques are variations on a theme – ask less and touch more. One of the problems that institutions often experience is the oft-repeated criticism: "The only time I hear from my alma mater is when they want money" or something to that effect. Ultimately, if that is the way people think about an institution, that is the fault of the institution, because institutions make very deliberate choices about how often and for what purpose they will contact constituents. If an institution contacts donors in a way that convinces them that they are viewed as nothing more than a checkbook, donors are going to recognize that – they are not stupid. In those cases, the institution has probably drilled that mindset into their donor's heads through years of contact that was designed only to explicitly extract money, and that institution needs to recognize that and realize first, that is not the way a supporter should be talking about the institution and second, the problem is one created by the institution and has been inadvertently reinforced by the institution as the negative opinion of the institution was presumably not one originally held by the donor or perspective donor. Obviously, at that point a different approach is necessary and the institution needs to recognize that "touching" constituents can and should include non-monetary requests – for opinions, insights, time, interaction … by asking potential donors not only to finance a project but also to participate in it and become an integral part of the developing project as a person, not just a purse.

The statistics clearly show that organizations, including colleges, are very bad at retaining donors and those studies also clearly show that the main reason why they are bad at retaining donors is because they poorly acknowledge gifts. For the life of me, this is very difficult to understand. Perhaps, there is this temptation to think "well, we have gotten their money, and so we do not need to do anything else because anything else we do after this is just wasted effort because they have already given the institution the money." However, nothing could be further from the truth. Leaving aside the fact that the institution owes its donors a certain amount of gratitude, the fact is that if a donor has thirty to maybe even fifty years of giving ahead of them and they have only made their first gift to an institution, the institution has in fact only received 1/40 or 1/50 or perhaps even 1/100 or 1/1,000,000 of the total lifetime gifts that the donor might eventually make to the institution. Ensuring that they make that second gift, and then that third gift, is the best way to capture all of those funds.

Perhaps there is something else at work, particularly in smaller organizations. When people express gratitude genuinely through a handwritten note or some other means of expressing sincerely held emotions, people leave themselves emotionally vulnerable through that process, and that is something that a lot of people do not want to do. People often do not want to make themselves emotionally vulnerable to other people, perhaps out of fear of rejection of their expression of gratitude and so have a habit of not exposing themselves emotionally to others, even in cases where it is clearly warranted, and even positive, and would move an important relationship forward. However, the truth is thanking people for their generosity should be one of the most natural and desirable activities that college administrators engage in because after all, everyone likes to be thanked. It also feels good to thank someone else, especially when it is done profusely and with genuine feeling. I would urge college administrators, not just fundraisers but any college administrator who is in a position to acknowledge a gift to thank a donor for their support. I have always been puzzled by organizations that invest in a planned giving program, knowing full well that that program will not yield a net positive return for five to eight years, and yet do not approach their first-time donor acknowledgments with the same sense of planning and long-range thinking.

In the end, when administrators approach first-time and small gift donors with the attitude that "I am going to make this a fantastic experience for this person so that they will come back next year to have another fantastic experience. I am going to ensure this institution is at the top of that donor's priority list," they will find two things to be true. The first is that, of course, donor retention will go up, and donations to the institution overall will increase. The second is that an attitude of gratitude will improve the quality of work-life for those employees who are part of the donor acknowledgment process. The more gratitude there is around us, the more celebration there is of donor (and other forms of community) support, the more people employed by the institution will feel worthy of that support, the more they will come to believe in the mission of the institution, because they see others from the outside the organization wanting to support and celebrate the institution publicly and repeatedly. This is a way of not just improving donor experiences, but actually improving the morale of the people employed by the institution.

Case Study: Strategic Planning as Outreach

In 2019, Independence Community College completed a lengthy strategic planning process, and there are important lessons to be learned from that process – strategies that worked well, situations that created problems for the institution, including problems that may not be avoidable during the strategic planning process.

The College went through a strategic planning process for a pretty simple reason: our current strategic plan was ending. Previously, the College had created a three-year strategic plan, which the College revised annually as part of a comprehensive review cycle, based on predetermined data the College used to measure progress toward the institutional goals outlined in its strategic plan. The Board of Trustees considered and revised the strategic plan annually. However, the three-year period for that strategic plan was coming to an end, requiring the drafting of a new strategic plan in the final year. In addition, the College's accreditors and other stakeholders, including the public and others, also assumed the College would continue to engage in long-term planning. As a result, the Board set out to create a new strategic plan for the College. Strategic planning can be an exciting process for an institution, especially because people can get bogged down with day-to-day operations and handling institutional emergencies that arise, making it feel like a luxury to even engage in short-term, one or two months, institutional planning. Strategic planning creates a formal opportunity to collectively plan for the future of the entire institution by engaging all departments of the institution, as well as the community that it serves and its high-level administrative leadership. While that obviously does not guarantee that institution will have perfect clarity to predict future challenges and opportunities, it does allow the institution the opportunity to consider institutional goals, and to dream of ways to reach those goals. Dreaming is always fun, and I enjoy strategic planning.

The College had been through periodic strategic planning, certainly since my arrival at the College in 2011. In 2012, I became involved in my first strategic plan at the College, which included a comprehensive process. The College involved quite a few subcommittees, and those subcommittees were populated by at least fifty or sixty people and focused on specific issues facing different areas of the College. There was widespread participation in developing that strategic plan, and it produced good results. However, often what comes with widespread participation is a strategic plan that includes a hodgepodge of goals suggested by very different constituencies, making the plan feel a little less focused because it includes such a wide range of projects and goals. Even so, the process itself has advantages, both because that approach helps engage quite a few members of the community and because it often involves a wide variety of people, and results in some pretty exciting new ideas.

Three years later, the College created another strategic plan, and this time the Board of Trustees of the College requested a different process for developing the strategic plan, one that required a very small focused workgroup. The College engaged about a dozen people, primarily employees of the College (including me). Because it was a small group of highly involved College employees, we were able to develop a much more focused plan that was centered around just three areas of excellence: academic excellence, service excellence, and support excellence. The Board endorsed it relatively quickly. Somewhat unsurprisingly, drafting a strategic plan with the assistance of such a small group of participants resulted in less than enthusiastic buy-in from members of the College's internal and external community. However, because our annual review process is pretty comprehensive and involves input from many departments, we found that over time, as the annual review and revisions occurred, there was more and more buy-in to the plan.

At the beginning of its next strategic planning cycle, the College began the process by holding a series of discussions, both with College employees and community members, to essentially get people thinking about strategic planning and to identify some of the main themes, not around items that College constituents wanted to see in an eventual plan, but instead perceptions about the process the College should use to create its next strategic planning process. During an open forum with College employees, we received feedback about what the process should look like. In addition, I had personal visits and discussions with eleven stakeholders, both inside and outside of the College (primarily outside of the College because I had already engaged in the open forum with employees). The purpose was really just to make sure that whatever process the College settled on was a process that was supported by the larger community.

As you might expect, some very specific themes emerged from those initial discussions, and those themes became the foundation for the process that we eventually used.

First, there was a widespread belief that the strategic planning process had to be inclusive and involve as many different stakeholder groups as possible. There were two groups of people that were especially vocal about creating an inclusive process – the people who simply held as a principle that inclusivity was a preferable way to go about strategic planning and those people who remembered the exclusivity of the previous strategic planning process and were not satisfied with that process and wanted to ensure that the upcoming process was open to more stakeholders.

The second theme that emerged was that whatever process we engaged in, it would have to be one that encouraged fundamentally new ideas, which is actually much more difficult than it sounds. People are only going to share and espouse new radical ideas when they feel safe enough to do so. My experience told me that people might feel threatened and be unwilling to consider radical ideas for a variety of reasons – because they felt a need to be as accommodating as possible to the views of the people around them or because and they did not want to rock the boat by espousing something new and seemingly strange. Even so, leadership at the College felt that, in order to remain competitive over the next five to ten years, the College ultimately needed to be able (whether or not it resulted in moving in a total new direction) to engage in a strategic planning process that encouraged people to come forward with fundamentally new ideas. Generally, an institution will always have some constituents that come forward with new ideas because there are always a few people who are not shy about doing that at all. However, the College was interested in engaging everyone, including its "quiet" constituents or those people that might not feel comfortable or might otherwise be unwilling to come forward with a new idea – not just the same people who always came forward with new ideas and suggestions for new College projects. Instead, the College wanted to create an environment that was supportive of and would encourage people with ideas that may seem very unusual, even if they were not the type of employee or community member who would normally push an unusual idea. The College has been in the community for about a century, which means a lot of tradition and a certain orientation toward the status quo, making it particularly important to encourage people to vocalize fundamentally new ideas rather than just suggesting a continuation of a certain method or perspective in the handling of situations or approach to opportunities out of respect of tradition or the status quo.

As for the third principle, which emerged again and again in these discussions, was the idea that the College had to find a way to avoid creating a final product that only reflected the views of those people that screamed the loudest. As anyone that has been through any kind of planning process or collaboration knows when there can be very dominant people in the room, people who express their views very forcefully and who have trouble coming to terms with the idea that compromise is inherent in a collaborative decision-making process (i.e., the idea that collaboration requires a certain kind of give and take, by giving up something or maybe just being overruled and accepting that). Some people have a tremendously tough time doing this, and while the College needed and wanted those people in the room because it did not want to shut them out of the process, it also needed to find a way to ensure that somehow the final product did not end up just being an accumulation of their ideas.

There was general agreement within the College that it should use an outside facilitator to assist with the strategic planning process. During previous strategic planning cycles, the College had used an in-house facilitator – in the first case, essentially the Board of Trustees and, in the second case, me. By the third strategic planning cycle, everybody wanted to try what is widely recognized as a best practice in strategic planning, which is to ensure that the coordinator of the entire process (i.e., the person who is leading the process) does not have a direct agenda and has a less direct connection to the institution. One of the benefits being that they are more willing to hear different perspectives, and to hear all points of view on a more equal footing, whereas somebody who has a very specific role at the institution may not be able to do that. Thus, the College elected to employ an outside facilitator.

The next suggestion that came out of the discussions around strategic planning process, a suggestion I fully supported, was the need to use data as a key component in the development of the College's strategic plan. Strategic planning for a small institution often boils down to people sitting around either reminiscing about the institution when they were a student there and how much they would like to return to that experience – or to see some element of that experience return to the institution – or focusing on the recitation of various anecdotes about those projects that are seen as being successful at the institution based on the experience they themselves have seen or about which they have heard positive comments. The plural of 'anecdote' is not 'data,' and ultimately a good strategic planning process needs to do a deep dive into the data, because very often, the data shows something unexpected, interesting, or counterintuitive.

As an example of how data can yield some pretty fascinating results, early in the process, the College engaged in extensive surveying of various groups, including current students, prospective students, high school students, alumni, community members, employees, and more. In its interpretation of the data, the College focused on quite a few different demographic groups, and one of the most interesting pieces of information that initially emerged within the data was that current students thought far better of the College than our graduates did, which was very surprising as it was generally assumed that current students would be caught up in whatever problem they might be experiencing at the institution, and so they might not rate their current experience as highly as someone that had already graduated. However, the College's survey data suggested exactly the opposite – current students gave the College much higher ratings – which concerned College leadership. That is, until it examined the survey data even more closely and segmented the ages of the alumni surveyed, and found that recent graduates actually gave the College very high ratings and that it was the graduates that had attended the College fifteen to twenty-five years earlier that were giving the College very low ratings, and dragging down the overall demographic response of College graduates. Examining the qualitative responses of these graduates, it became apparent that the low ratings stemmed from the fact that, at the time they attended the College, community college credits did not transfer nearly as well to universities as they do now, and most of the students providing low ratings were transfer students. It turns out that the reason for the low ratings had much more to do with these graduates' own experience, including having a considerable number of their credits not transfer to their next institution, and erroneously believing that situation continued to exist for current students at the College. As a result, these survey ratings reflected both disappointments around their own experiences and their assumptions about the quality or the transferability of education at the College at the time of the survey. It turned out that they were wrong about that, but it was deeply coloring their responses and changing the overall result for the entire alumni group. Ultimately, the College discovered that what it thought was something very troubling actually reflected an improvement at the College that had occurred over the past couple of decades.

In furtherance of its goal to create an inclusive well-designed strategic planning process, the College created the Strategic Planning Process Committee: a group of people at the college (three professionals) with two things in common: 1) background and training in strategic planning and 2) a position with the College outside of upper administration to avoid the appearance that the process was being controlled either by senior administration officials or the Board. The Strategic Planning Process Committee developed an excellent process for creating the College's strategic plan. They recommended a data-gathering phase of about two months that would include both established data about the College, based on the information the College reported to the federal and state government, combined with comprehensive surveys and listening sessions with various College constituencies. For surveys, the College used a combination of electronic surveys distributed to alumni nationwide and surveys administered to the residents of the College's service area, regardless of whether they were alumni of the College or not. The College also directly surveyed prospective students (i.e., high school students in the service area who were considering a college) to gain insights into prospective students' thoughts about the direction in which the College should be headed within the next few years.

The comprehensive surveys sent to alumni, residents and high school students were very deliberately structured. The surveys focused on the College's mission and vision statements, breaking them into their various components, and asked people how well the College was meeting each component on a scale of one to five. Finally, the survey ended with an open-ended question to allow respondents to provide open-ended feedback to the College even if it was not directly related to a question specifically included in the survey. These open-ended responses allowed the College to better identify the perceived gaps between what the College was supposed to be doing or had promised it would do, and what it was actually doing.

The College also engaged in listening sessions led by College trained facilitators. This second step created two halves of the conversation – complain first, brainstorm second – thereby giving people the opportunity to get the negativity out of their systems before moving on to dreaming and creating productive solutions and suggestions. These listening sessions were fascinating because they were quite structured, ensuring that these sessions did not turn into an opportunity for College constituents to focus solely on the negative. Instead, the people who attended the sessions were asked to respond individually to specific questions about the College before splitting off into small groups to discuss and endorse collective responses to the questions, which were presented to all the groups as well as the listening session facilitators. Like the surveys, these sessions allowed the College to identify the specific areas where respondents thought there was a gap between what the College was supposed to be doing or had promised it would do, and what it was actually doing.

I use the word "gap" very deliberately because the next step in the strategic planning process involved the creation of a group the College referred to as the Gap Analysis Committee. The Gap Analysis Committee was made up of four community members, two faculty, two staff, two board members, and me as an ex officio member and was led by the strategic planning coordinator (aka, the outside facilitator described previously). For that role, the College managed to snag an amazing alumnus retired from the financial services industry.

The Gap Analysis Committee was responsible for examining the quantitative and qualitative data received from federal and state reports, the survey responses, and the listening responses, and to essentially identify the areas in which there was the most significant and/or largest perceived gap between what the College said it would do and what it was actually doing. The Gap Analysis Committee's job was also to determine whether that gap was real or merely perceived by determining, for example, whether an issue stemmed from an actual operational defect or a potential marketing issue.

The Gap Analysis Committee was not perfect in its makeup or in the execution of its role. Its facilitator, although highly skilled, was from a completely different industry and had no higher education experience. The community members who served on the Gap Analysis Committee were primarily from industry, and the result was not particularly diverse in perspective. The faculty representative elected by the faculty was selected for his mathematical skills, and otherwise, his input in the process was modest. I was only ex-officio, and would have liked to have had more influence over the final result, at least in part because being the president of the College and being on the committee automatically assigned me a lot of responsibility for the result, even though in practice I had limited influence over that result.

Before the Gap Analysis Committee could present its conclusions to the College community, it had to complete one additional step: examine the mission and the vision of the College and decide whether to form a group to alter that mission and vision. In this case, the Gap Analysis Committee decided it was satisfied with the current mission and vision and elected to leave those untouched. That said, every strategic planning process should provide the opportunity for an alteration of the mission or vision of the institution as it sees fit. In this case, the College elected to leave it alone.

At that point, the Gap Analysis Committee, having identified the various areas where the largest or most important gaps existed, formed workgroups assigned to focus on each one of those gaps, each of which spent about a month and a half creating solutions in those particular areas. The workgroups were charged very specifically – the Gap Analysis Committee provided each workgroup with detailed information about the gap identified and what each workgroup needed to consider, and the type of output expected from each group (with deadlines for completion). The College also placed resources at the disposal of each workgroup, including the assistance of the College's institutional researcher and the information available from various administrators with experience in different areas of College operations. In addition, workgroups were encouraged to seek information or community resources, even if they were external to the institution.

Each of the workgroups completed its work as assigned, and the results were provided to the Gap Analysis Committee for review. The purpose of doing so was that each of the workgroups did their work in isolation, and as a result, might potentially produce suggestions that did not complement the suggestions of other workgroups very well. By allowing the Gap Analysis Committee to review all the suggestions from each of the workgroups, the College could ensure that the final recommendations to the Board of Trustees were coherent, complementary, and complete. As such, all of the workgroup members met with the entire Gap Analysis Committee to present the results of each workgroup's final recommendations, which was followed by a discussion about how these recommendations might be reconciled with one another. At that point, the Gap Analysis Committee took a few weeks to create a final set of recommendations that were, essentially, a sort of an amalgam of what had been the workgroup products.

This set of recommendations was ultimately provided to the Board of Trustees. At that point, the Gap Analysis Committee's mission had been fulfilled as the final stages of the process required oversight by the College's Board of Trustees. After all, in the end, final approval of the strategic plan belonged to the Board of Trustees. Once the strategic planning recommendations from the Gap Analysis Committee were turned over to the Board, the plan was released to the public, and the College entered its public comment period, during which members of the community and employees of the College had the opportunity to comment on the recommendations. The Board provided the public with two opportunities for public comment as the Board addressed the strategic plan during two separate Board meetings, one to address the recommendations of the Gap Analysis Committee and another to review a final version of the strategic plan.

At this point, however, employees expressed concern to the Board about some of the components of the plan. They saw these components as either impractical or a reflection of the strong community influence over the plan, which had the effect of reducing employee influence and input into the strategic plan. The Board created a small team of employees to suggest changes for the Board to review. The changes proposed by this group were excellent, thoughtful, and amenable to the community, and the final draft was approved by the Board of Trustees in May of 2019.

The creation of the College's strategic plan spanned eight months and involved the perspectives of over six hundred people, including employees, current students, community members, high school students, and alumni. The result was a comprehensive plan that positions the College to successfully enter its second century of existence in 2025. I will not discuss the details of the strategic plan itself, since this book is not about the specifics of the College or its strategic plan but rather the process it used to create one. However, the process used by the College was remarkably inclusive. Despite being a small school in a small rural corner of the state, the College managed to engage with over six hundred of its constituents in the development of its strategic plan – some in workgroups, some as members of the exclusive Gap Analysis Committee, some via the survey responses they provided to the College, and some as attendees at College strategic planning listening sessions. In the end, the College created an inclusive process that it could be proud of, in the sense that as a community college, it listened carefully to the community it serves before developing its strategic plan.

It is the nature of strategic planning that not everyone will agree with the end result – I have never seen a strategic plan where everybody involved liked the result. Even so, I have found that the process itself really matters in terms of people's willingness to accept a strategic plan with which they might not entirely agree. For this reason, a very crucial component of strategic planning is creating an inclusive process that is as free from any agenda as possible, so that people will have confidence that, whatever the outcome of the process, the process itself was transparent, and the institution listened carefully to its constituents. I feel pleased with the process that we used because people have told me again and again that they either enjoyed the process, or that they could see that we were working very hard to make it inclusive and to make sure that all voices, even the quiet ones, were heard.

Section 2

Innovation and Experimentation

CHAPTER 1

The Mindset to Create Opportunities

People familiar with the College know that it did a lot of new things, and that in some sense it seemed to have a reasonably healthy appetite for risk. Of course, I do not want to be thought of as reckless, and so I thought I might begin by describing how the mindset adopted at the College lent itself to seeing and seizing opportunities.

For starters, the College adopted and applied the Ice House Entrepreneurship program created by the Entrepreneurial Learning Initiative (ELI), an organization that I have referenced in previous publications and in several of my podcasts. ELI is run by Gary Schoeniger, who is an articulate advocate for entrepreneurship, and if you have not yet examined the curriculum ELI offers, I urge you to do so. Although the program has many beneficial elements, I find its definition of entrepreneurship to be the most helpful. It embraces a broad understanding of an entrepreneur as one who solves the problems of others, which has several advantages for community colleges. First, it does not confine entrepreneurship to the business department or related curriculum – something that is seen very frequently in colleges. Second, it does not rule out students who do not see themselves as business majors, which is one of the significant drawbacks of tying the entrepreneurship curriculum directly to a business program. Finally, and most importantly, it allows the community college to better serve the local community.

The values that ELI encourages its students to emulate and which it seeks to exemplify itself are these (read this list carefully):

- Deliver Exceptional Service
- Challenge Our Assumptions
- Listen to Understand
- Be a Resourceful Problem Solver
- Be Useful, Add Value
- Do the Right Thing
- Work Hard, Eat Well, Be Well
- Reflect, Learn, and Grow

In 2018, Gary Schoeniger published a short piece entitled "How to Recognize Opportunities that Others Overlook" that resonated with me. The projects engaged in at the College were not really about seizing risk but rather focusing on seizing opportunities, and this article is a good jumping-off place for a discussion of what it means for an organization to have an entrepreneurial mindset.

In his article, Schoeniger asks, "so what exactly is a mindset?" and then responds by defining a mindset as the "underlying beliefs, tacit assumptions and thought processes that influence our behavior." Schoeniger points out that while our mindsets help us spot opportunities, they can "trap us in self-defeating cycles." Schoeniger, who travels extensively in his work and interviews many entrepreneurs, writes in his article, "So what are the underlying assumptions that enable entrepreneurs to recognize opportunities that others overlook? Having interviewed hundreds of entrepreneurs across the globe, there seems to be one universal assumption that drives their behavior, which is an assumption that by solving problems for others, they can empower themselves." I am going to repeat that: *By solving problems for others, they can empower themselves.* Schoeniger knows that solving problems for others is just part of the equation. Entrepreneurial leaders have got to be in a position to see what those solutions might be, which can be difficult. Schoeniger points to an excellent book, "Seeing What Others Don't: The

Risk and Reward

Remarkable Ways We Gain Insights" by Gary Klein, a cognitive psychologist. Klein studies how people make decisions in complex and demanding real-world situations and defines a mindset as "a belief that orients the way we handle situations, a way we sort out what's going on, what we should do." Klein describes the challenge that many organizations face: the more organizations rely on rules, the more they codify the workplace, the more organizations define what it is that they do, the less likely employees are to have insights about what they *could* do. Those people who can get over that psychological constraint are going to be much more easily able to see what they could do for others and thus empower themselves.

Let me digress for a moment and say that I was already primed to agree with elements of Schoeniger's program. Not because I had any special knowledge of, or expertise in, entrepreneurship, but because as described in the introduction to this book, I subscribe to the idea that creating good ongoing *systems* should be the true objects of institutions, and that chasing large, singular goals is not the best way to operate. In my experience, large goals lead to underachievement for three reasons: First, most large goals take time to achieve, and there is no way to know whether, over time, a specific large goal will continue to be appropriate for an institution. Second, a focus on a specific goal creates a sort of blindness to alternate, better goals. Third, truly lofty goals require the creation of systems to meet those goals, and it is better to invest in a system that will not be obsolete once a goal is achieved, by developing a system that remains and continues to serve the institution well regardless of the individual goals it adopts for itself.

Because I come from this systems-oriented mindset, which ideally remains open to new long and short-term goals as well as new measurements of progress, Schoeniger's entrepreneurial program, which encourages a mindset of responsivity to emerging opportunities, resonated with me. I believe one of the reasons Independence Community College was successful, why it was objectively the best community college in Kansas (despite being the smallest community college in the state), was because a critical mass of employees had this entrepreneurial mindset. To be clear, that does not mean that they had formal training in that mindset – some of them did through participating in the Ice House Entrepreneurship program offered by Schoeniger – but many of them had no formal training in entrepreneurship at all. Instead, they had developed a mindset of seizing opportunity through the course of their lives, and the impact of that showed in the way that the College capitalized, not just on the good things that came its way, but on the bad things as well, beginning with the origins of Fab Lab ICC.

As I have described on my podcast, when I came to Independence Community College in 2011, the College had introductory engineering programs on the books and an engineering professor, but no completers (i.e., students who were actually completing the engineering programs at the College). The facility in which the programs were housed was impressive in many ways. It was a very large, very nice space, and it was actually the newest building on our campus, but it was nearly totally unused. The building itself had been built and donated by the aerospace company Cessna, and, as a result, the lab space was an engineer's dream, a sort of a blank canvas for a lab. It had everything – high voltage, high ceilings, compressed air – all sorts of great infrastructure – but the space really was not being used for anything, and no, I am not being flippant, the professor was actually using the lab space to store his boat trailer!

By coincidence, the College also had an entrepreneurship program that had no physical home. The program was successful, and had resulted in developing successful businesses in Independence, Kansas. I felt that the person who was directing that entrepreneurship program, Jim Correll, was the right person to convert the engineering space in an entrepreneurial way. So, I met with Jim and made him a proposal: Independence Community College would turn the building over to him for the creation of its very own Fab Lab. (For those who may not be aware, some maker spaces are called "Fab Labs," which simply means that the organizers of the maker space have been granted a license from Fab Lab International to use the name "Fab Lab" and to become part of an international network of maker spaces. Independence Community College obtained that license, and as a result, its maker space is officially called Fab Lab ICC.)

Fab Lab ICC is a creative space that provides community and student access to advanced manufacturing and digital fabrication tools for learning both academic and vocational skills. People tend to think of it as something that is strictly vocational, but it does not need to be that way at all. For example, a Fab Lab can dramatically increase the quality of the art program at a college by providing whole new ways for students to create both 2D and 3D designs. Fab Lab ICC is one of about five hundred MIT-chartered labs in more than twenty-seven countries and was the first Fab Lab developed at a Kansas community college.

Fab Lab ICC hosts activities, classes, and seminars, not just on how to use the equipment there, but also to provide training, encourage creativity, and assist with design. Access is available to pretty much everybody – students, businesses, community members – and the facility is heavily used. It has been almost five years since the College first created the Fab Lab, and it has flourished. I think it is quite amazing in terms of both the depth and the breadth of what Fab Lab ICC has offered, not just to the community but to the entire state of Kansas. During my tenure at the College, Fab Lab ICC created a quarterly program to build prosthetic hands for disabled children and summer camps for middle school girls to learn about and engage in STEM related activities. It helped entrepreneurs bring projects to the market. It provided a working space for multiple local organizations to create and to dream. It had an outreach program to bring some of the equipment of the Fab Lab out to our service area instead of making people come to it. It embraced solar power and became the first Fab Lab in the world to operate substantially on solar energy. It enlarged the curricular offerings at the College by creating courses intended primarily for other, non-entrepreneurship majors unrelated to business. It grew in physical size – a federal grant from the Economic Development Authority allowed it to build an entirely new building next to the original facility.

All of these successes were transforming not only for the College but also for the larger community. When the College did an environmental scan for strategic planning purposes at the College, one hundred percent of the people interviewed (sixty-four randomly selected local people) mentioned the Fab Lab positively. I challenge you to think of something at your own school that one hundred percent of randomly selected survey respondents would independently identify as something they appreciate.

While Fab Lab ICC is staffed and operated by people who are formally trained in the entrepreneurial mindset, I think there are lots of other examples of ways that people at the College have been able to visualize and seize new opportunities simply because they have the mindset, despite not having the formal training.

The first example that comes to my mind relates to the on-campus turf practice field that was built during my tenure at the College. Although I will provide more details about the unique opportunities and challenges involved in this project in the upcoming chapter related to *Last Chance U* and in the section dealing with crisis, suffice it to say that building this practice field was part of a long-range institutional plan, which involved badly-needed, expensive new facilities for which an institution absolutely must plan. The long-range plan was part of a campus-wide collaborative process that was driven by a need to improve facilities over time in a responsible way. Those needs were supported by data that identified the need from both a continuous improvement and a student safety standpoint. After careful consideration of potential funding sources, it was determined that a multi-use turf practice field would be built sometime between 2019 and 2021, likely as part of a larger capital campaign. But then, in Spring 2018, a situation arose out of left field that College leadership and athletics personnel did not expect. The College was renting a different turf field for football practice, and the landlord of that turf field, citing concerns about the wear and tear on their field, exercised their option to cancel the College's lease. They offered a new lease that allowed the use of the field only for competition, which left the

Risk and Reward

College with no turf practice facility, and in fact, no full-size practice facility at all! Our secondary practice facility was a small grass field on campus, which was both smaller than regulation size and, because it was not our primary practice area, was in fairly poor shape prior to the cancellation of the lease.

Essentially, a series of events unfolded fairly rapidly, and what is important to note is they unfolded rapidly for one important, systemic reason, which is that we had done a great deal of planning beforehand and thus could re-open that research when-the urgency arose to complete the project. But equally important was the fact that this was not seen as an obstacle by our athletic department, which immediately saw the situation as an opportunity to engage donors in large part because of, rather than despite, the urgency created by the cancellation of the lease. As a result, not only was the project completed in record time, but it was also completed under budget. As of the time of this writing, eighty-five percent of the project has been privately funded. The financing of the project will occur over an eight-year period, which means the college has an additional eight years to raise the other fifteen percent, which it will do easily. The real reason the College was able to complete the project was that its leadership saw the situation as a problem, but also as an opportunity to do something that it had recognized years ago needed to be done. Because the College had been proactive in its research, and had the ability to visualize an opportunity where others might have only seen a problem, when time became unexpectedly tight, the College as both able and ready to approach donors with a full-fledged plan and could make the entire project, including construction, happen in a very short time.

In both of these situations – Fab Lab ICC and the multi-use use turf athletic field – College personnel worked together to respond to a problem in a unique way. Using an entrepreneurial mindset allowed the College to respond in a certain way – a way that recognizes solutions, possibilities and visualizes a way to move forward – not backward, not sideways, not merely in reactive mode, not just fight or flight. Instead, the

College was able to say, "no, wait a second, this is a problem, but there are a bunch of solutions to that problem, and some of those solutions might actually allow the College move forward in a meaningful way, so let's take a look at those possibilities."

Another great example of the entrepreneurial mindset in action at Independence Community College, occurred when the Higher Learning Commission placed the College on notice. For readers who are not familiar with the term "on notice," it means that although an institution is fully accredited and fully meets the criteria for accreditation, the accreditor believes that some academic or non-academic practices at the institution, if they continue, may cause the institution at some time in the future to fail to meet the standards for accreditation. There were a narrow set of practices at the College that, in the accreditor's eyes, met that criteria. One of those practices was program review, which was being performed very sporadically and was essentially falling farther and farther behind in the kind of regular review that the accreditors expected. Over the next two years, the process was completely overhauled. All programs were reviewed–and brought up-to-date in their review cycles. Program review became the work of a permanent institutionalized committee, staffed with an appropriate membership. The College satisfied accreditation requirements around program review with both the completion of outdated program reviews and the overhaul of the ways in which program reviews are completed, such that they are now very comprehensive and offered employees, the public, and the Board of Trustees (in some cases for the first time) a detailed look at curricula outcomes and academic resource needs. We were proud of this evolution. But why did this happen? The College was, of course, prompted to do it by its accreditors, but the commitment, the opportunity was not just to meet their requirements but to exceed them: to say yes, program review definitely does need help, and yes we can go beyond simply catching up in the review schedule, which is primarily what the accreditors wanted, by correcting everything that is going wrong with program review to make it a much more comprehensive review. The College can codify the process in a much better way by making it so that the process is not dependent on the identity of the person leading the academic part of the school. In other words, we can make it so that it is somewhat impervious to employee turnover, and the College can come out of this with a much, much better process.

I would argue that the College had a mindset to use the opportunity provided by the accreditation process to move beyond simply meeting the bare minimum expectations of Higher Learning Commission, by leveraging the opportunity and buy-in to overhaul the entire process for the good of the institution. While academic program review may not be one of the sexier things that college administrators discuss, it is important to remember that a college is first and foremost a school. The central thing that we offer is the education primarily exemplified by the academic programs that we offer, and careful review and continuous improvement of those programs means serving our students better and better and better. So, I am particularly proud of that project because even more so than the other two examples that I have mentioned, it strikes at the very core of our traditional academic mission, and required a concerted effort to make it better.

I could give many other examples, but I will focus on just one more: when the College revamped its William Inge Theatre Festival, which is hosted every year on the Independence Community College campus, and which is the official theater festival of the state of Kansas. That festival, which was the first theatre festival in the United States to specifically honor playwrights, has been completely retooled to preserve that heritage while refocusing on female playwrights and playwrights of color, both of whom have sadly been largely ignored by the artistic community, in terms of recognizing the quality of their work. Chapter Three of this section includes excerpts from an interview with the person who led that effort, Producing Director Hannah Joyce-Hoven.

Clearly, the entrepreneurial mindset is not about "never wasting a crisis," but instead recognizing that there are many ways to utilize a crisis. Some of these opportunities are noble while others are not so noble. Entrepreneurial mindset is about making a systemic commitment to continuous improvement and fostering an organizational mindset in which people are encouraged to be open-minded enough, and the institution nimble enough, to recognize and seize opportunities that present themselves – in ways that are both noble and beneficial to the institution and its mission. Relying on the idea that "opportunities present themselves" makes it sound like an entrepreneurial mindset involves passive activity, as if the opportunities are just there and just have to be seen. Honestly, sometimes that may be true, but many times it is not.

Instead, what is really exciting is when a group of creative people get together and combine a set of opportunities (sometimes disguised as problems) to create something truly new, something that arguably did not exist until those people decided to work together to create something: a solution that creates real value because it is better – a step, two steps, ten steps better – than a more ordinary way of approaching the situation would have been. The artificial turf field project was like that – various employees came together to combined multiple factors – the renegotiation of a lease resulting in the loss of access to a stadium practice field, the inclination and capacity of our donors, the demonstrated liability of a grass field, and an odd circumstance – the Atlanta Falcons cutting their turf too short for the specifications of a professional football field and needing to unload a "used" but brand-new turf surface. In that circumstance, having an abundance mentality, instead of a scarcity mentality, allowed College employees to see the opportunity in the midst of a negative situation and to convey that vision to supporters. Likewise, a series of events led the College to getting a federal grant from the Economic Development Authority, which allowed the College to build an entirely new building next to the original Fab Lab ICC. In that situation, factors that appeared disparate – the grant from the DEA, the relationship the Fab Lab ICC leaders had built with the decision-makers through their previous good work, the availability of adjacent land, the demonstrable success of the Fab Lab ICC up to that point, the detailed plans for the future, including our commitment to substantial future resources – all worked together to create the perfect opportunity to move a project forward because... a successful organization has leaders that are able to see that the organization already owns all of the pieces to the puzzle.

CHAPTER 2

Entrepreneurship and Maker Spaces

It is crucial that community colleges not only produce entrepreneurs but also are entrepreneurial themselves. At Independence Community College, we fostered an environment of entrepreneurship from which both the College and the community benefited a great deal.

What does the term entrepreneur actually mean? When asked about the meaning behind the term entrepreneur, most people respond with phrases like "small businessperson," "self-employed," and "a profit-seeker." However, the perception of entrepreneurs as primarily people going into business for themselves and thus as businesspeople has actually been detrimental to entrepreneurship education, and detrimental to entrepreneurs because it creates too narrow of a focus. Colleges have likewise failed to settle on a clear understanding of the meaning of the term entrepreneur although they do tend to lean toward similar descriptions.

In preparing for this book, I visited the websites of colleges that brand themselves as entrepreneurial. I found a wide range of entrepreneurial branding including a description about producing graduates who understand how to market the products and services they have produced to business management training to a focus on some area of economics education. Although there are very, very wide-ranging possible descriptions for entrepreneurship, most descriptions were also pretty limiting and likely contribute to significantly limiting those who see themselves as entrepreneurs or as being entrepreneurial. A community college that accepts narrow definitions of entrepreneurship is going to run into familiar trouble, by significantly limiting the number and types of students for whom entrepreneurship curriculum might be attractive. More importantly, those entrepreneurship programs are likely going to produce graduates who are, on the whole, not actually very entrepreneurial.

Why is it so critical that community colleges be entrepreneurial? Most importantly, it allows the community college to better serve the local community. If a community college views itself as entrepreneurial and able to solve the problems of its constituents, it is naturally going to be far more responsive to the community it serves. As community college leadership knows, and as the name implies, colleges have a special obligation to meet the needs of their communities. By embracing an entrepreneurial mindset, an institution embraces the opportunity to solve the problems of others and is one of the most effective ways for creating strong bonds within the community itself. Let me remind you of a previously discussed example of this: When Independence Community College did an environmental scan for one part of our strategic planning a number of years ago, we interviewed sixty-four community members taken from a broad variety of demographics – business people, homemakers, students, retirees, etc. – and one hundred percent of the people interviewed favorably referenced Fab Lab ICC (which is run by the Entrepreneurship Program) and more significantly they did this unprompted in response to general open-ended questions in the survey. Again, I challenge you to think of something at your own school that one hundred percent of randomly selected survey respondents would spontaneously identify as something they value and appreciate.

The Secret to a Successful Maker Space

What made the maker space (Fab Lab ICC) so successful, and how can other institutions replicate it?

Maker spaces are typically places where people can work collaboratively to create physical objects using tools ranging from low-tech (like a wrench) to high-tech (like a 3D printer). However, in practice, maker spaces have become much more than that – their computing capabilities make possible the creation of virtual objects, and their collaborative environments often encourage people to go beyond fabrication and venture into the areas of marketing, business development, and entrepreneurship. Maker spaces are often used as incubators and accelerators for business start-ups.

The maker space is often an integral part of college entrepreneurship programs. In fact, there are nearly a thousand maker spaces in the United States, and the majority of them are housed in educational institutions. Yet, as important as it is for entrepreneurship programs to create flourishing maker spaces, in many cases, many institutions struggle to create productive maker spaces, and to ensure they are successful enough to reach their full potential in serving students and the community. There are many more unfinished maker spaces in the United States than there are finished ones – many, many colleges, communities, and school districts have plans to create a maker space, or have actually started to create one, and then found that the process can be challenging.

I would like to offer my theory for why educational institutions struggle to create vibrant maker spaces. I am personally acquainted with four maker spaces that have been trying to get off the ground, unsuccessfully, for three years or more and four others which have opened but serve very small and/or very narrow audiences. All eight of these maker spaces suffer from the same problem, a shallowness in either their mission or the execution of their mission, which causes supporters or users to think of them in terms of only the whiz-bang equipment inside. The result is failure. The success of maker spaces, whether in the developmental stage or the operational stage, is entirely dependent on the mindset of its people. For most people, creativity is a novel experience and therefore a bit frightening, and for many people, working with their hands is also novel and frightening. Machines do not cure this fright – people do.

Recall, when I came to Independence Community College in 2011, the College had engineering programs on the books and a large lab space that was almost entirely unused. Coincidentally, the College also had an entrepreneurship program that had no physical home on campus. So, I met with the director of the entrepreneurship program, Jim Correll, and proposed that we turn the building over to his program and create Fab Lab ICC if he would direct that project. Believe me, Jim Correll did not need any convincing – he was all over it. Over the next six months, with a little help from me, Correll raised donations of both money and gifts to equip the new lab. The College also made some basic investments in the infrastructure of the lab and we were off to the races. We hired a person named Tim Haynes to be the manager of the lab. Tim Haynes was already an employee at the College – he worked in the library – but I believed that his real heart was in the traditional mission of the maker space.

Five years later, the Fab Lab ICC has flourished. I do not make that judgment lightly – the lab's accomplishments over that time have been amazing in both their depth and breadth. In addition to the accomplishments mentioned earlier (a quarterly program to build prosthetic hands for disabled children, a summer camp for middle school girls to engage in interactive STEM activities, a working space for multiple local organizations to create and dream, an outreach program that brings some of the equipment of the Fab Lab out to our service area instead of making people come to us, etc.), the real change has been the awareness and self-efficacy that we have brought to the people of the community. Recall the example I gave earlier: there was only one positive attribute of the college mentioned by one hundred percent of respondents to a survey – the Fab Lab. We had never seen a result like this before. Success stories regarding publicly funded organizations, especially educational institutions, also tend to be divisive – success in sports antagonizes those who do not like sports, success in the arts antagonizes people who do not care for public funding of the arts, and so on. The Fab Lab seemed to be largely immune from criticism. Why?

I believe that the main reason for the success of the Fab Lab was the entrepreneurial mindset of the people running it. The staff at Fab Lab

ICC have wholly internalized the values of the Ice House Entrepreneurial Program, and it is this mindset that is at the core of the success of the lab. I am sure anyone who thinks for a moment about the ideals of the entrepreneurial mindset, and envisions an organization that exemplifies them, would find it easy to see why people who use Fab Lab ICC feel well-served and challenged, and why the community considers the lab to be a real difference-maker. Although the sophisticated machines at the lab are exciting, I believe strongly that the success of the lab has nearly nothing to do with them. A maker space with 3D printers can open in a community, but unless the staff engages in dedicated outreach and provides genuine service to users, the maker space will remain a small niche business that serves a tiny group of dedicated hobbyists who do not need help with tools or design. Most people need help, and providing that guidance is what makes the difference in a maker space, not the fancy printers or sophisticated machinery.

Lessons Learned

First, an institution should structure its entrepreneurship program in such a way that any major can earn an entrepreneurial credential as part of their degree. Easy to say, hard to do because the institution would also need to do the next two things, which require a disruption of the status quo.

Second, the institution needs to encourage the entrepreneurship program to be structurally separate from the business program or the business school. At Independence Community College, the entrepreneurship program is structurally unrelated to the business-related programs, even though it often includes a focus on mentoring businesspeople.

Third, an institution needs to adopt a specific definition of entrepreneurship that is sufficiently broad to allow anyone to see themselves as an entrepreneur if they are so inclined. Independence Community College developed its entrepreneurship program around the definition created by ELI, but there are certainly other ways to approach this.

Risk and Reward

Fourth, in recognition that by using a broad definition of entrepreneurship, which is at odds with modern cultural assumptions about entrepreneurs, an institution must put itself in a position to conduct specific outreach to students and other groups that might not fit the traditional cultural model of entrepreneurship. In so doing, an institution can refute the assumptions that support automatically viewing entrepreneurs in a very narrow way. Through outreach and education, an institution can help people think about entrepreneurs in a broader way, one that is more appealing to people and has a broader audience in a way that is very deliberate and thorough in overcoming the cultural bias we have about entrepreneurship.

Finally, as I described earlier, the staff must engage in dedicated outreach and provide genuine service to users. Most people need help, and providing that guidance is what makes the difference in a maker space, and more generally, in entrepreneurship.

The result will be entrepreneurial graduates who apply their talents to a wide variety of fields and a community college that is better positioned to serve its community. Plus, as the needs of the community change, an entrepreneurial college will be better equipped to meet those needs and solve problems – because the truth is the community WILL change, and having an entrepreneurial mindset will allow a college to not only change with the community, but also to change in ways that help the community address its own changes. A college that has a culture of not just solving problems but also seeking problems to solve will be in the best position to recognize and address future changes and challenges. For example, in a small community of modest means like Independence, fostering small businesses that could grow was very desirable, and so the entrepreneurship program focused on creating real, small businesses. To this day, many of the most successful small businesses in the community were started and run by graduates of the College's entrepreneurship program.

CHAPTER 3

Re-imagining: Conversations with Academics Creating Change

Jim Correll and Tim Haynes – The Guys Who Run the ICC Fab Lab

In preparation for this book, I asked Jim Correll and Tim Haynes to be guests on my podcast. My interview with them (slightly edited for length and clarity) is an excellent glimpse into the mindset of two service-oriented people dedicated to the entrepreneurial mindset and to helping other rural communities ignite their own entrepreneurial passions through the development of maker spaces.

Dan: I've got the two bosses of the Fab Lab here with me today, Tim Hanes and Jim Correll. Jim Correll is, I guess his official title is, Jim, tell me...

Jim: Director... Director of Fab Lab ICC.

Dan: Director of Fab Lab ICC and Tim Hanes?

Tim: I am the Fab Lab Manager. Jim is my boss.

Dan: (Laughs) He's like, "just want to make that relationship clear there." (Tim laughs.) So this is kind of a wild place. Not two minutes ago, Jim poked his head in the door and said, "either one of you guys got away to light a fire?" So neither one of us did, so I don't know what he did, and I don't know why the person wanted to light a fire. In the last podcast, I told you all about Fab Lab ICC and their work with local entrepreneurs and the mindset here, but I thought you might like to hear it from the horse's mouth. So I've got the two horses here, and you're going to hear it from their mouths. So my first question for you is this, I've claimed that the Fab Lab is successful, but how do you measure its success?

Jim: Well, we measure it by the reactions we see when people come in and learn how to do things that they didn't think they were able to do, but just the fact that we've had probably going on 21,000 or 22,000 visits in the four and a half years we've been open I think, is kind of an indicator, and we've had three or four entrepreneurs that have started out working in the Fab Lab and then gotten so busy that they bought their own equipment and went out on their own. So I guess success is on a lot of different levels because we deal with a lot of different types of users from K-12 kids up through a few college students and then the community members and entrepreneurs.

Tim: I'll add that it's also in the number of lives changed, and that doesn't always take a form that lends itself well to statistics or numbers. A lot of that is anecdotal. A lot of that is just what you feel when you interact with someone and they finally, grow some wings and learn to kind of fly in the Fab Lab a little bit, do things on their own, maybe for the first time they've ever done [it] before. I mean, there's a number of ways we could measure success that aren't easy to track. There are high schools that come on field trips here from hours away, and then there are high schools who don't come on field trips here that are 15 minutes away. How do you measure that success? You know, the word is getting out really far and yet still sometimes it feels like it's difficult to make in-roads. I don't know how to reconcile those.

Dan: It's fascinating…of course, I'm hearing your answers to my questions for the first time, but both of you, when I asked you the question about how you measured the success of the Fab Lab, both of you talked in terms of the people that you were impacting. So in the original podcast about Fab Lab ICC, I talked about how it wasn't the sexy machines, it was the way that you were interacting with people. And I noticed that even though, for example, you guys just built an addition onto this place that more than doubled the size of the place, not one of you mentioned that as a measure of your success. Not one of you mentioned the donations you have received or anything like that. Your answer from both of you was one hundred percent about the people that you're working with.

Jim: I think we have, we may both have a different way of looking at that because for us, the kind of the number one goal is to change the way people think, and even to change a few lives here and there. I think one of the reasons that the donations have come in and that the building has been built is just because when other people see that, when they see a bunch of kids in here and see how they're engaged, and they come alive, they liked that, and they'll donate money for it. So yes, it's been really phenomenal – the amount of money that we've had donated and that we were able to put this new building up, but we still kind of think of it in terms of the human element and how we changed the way people view themselves.

Tim: Yeah, very much so. I think it's sometimes intimidating to see just all the space unless somebody is using it because it's not always easy to visualize yourself. I'm utilizing all the resources here. If you don't see anyone else doing that, I think sometimes it takes a little bit of a visual stimulus, a little bit of a model. Somebody that's doing a process or interacting with a machine or even some software in order to see that yes, it's possible and people are using the Fab Lab to do what they need to do and even if they don't know how to do it today, they can learn because somebody else learned and many people have in the past here.

Dan: Well, speaking of many people, let me give you an opportunity. What success story of the lab is most significant to you?

Tim: For me, it's probably the high school student who was coming here for summer, basically summer school, a couple summers, and finally decided to launch a little side business, laser etching, and has become successful enough that he's considering doing that full time. He's also a college student, has graduated high school and moved on to Pitt State, but we still see him back here regularly. He still stays engaged with us, and he always was going to be successful. But I think his vision of what success means for him is a little different after coming to the Fab Lab.

Dan: Jim?

Jim: I think one of mine is probably the salon owner downtown that didn't know anything about fabrication equipment or any of that. She knew how to do hair and nails, and she learned how to do enough to construct her own sign for above her awning downtown. And now she's re-done all her vinyl's and she almost tears up a little bit when she talks about that. And so seeing that increase in self-confidence and people as they've, as they learned to do things and in this case, it's a small business owner who saved quite a bit of money, probably a few thousand dollars, by doing that work herself. That's pretty powerful for me.

Tim: And I'll just kind of add to what Jim said. It's really cools for us as the director and the manager of the Fab Lab to be able to share in these case studies. It's almost never the case that I will interact with somebody in isolation. And Jim won't interact with them or vice versa, that Jim will interact with somebody and I won't. It's very rarely the case that one of us gets to enjoy success with a member or a Fab Lab user in some capacity, and the other one won't get to share in that success story. We get to do both, and so I think we get to high five a lot when it comes to that sort of thing, and that charges us up.

Dan: That does sound pretty cool. Now one thing I did not talk about in the last Fab Lab episode was that I've been to plenty of other labs, and I know you have too. But in terms of the amount of time that a lab focuses on the different parts of what it does, there's something disproportionate about this Fab Lab, which is that it appears to me you spend far more time than most Fab Labs procreating and trying to create new Fab Labs elsewhere, new maker spaces. You have these boot camps where these people come in from other communities and learn about how to put a maker space in their community, and you're very focused on that. And I just, I think I'd like you to talk about maybe two things. One, all of us have sort of observed how other communities struggle to put in maker spaces, and two, I guess I'd like to talk about why you feel so focused on helping other people create maker spaces rather than focusing on just this one.

Jim: Well, I'll lead off, and then I'm sure Tim will have something to add. We learned about the combination of entrepreneurial thinking and the making itself, and what a powerful tool that can be in encouraging entrepreneurship in a small town. All these rural communities across America are shrinking, and nobody can seem to figure out what to do to reverse that. For fifty years, we've told the youth of these communities, I have to go somewhere else to have opportunities. And yet we see that in most of the community there's still people with money. They still have problems to solve, and there's still room for small businesses to start. And so once we learn what a powerful combination, the entrepreneurship and the maker space was, we started believing that every rural community [needed] to have one, and it's not just the equipment, but it's the sort of comradery and the increase in self-advocacy that everybody gets working and it's almost a way to build community pride. And so as we discovered that on our own, we became passionate about trying to help other communities figure out how to start maker spaces. And then we're very privileged because Network Kansas, which is a remarkable story in itself, is a unique program among the United States for promoting entrepreneurship within Kansas. They see what we've done here, and they've made us one of their certified programs. So I'm there helping us try to spread this, how to do this around Kansas.

Tim: And I'll think, I think that it's really a movement that needs to go viral to a greater extent than it has. There are over 1600 Fab Labs that are part of the International Fab Lab network right now and there are other private maker spaces that aren't part of that network. We happened to be a part of that network. We are one of the 1600; when we first started our Fab Lab, I think that count was around 600 globally. So it's, it's grown by leaps and bounds just in the four years that we've been open. But there is no glory in it necessarily for us personally. There's just this imperative for us to remain sort of mission-driven and our mission really is to spread innovation and hope, among the other activities that we do to achieve those goals, and to fulfill that mission and part of that mission, involves spreading it far and wide. How can we really spread it far and wide just on our own? You know, it would make a whole lot more sense for us, for the Fab Labs to go viral in our region. And so we show people how we did it in, in, in the hope that they might be able to replicate our success at some scale and, and also to communicate just how little it really takes to start a Fab Lab. You don't have to do it the way that we did it. There are many ways to do it, and none of those ways have to be exceedingly expensive or time-consuming.

Dan: Can you tell us a little bit about that? I mean, what is sort of the bare minimum you could do in order to create a maker space?

Tim: I guess, I guess I'll kind of let Jim weigh in on that. I think it doesn't take a whole lot of equipment. Maybe one or two affordable machines, maybe a 3D printer, maybe a laser, and really just a space borrowed or, otherwise temporarily occupied.

Jim: I would agree with that. The 3D printers are whatever everybody wants in a maker space and they actually aren't as creative as a bunch of the other machines, but they are affordable especially now. And then the laser is one of the most popular machines, so I've told people…

Dan: Can you just tell people what this laser does?

Jim: The laser – the ones that we have and the ones that are affordable are not big industrial lasers that will cut through quarter-inch plate steel, but these will cut nonmetallic materials like wood and leather and acrylic and then they a laser etch or burn basically designs and letters and things into the service so they can cut shapes out and burn letters and artwork into services. And that's what makes them so popular that the computer treats them sort of like a printer and so it's a little bit more complicated than learning to print something, but it's not, it's not as complicated as learning to use some of the other machines. So we tell small communities, many of the small communities still have a library, so we tell them that for let's say $20,000 even they could put a laser in a 3D printer in the local library – and that gets [it] started.

And then now a quick story of a woman in western Kansas, and I'm in a town called Jetmore, and this is a problem, and in a lot of communities people think that maker spaces are just for geeks to go to make stuff, so they don't see the potential – it has an effect on everybody. So, she came to our boot camp, and she went back to her small town, which is probably only I think three or four thousand people and she started telling everybody they needed a maker space, and everybody was saying, well what is that and who would use it? So then she bought a couple of pieces of equipment, I think Network Kansas actually helped her do that. She bought a couple of pieces of equipment, and then she had a little boot camp for some youth in the summer in that little town. Now the youth are all on fire, and that fire is spreading to the parents, and so people are starting to get it, and that they don't even have a space yet. But they just did it in the local rec center I think or something. We're going to add that to our strategy because people won't know what it is, and getting the kids started on it is a way to help that spread.

And I got one last week. I get a lot of inquiries from community colleges around the United States that want to put in a maker space, or many times they'll say we want to partner with our city to put in a maker space, and then they say they're going to do a community needs assessment. And I have to figure out a way tactfully to say I'm not sure that'll be very helpful because in most communities they're not going to know what you're talking about, so they're not going to know what kind of equipment they'll want, because they don't even know what a maker space is and the one that I talked to most recently was in Wyoming, I think. In Kansas, most of the communities don't know what maker spaces are, but I know that that's pretty common and maybe that'll change over the years. But people that do want to know what maker spaces are, tend to think, they're just for the sort of geeky nerds, and they're really not, they're really for everybody.

Tim: And even if you think you have a good idea of what a maker space is, it's also possible that if you're trying to start a maker space, you may think there's a certain set of criteria. What defines a maker space? And moreover, what defines the people who use or the people who work at a maker space? I didn't know what a maker space was really when I started working at the Fab Lab, and looking back, I can see it didn't matter that I didn't know really what a maker's space was. You figure it out as you go. And I think what value we bring to the community, what value we bring to ICC, to the region of southeast Kansas has changed over the years too – and that's okay. I think that's the way it should be. What it shows is that we're not static or dynamic. We're continuing to adapt, and effectively we are adapting to become more closely aligned with what people want us to do.

Dan: Okay. One last question for you guys. So close your eyes and imagine what does the Fab Lab look like in five years now? I say five years, but you know, if you'd prefer a different timeframe, ten years, that's okay too. I'm really just wondering what the end-game is here and you know, maybe if you're ever-changing, as Tim said, you know, there's, there's no ultimate end game, but take a five-year horizon. What do you hope to be offering then? What does the Fab Lab look like?

Jim: I'll start, then Tim can weigh in, and we already just within the last month have had somebody with a pretty good size office say, "if you ever expand again, we would like to move our office and be a part of that." So my five-year vision and

Risk and Reward

by the way, well it's two things. We try not to have a firm vision because we want to stay flexible for the opportunities that come forward but right now I could see a small, almost strip mall type of a building going up adjacent to the Fab Lab where we could have some retail spaces and possibly some office spaces because I think more people will want to be a part of this and be a part of this atmosphere that's out here. And the other thing that I think would be cool is to have some container stores and container buildings. Like there's a thing called the Box Yard in Tulsa, which is a whole small shopping center that's made up of shipping containers and there's many, many small shops and one of them is, has several of these put together, and there's a bar on the upper level and the restaurant. So that's something that you could kind of move in and do experimental retail. And the other thing I'll add is maybe a facility either here or somewhere else in town where once the business got their prototyping done and started selling, they're selling their product. They would maybe have a place to go for another year or two and then do manufacturing runs before they actually have to acquire a building and their own equipment and all that kind of stuff so they can do some light production runs in the Fab Lab, but eventually, they run out of capacity. So if we had somewhere where we could move them for phase two, I think that'd be pretty cool.

Dan: Tim, would you like to describe a dream that completely conflicts with what Jim just told us? [Laughs]

Tim: Nothing that conflicts, we try not to contradict each other when, when we can avoid it. [Smiles] In this case, I think his vision and mine can coincide quite nicely. My vision is that, you know, every day of the school week we are just flooded with schools, with K-12 students who come in here for after school programs and they are, you know, more or less

156

supervised, but really self-directed in the kinds of activities that they do out here. I'd like to have more, sort of hands-on basic skills, like leatherworking, more woodworking, and I'm talking small scale stuff like birdhouses and things like that. I'd love to have some sort of canned activities that are sort of modular, like, for example, a shoe-making kit or a birdhouse kit or something that can be done in a sort of fixed amount of time. A lot of the projects out here are so free form, it's very difficult, and that's not a bad thing, but it's very difficult to see exactly how long it's going to take to finish a project and if we had some more activities and more offerings, like little kits, DIY kits, it might engage a different kind of person and it might help take the training wheels off of, of people's creativity a little bit faster. If they could just get one or two successes under their belt. And I'd love to see more, more youth out here.

Jim: That's really good. And I'd like to add a couple things to that because I don't remember if you covered it in your other podcast or not. But one of the things that we learned is not only the young people, but many of the adults too, they can't do things with their hands. So our Fab Lab is not just for digital fabrication. Our Fab Lab always includes handwork too because the kids don't know how to use hand tools and you're still going to have to be able to do those if you're going to be very independent when you're an adult. So all those things Tim just said, are good.

And there's another thing I'm going to predict that within five years the world of academia will have discovered and embraced the power of experiential learning and that means that our Fab Lab and other Fab Labs as far as having tutoring centers and even a class for homeschool kids where it's all project-based and people are learning their math and science to making things. Kids, when they are on fire to make

Risk and Reward

something they're interested in, will learn whatever they need to learn to make it work – and there's a huge potential in that.

Tim: I'll agree. It's really a lot easier to teach any math concept really by application. And I think there's some strong connection between a hands-on project where you're actually using your and not necessarily just clicking a mouse and typing keys on a computer, but actually using your hands to craft something it, it helps those concepts really sink in. You know, one example is when I show somebody the software that runs our CNC plasma cutter, for example, there is an origin and they have to understand coordinate plane geometry in order to make that thing function. And they may hate geometry, but everybody enjoys cutting out a sign. Everybody enjoys making some plasma-cut metal art. So if you have to understand a little bit of coordinate plane geometry just to do a basic project, they will even enjoy it so much. Most of them will go to the next step and learn some more advanced concepts of geometry to make it a more advanced CNC Plasma-cut project. That is the way we ought to be teaching math concepts, and it's fun.

Jim: I might just add that there are, there are schools and classes around the country that have dumped the drilling and continuous practice for standardized testing and just turn the students loose with project-based learning, and they not only were excited about it, but they did just as good or better on the standardized tests as the other kids who were stuck with drilling for them all the time. Anyway. So this maybe is really something that I think we're just beginning to understand the way that it could promote learning.

Tim: And it's extremely uncomfortable, I think, for students who are steeped in a more traditional classroom learning environment where they're told to sit down and be quiet and listen to the expert at the front of the room tell them exactly what they need to know so that they can pass a test. Now we don't do it here that way, and I think that it's uncomfortable at first for students who were raised the other way or who have gone through the k-12 school system without much hands-on learning experience. But once they get a taste of how it's different out here at the Fab Lab, most of them will make sort of sidebar comments like, "man, I wish school were more like this." And it begs the question, what if school were more like Fab Lab? What if Fab Lab were school? Some places are starting to get that, and other places aren't. Ultimately, I think the future looks quite a bit different. I think Fab Labs are the future of school and we may come to a point in the future when schools that do it the traditional way, the old way, are just going to be left behind.

The Rebirth of the William Inge Theatre Festival: A Conversation with Producing Director Hannah Joyce-Hoven

Innovation and entrepreneurship can be displayed in many ways. One of the displays of innovation and entrepreneurship that I am most proud of from my time at Independence Community College involved the re-imagining of the William Inge Theatre Festival. When I came to the College, the festival was struggling in many ways: it lacked artistic direction, attendance was falling (particularly locally), it was not financially sustainable, it was not creating enrollment in the College's theatre program, and it was not contributing as much as it could to the culture of the community. From 2012-2018, the festival was transformed into a much more relevant, much more successful, and much more sustainable festival. I am so grateful to Hannah Joyce-Hoven, the producing director of the festival and what follows is a partial transcript from a podcast interview with her, which provides the reader with insights into the innovative methods she used to lead the team that tackled the problems facing the College's William Inge Theatre Festival and how those methods forever changed the festival.

<u>Risk and Reward</u>

Dan: I'm here with Hannah Joyce Hoven, a person who I think of as a dear friend because I have known her for a very long time. When I came to ICC in 2011, she was already an employee here and had been an employee here for, I would say, at least two or three years…

Hannah: Since 2004.

Dan: Her husband was an English teacher at the same time, her husband, Matt, and so I've known her ever since then. So, so that means I've known you for eight years.

Hannah: [Laughs] Yeah.

Dan: So what I'm going to do first is I'm going to embarrass Hannah by making her sit there while I read who she is, a little bit about her, her biography, which is pretty remarkable. [Hannah laughs.] She's professionally speaking, she's a pretty incredible person and that's why she is the Artistic Director of the William Inge Theater Festival here at Independence Community College. Hannah Joyce Hoven is the Director of Membership Programs at the Playwrights' Center in Minneapolis and the Producing Director of the William Inge Theater Festival in Independence here. She is the ultimate playwright fan girl. Hannah has helped to develop the new work of some of the country's finest playwrights, among them Caridad Svich, Alice Tuan, and E.M. Lewis. Prior to joining the playwrights' team, she was the Director of Operations at the William Inge Center for the arts, which is where I met her originally. In her time at the Inge Center, Hannah was on the executive producing team for twelve festivals (we have an annual festival here at the William Inge Theater Festival honoring visionary American Playwrights) [where she] co-produced over forty new play development workshops with playwrights from across the country and hosted hundreds of guests, theater

160

artists on the center's campus. Originally from Saint Louis, Hannah has worked and performed with a number of theater companies throughout the Midwest, including the Repertory Theatre of St. Louis, the St. Louis Shakespeare Company, and the Prison Performing Arts, which is intriguing. Hannah serves on the Board of the William Inge Festival Foundation. Her education and training include a Bachelor of Arts from Wheaton College, the Lincoln Center Education Teaching Artists Certification, and yoga teacher training. She is also an actor, singer, and Yogi – and I have seen her do all three of those things. Hannah, welcome to the podcast.

Hannah: Thank you very much. I'm happy to be here.

Dan: I thought maybe I described that you are the Artistic Director of the William Inge Theater Festival. Now this is a little complicated for somebody who isn't associated with ICC, but there are actually two entities here with sort of similar names, and to make it worse, one entity is embedded in the other. There is something here called the William Inge Center for the Arts, and that is an organization, and but that center for the arts, one of their primary responsibilities is that they put on the William Inge Theater Festival, an annual event which is the official state theater festival of the State of Kansas. Hannah is the artistic director actually, Hannah, I say you're the artistic director. But is that the actual official title?

Hannah: I think the official title is Producing Director, but it made… they are sort of kind of the same.

Dan: Yeah, I think, right. I think it changed; I think maybe a year or two ago because when I came here for the longest time it was the artistic director and I think they actually changed the name to better reflect what the person was actually

Risk and Reward

	doing. Sorry, I'll change the name to producing director.
Hannah:	Correct.
Dan:	You've been here a lot longer than I have, and you've been associated with the festival for a lot longer than I have. Could you just tell our listeners a little bit about what the William Inge Theater Festival is? How it came to be and a little bit about William Inge himself perhaps?
Hannah:	Yes. I would be happy to. William Inge, who was a playwright and a screenwriter, and he really hit the world scene on the theater scene in the fifties and sixties; he had plays on Broadway. He had films, his screenplay "Splendor in the Grass," featured Natalie Wood and Warren Beatty. And that was sort of their first, I would say for Warren Beatty. It kind of made his career take off after that. He had a screenplay called "Bus Stop" that featured Marilyn Monroe, and he had a number of plays that did really well on Broadway, including "Dark at the Top of the Stairs," "Picnic," which many high schools and colleges have done over the years, all over the country. Most recently, they did a revival of his play "Come Back, Little Sheba" on Broadway, but I think that was five, four more years ago. So William Inge had an incredible career. He was inspired by Tennessee Williams when Inge was living and working in Saint Louis, and working for the St Louis Post as the theater critic, and he saw "A Glass Menagerie" and was blown away by it. And so he met Tennessee Williams afterward, and they talked. Tennessee is actually who encouraged him to start writing plays. So he did, and he became quite successful. William Inge was a closeted gay man back in the fifties and sixties, and that was a really difficult time to be gay, and he never really found a way to live that way authentically. So he was very depressed, and in his later years, he was having some plays, but they weren't getting great reviews, and he started

to feel like he didn't have anything more to give in terms of the theater. And so tragically he took his life, but William Inge had a really big impact on a lot of people over his career, including people in the town of Independence where he grew up. One of his former classmates, who was also on faculty at Independence Community College at the time, she wanted to somehow honor his life and his legacy here in his hometown.

Dan: That's Margaret Goheen?

Hannah: Yes. And William Inge's sister during that same period decided that she wanted to donate all of Inge's books and his artwork and his collections and his plays, both finished and unfinished, to the Community College, Independence Community College here where he also attended and so the donation of what is now known as the Inge Collection, and Margaret Goheen's desire to celebrate Inge was the beginning of this seed of the William Inge Theater Festival. Margaret, who was also teaching theater, happened to have a connection to Jerome Lawrence, who was also a playwright. The two of them worked together to decide what would be a fitting way to celebrate Inge and they decided together that maybe if at the point in his career where he had taken his life, if he had been given some recognition, if someone had said, your work matters, keep writing, that he would have felt like he could continue. So that was sort of the spirit in which the festival began, that they would celebrate playwrights who'd had a long career in theater, who had a significant impact, but who weren't being celebrated as much anymore because they were getting older, but who were still working to give them a recognition at that moment in their career and tell them, keep going. We see you; we see your work and, and we love you.

Risk and Reward

Dan: Now this, this festival occurred every year for how many years? Thirty?

Hannah: Thirty-eight. So we're about to start our 38th annual festival here in just a few more weeks. And over the years we've honored some incredible playwrights, people who many will recognize: Neil Simon, Stevens Sondheim, Arthur Miller, August Wilson, Paula Vogel, Wendy Wasserstein, the list goes on and on. There's some just really incredible playwrights, and they all come to Independence, Kansas.

Dan: And that totally blows me away that it hosts the official state theater festival because of course, you know, Kansas like many other states, has much larger cities that have large universities in them and can be, you know, are very, very cultural places, and instead of the state theater festival existing in one of those places, it's here in Independence, which kind of always surprises me.

Hannah: Oh, it's incredible. It's really amazing. Yeah.

Dan: Yeah. Well, thirty-eight years. Okay, so let me tell you a story. When I came here, the first year I was president here, I had a meeting during the Inge Festival, which by the way, occurs at sort of the end of the academic year. It varies a little from year to year, but it's, it's sort of toward the end of what academics think of as the year. And the executive board of the Inge Festival Foundation asked to meet with me, right here in the office where Hannah and I are sitting, and we sat down, and I remember that these people were actually, every one of them, was from out of town – I think all of them at the time were from the east coast. So these were not local people that I meet with regularly, and they sat down. So we got acquainted for a few minutes and then the person at the time who was the president of the foundation, he, he looked at me, and he said, "Now, the most important thing you have to understand is that in ten years there will be no festival." Hannah, by the way, just raised her eyebrows. [Hannah laughs.] I said, what do you mean? And he was very frank. He said, "Look, look at me. I'm not getting any younger. And look at the other people in this room. We're not getting any younger either and in another ten years the people who go to this festival, who originally started going to this festival because they were in some way, peers of William Inge, thirty-something years ago, those people in another ten years, we're all going to need new hips or new knees. Traveling to Independence, Kansas, in the spring is not something we can all manage to do. When I look at who's coming to this festival, it feels like it's the same people coming each year, and there are fewer and fewer of them every year." And he said, so unless something is done about that in ten years, there will be no more festival. I took that to heart. It's eight years now, and I still remember that exact speech he gave me and I'm thinking to myself, okay, it's eight years later and unless the festival is going to go away due to lack of attendance in two years, that it seems like he was wrong. Well, he wasn't wrong at the time. His concern was genuine, and his concern was appropriate for the circumstances that he saw. But Hannah is one of the people who has been part of the effort. She has worked, I think, every year on the festival, right?

Hannah: Yeah. Except for one, just one year.

Dan: She has been part of the effort to basically take something that began in one context, and that context may not have a market indefinitely. And basically, she's been part of the effort to continue to reimagine the festival in ways that will bring what is so interesting and fun about playwriting to a wider and wider audience. So with that long setup, I thought it might be helpful since ultimately, this podcast is about

Risk and Reward

how educational institutions can administratively, address challenges they face. I thought it might be interesting to have Hannah talk a little bit about the kinds of changes that have occurred in the festival. Not just since she's been the artistic director, because remember she worked on the festival even before that, but really what's been done over the last four years or so, in which we've really made a concerted effort to alter the trajectory of the festival in order to create markets. And now I'm probably stealing her thunder at that point. So, Hannah, can you tell us a little bit about your efforts in that area?

Hannah: Yes. So I know who you were talking about and I won't name any names, but I will say that the concern was real, not imagined and I think that a lot of theaters across the country are facing this very thing. We giggle and laugh about the gray hairs who show up at theater productions but what's true about that is that we have built our theaters to serve a specific audience and that audience is aging out and over time that audience, who is well-educated, has money, likes to see specific kinds of plays, won't be with us anymore. And so what, what does the theater as a whole across the country do about that? And this is a conversation that is not just happening, you know, between you and I right now, but in these major theaters across the country and the answer is really going to have to be a creative problem-solving answer.

And I think a lot of what I believe and am discovering working with playwrights my entire career, which has been really special, is that the stories we see on stage have to matter to the people who are in the audiences. Although we all love Shakespeare, he's not necessarily speaking to the hearts and minds of the young people who are growing up or even the, you know, middle-aged folks who are possibly going to be in our audiences. There are so many stories. There are so many perspectives that we all want to see right now. We are living in a divided country, and if we can't find common ground across our sides, which seem to be two sides in every situation, then we're not going to make it as a society very well. And storytelling plays, in particular because they are alive and on stage, have these universal truths that we can all identify with. And I believe that the power of new plays is that they can bring us together, they can show us these universal truths in a way that allow us to have empathy for people who may not have the same political views or cultural views that as we do. And I also believe that plays and stories are going to show us the way forward in this really difficult and divided time.

Dan: So how, how has that manifested itself? Of course, I agree with what you're saying, and I've observed the truth of what you're saying the entire time that I've been here. I know that has led to some very conscious changes in the festival. What are those?

Hannah: Yeah, so there have been a few different ways that we are kind of activating these beliefs. We have a new play lab that we started a few years ago. And so in the afternoons, during the festival days, we're now featuring new plays by playwrights who've written these plays in there coming from around the country, and they're on a variety of different topics and things like that, but they're short ten minute to thirty-minute plays, and we're bringing actors from around the region. So it's a great opportunity to see a lot of new plays and a very short amount of time, and it's engaging artists.

So let me back up and say that we for a long time, the Inge Festival liked to bring professional theater artists from LA and New York and Chicago and we like to pull from these bigger cities but what was happening was that people were coming and enjoying the heck out of the festival and really talking about it all over.

And we started getting this great national reputation, but it didn't really feel viable for all of these national theater artists to come all the way to Kansas unless we were footing the bill and bringing them out there to do something specific. So what we started doing over the last few years is engaging artists in the region. We are in this, I sort of described, we're in this tiny little town, but independence, Kansas is in the corner of Kansas where Missouri and Arkansas and Oklahoma and Kansas all come together. And so we've started pulling artists from St. Louis, from Minneapolis, which is, this is a little north of us from Kansas City, from Tulsa, so all kind of around our region. So that not only do they fall in love with the festival and they have an opportunity to perform in these new plays, but then they come back again the next year, and they bring their friends because it's driving distance and they love the festival.

Dan: I should probably mention, you know, you reminded me of something when you said that it's not necessarily financially feasible for people to come from far away. Playwriting is not lucrative. Acting on stage for the most part is not lucrative. And so part of the challenge of the festival is that the very people who are supplying that beautiful raw material of the festival are not in a position to provide it without help. Is that a good way to put it?

Hannah: Yeah, that's true. Yes. Yes, absolutely. We've had some incredible artists on that stage though – you'll see on TV and movies and television shows and commercials popping up all the time. And that's sort of the beauty of what we do at the festival is that we have all of these regional artists who nobody would recognize unless they go to the theater, but then you also have that all mixed in with these people they have seen on screen and they're all incredibly talented and just so happy to be here. So you're rubbing elbows with famous folks and regional folks who you can go see up in Kansas City, you know, and a month from now in a play on a main stage. So it's pretty special. The other thing that we've started doing is to engage our local community in a new way that we haven't done for a long time. The festival kind of felt like an elite festival for theater lovers up on the hill where the College was. We catered all of the meals. We had everything in one location, and the prices for tickets were really high. So it was going to cost you a lot of money to come, and you might not know enough about theater to feel comfortable showing up for some of the events and it was really unfortunate because we have a community here that loves its theater.

Dan: I'm delighted you're here with me. I've been looking forward to interviewing you. I asked her to interview for this podcast, it had to be at least a month or two ago, and I've been looking forward to it ever since because I think you've just done amazing work here. I feel like I'm talking to somebody, this sounds completely corny, I feel like I'm talking to somebody who actually was part of what made my family like living in Kansas, because when we moved here from New York, one of the most amazing parts of being in Independence was this theater presence that my two young daughters were particularly captivated by. So I just feel like I owe Hannah this debt. So I'm so delighted you're here, and I appreciate it tremendously. Good luck with the festival this year.

Hannah: Thank you so much. I appreciate that.

CHAPTER 4

Three Immediate Opportunities for Your Institution

A New Way to Recruit Outstanding Students

There is a natural extension of this focus on entrepreneurship – an opportunity for colleges to reward entrepreneurial student activities. Yet, few (if any) higher education institutions are taking advantage of a means to award credit, generate revenue, provide students with a genuine and distinctive credential as well as recruit absolutely outstanding students. First discussed in an article I published on the blog of the National Association for Community College Entrepreneurship (NACCE), I would like to enlarge on the topic here, specifically one of the most significant missed recruiting and credentialing opportunities for higher education involving on-going entrepreneurial activity by students (i.e., entrepreneurial activity that is not assigned by faculty).

Currently, there are many institutions that offer credit for entrepreneurial activity to the obvious candidates: 1) within a traditional course in which either group or individual entrepreneur projects are assigned as part of the class; 2) as part of directed study in which a student proposes an entrepreneurial project and works directly with a faculty member; or 3) through a credit-bearing internship in which a student is working directly with an entrepreneur. While colleges do use these different methods to award credit to students, many activities, like entrepreneurial club membership, are extracurricular and, thus, by definition, not going to be a candidate for academic credit. To a certain extent, the opportunities for credit also depend on institutions' interest in entrepreneurship – no surprise there, of course – but it also depends on institutions' definition of what constitutes entrepreneurial activity. Overwhelmingly, entrepreneurs are seen as individuals going into business for themselves and as businesspeople. As I mentioned earlier, this conception has been detrimental to entrepreneurship education and to entrepreneurs themselves. The broader the definition used by a college, the more opportunities there will be for students to engage in activities that meet that broad definition. The narrowness of definition of entrepreneurship used by colleges is a real missed opportunity for those institutions.

Of the one hundred and ninety-six schools canvased for my research, none specifically offer students credit for preexisting and on-going independent entrepreneurial activities, and none recruit students based explicitly on knowledge of their entrepreneurial activity. Let me use a real-life example: Laura is a nineteen-year-old sophomore at a large midwestern university that stresses entrepreneurship through traditional programs, primarily in its business division. Laura is an art major who is quite entrepreneurial: She places her paintings for sale on internet art sites and on Facebook. She receives commissions for new artworks from people across the country. She designs earrings for sale at a local store. To support these ventures, she has to maintain a supply inventory of the raw materials that she uses for both the paintings and the jewelry and she has to price her products appropriately, pricing them wholesale, in the case of items that are being resold in the store, and retail, in the case of items she is selling directly to the consumer. In other words, she is responsible for the design, production, marketing, packaging, pricing and sale of her work. She also must continuously create new designs based on established market preferences as demonstrated from prior sales.

Laura's college has an entrepreneurship program and an entrepreneur's club. They have elaborate maker spaces, extensive corporate internship opportunities, and respected business programs, but there is no accommodation for an art major who seeks credit for engaging in such thorough, albeit independent, entrepreneurial activity. When Laura graduates and wants to put her art skills to work for a company, perhaps as a graphic designer, I believe that company would be impressed to know about the entrepreneurial work she did while in college. Of course, there is nothing stopping Laura from describing this to a prospective employer, but credit on her transcript gives the work a credibility and a status that mere description will never achieve, and it could very well distinguish Laura from other applicants.

What obstacle stands in the way of institutions giving credit for this kind of entrepreneurial activity? The primary issue appears to be timeframe: unless specifically asked to limit their work to a single element of the life cycle of their business, product or service, most of the work performed by student entrepreneurs spans beyond a single quarter, semester, or in some cases, even academic year. A secondary issue involves instructor buy-in; the broader the type of activity that qualifies as entrepreneurial, the more varied the experience, expertise, and qualifications faculty assisting the student in the entrepreneurial process need to have in order to participate and evaluate student activity fully.

But these problems are surmountable. Higher education institutions already break majors into components and offer classes about each component on the assumption that once the various components have been completed, the entire major has been mastered. Institutions could approach entrepreneurial activity the same way, although in many cases, they would need to consider giving credit for work that has already been completed. This is not substantially different from the concept of transferring credit that has been completed at another school, with the only real difference being that an appropriate faculty member would need to examine the work completed in the past. When a student transfers work from another institution, the assumption is that the first institution has essentially certified the quality and the appropriateness of it, and so the evaluative component has already been done. The process I am proposing would simply require that students receiving credit for entrepreneurial activity, whether it is completed prior to or while attending the institution, coordinate with an appropriately qualified academic to evaluative the entrepreneurial work. Because the institution would still have the opportunity to charge students for the evaluation of the students' entrepreneurial work, it would not have to give the credit away for free. However, it would still allow students to receive academic credit for entrepreneurial activity.

Presumably, this setup would require institutions to ensure that appropriately qualified academics continue to participate in, and evaluate, students' entrepreneurial activity on an on-going basis. Personally, I would advocate that at least some of the entrepreneurial work be done while students attend the institution, engaging with and learning from the entrepreneurship program at the institution and that colleges not award credit based solely on entrepreneurial activities performed by students long ago. So, in the case of Laura, it would make sense to give her credit for recent work that could be quickly evaluated, but in the case of an entrepreneurial project she started ten years ago, did for five years and then stopped, it would be very, very difficult, five years later, for an institution to adequately evaluate or engage the student in further academic instruction with regard to that work. While it is not impossible to evaluate a long finished entrepreneurial project in some cases, generally, if students are truly interested in the entrepreneurial activity, one presumes that interest and activity will be continuing and on-going.

Students' continuing and on-going interest in entrepreneurial activity is highly relevant to this discussion because what I am suggesting is that institutions are not only missing out on the opportunity to award credit and increase revenue but also that prospective students could be identified and recruited based on this previously established entrepreneurial interest and activity. Based on my own personal antidotal experience (not data), students who engage in an on-going entrepreneurial activity tend to be very good students. They tend to be self-starters. They tend to be independently minded. They tend to be original thinkers. They tend to be high energy. All of which is exactly the kinds of attributes that institutions are seeking in students attending their colleges. My recommendation – adopt entrepreneurial activity as a screening component for new students, in a way that actually looks for students based on whether they are engaged in on-going entrepreneurial activity. I would go even further and suggest that colleges accept students based on their entrepreneurial activity, which I think probably indicates far more about a student than many of the other things that admissions departments typically consider in their decision whether to accept students into their programs. Of course, what is needed here is real research through controlled experiments in which a sufficiently large institution recruits, accepts and tracks students based perhaps solely on their entrepreneurial activity and then compares those students to other students who were recruited and accepted into similar programs based on the traditional criteria that the institution was already using.

Distinguishing Entrepreneurship Programs with Effective Internships

There are at least three hundred baccalaureate-granting institutions in the United States that provide entrepreneurship programs of some type. In the community college arena, NACCE's data shows that out of the 1,195 public, private, and tribal colleges across the country, sixty-six percent offer at least one course in entrepreneurship, while fourteen percent offer a degree program in the subject. Another nineteen percent offer certifications in entrepreneurship, while twenty percent have some type of small business development center. Given the number of institutions that have entrepreneurship programs of some kind, the scarcity of internship programs in which students work one-on-one with entrepreneurs is surprising.

Internships are particularly rare at community colleges. An internship requires time, something that is inherently in shorter supply for students seeking a degree of about sixty credit hours (or, in the case of a certificate, often substantially less). Additionally, internships are typically higher-level student activities from which students will derive the most benefit if they already have acquired a body of knowledge – which is why internships usually occur late in the course sequence of an academic program.

But internships at baccalaureate institutions appear to have some common features that present real opportunities for schools to provide impactful experiences for students. In preparation for this book, I surveyed fifty institutions with entrepreneurship majors, selected randomly from the entire list of institutions that offer such a major. Some findings:

- Of those surveyed, ninety-four percent of the institutions either house their entrepreneurship programs in their business school or allow their business faculty to oversee or coordinate the programs;
- Over two-thirds of the programs described themselves as appropriate for students who may wish to start their own business, work in a family-owned business, or work for smaller businesses;
- In practice, a substantial number of students enrolled in entrepreneurship programs actually plan to take over an existing family business, with the second-largest group being students who plan to start a business in a specific area and are taking a minor or second major in entrepreneurship to complement a first major; and
- Many institutions allow the internship requirement to be satisfied through work in students' existing family business so long as that work is evaluated and approved first.

Although one might think that an internship in entrepreneurship would involve students working one-on-one with an entrepreneur, in most cases, the internship was indistinguishable from a generic business internship, with the possible exception of an internship in an existing family business. Even in those cases, students seem less likely to be exposed to particularly new ideas or new ways of doing business, since the internship is carried out in the presence of family with whom the student has likely worked for years.

These issues were not universal – some programs actively strive to create a personalized, one-on-one internship distinct from curricula experienced by the rest of its business majors. Those programs tended to be at smaller institutions with entrepreneurship programs that were less enmeshed within traditional business programs. However, my research suggests that many, if not most, institutions are failing to provide genuinely distinctive entrepreneurship internships for their students.

An ideal entrepreneurship internship would have the following elements:

- Some portion of the program would involve time spent one-on-one with an entrepreneur and would focus on the creative process of entrepreneurship;

- Entrepreneurs would be assigned to students in a way that deliberately ensures that internships involve businesses or projects outside of students' comfort zones to avoid repeating students' previous entrepreneurial experiences by focusing on creating an environment that encourages the experience of new ones; and

- Entrepreneurs would need to fully appreciate that internships exist primarily for the welfare of the student, and as such, students need to be given meaningful work and responsibilities.

If community colleges were to provide these types of internships, it would be a win-win for the student, the institution, and the entrepreneur because doing so not only represents a marketing opportunity for colleges that provide quality internships, but it also points the way for existing programs looking for a straightforward way to improve.

Seeking Support from Entrepreneurs

The entrepreneurship program and Fab Lab at Independence Community College are amazing, and I am proud of the related programming the College provides. I am proud that nearly every piece of equipment in the building and much of the building itself was paid for with external funds, much of that coming from entrepreneurs who support the lab. Presidents spend a great deal of time fundraising, and luckily, soliciting support from entrepreneurs is one of the most enjoyable aspects of the fundraising role. I truly enjoy fundraising in part because I find spending time with donors to be a way of getting a glimpse into the fascinating lives of other people who have often done very, very interesting things. I feel fortunate that my job involves spending time with those folks, and entrepreneurs are among the most interesting and fun people to be around and with whom to work. After all, they tend to be very independent thinkers, have a natural curiosity and a sincere desire to help others. Who would *not* want to be around people like that?

Over the past fifteen years of working with entrepreneurs, I have found that there are specific approaches for specific types of philanthropic support that can be very effective and that tend to resonate well with entrepreneurs. I have received a fair number of questions about fundraising issues, some in response to a recent blog post I published on NACCE (a great organization, with a great website full of useful resources – do yourself a favor and check it out) about creating solicitations that resonate with entrepreneurs, an exceptional class of donor requiring a very specific approach to fundraising.

First, understand that philanthropic support can be categorized as annual gifts (typically modest, but if the relationship is appropriately maintained, they can be expected to be recurring) or major gifts (as the name implies, these are typically larger in amount but also tend to be more sporadic). Endowed gifts (a subcategory of major gifts and generally a much rarer type of gift because they have to be quite large in order to be impactful on an annual basis) differ from a single major gift that is *not* endowed (e.g., a single gift of $100,000 designated for a specific purpose, which after it has been spent on that purpose is gone) because an endowed gift goes into a special type of account in which the principal remains untouched instead generating some sort of return, most of which is used to support the purpose of the endowed gift. Since the return is obviously much smaller than the original gift, an endowed gift generates a smaller amount of money to spend annually. However, since the principal remains untouched, the lifetime of the gift is essentially infinite, and so the total amount of the gift is dramatically higher than the amount of the original gift itself.

I am not going focus specifically on *annual* gifts from entrepreneurs, but I will just say that when a president and entrepreneurship program's employees fully engage interested local entrepreneurs, annual support is a natural consequence because engagement is something that tends to inherently produce support from people that have the resources to offer it, and very often those annual gifts are just one likely consequence of an on-going relationship. But in the case of major gifts from entrepreneurs, whether endowed or not, the timing often reflects the sporadic nature of discretionary income for entrepreneurs. Those entrepreneurs who are businesspeople tend to have much greater fluctuations in their income, and therefore in their discretionary income, than someone who simply receives a regular salary because entrepreneurs' ability to support local programs often fluctuates as the successes of their individual business ventures wax and wane.

Gifts can be made in the form of cash or gifts in kind (e.g., goods, services, time) and are generally most desirable when they enable a donor to provide support in a way that the donor just could not otherwise. A great real-life example of a gift-in-kind donation (that that also ended up being a recurring gift) was a donation made to Alfred State College's forensic program that originated from a surprising source. The Drug Enforcement Administration (DEA), a federal agency in no position to provide cash support to Alfred State, was able and willing to donate fully usable equipment that was five or more years old. The gift originally came about as my research uncovered that policies required that the DEA's lab testing equipment be less than five years old to maintain the integrity of the testing and the credibility of the subsequent testimony in criminal cases, which meant the DEA was regularly getting rid of equipment and, as it turned out, getting rid of the equipment was actually fairly costly for the DEA. Having already developed a relationship with the director of the local DEA Lab, Alfred State's Forensic Science department was able to offer a basic explanation of its needs and to suggest helping the DEA reduce its costs by taking this equipment for the program. Although the equipment was five or more years old, it was well-maintained, looked brand new, and was perfectly suitable for our forensics program. As a result of the gift-in-kind, the forensics program received millions of dollars' worth of equipment that the program could never have afforded on its own. (Of course, there are specific processes to follow in order to compete for such gifts, both for an institution and for donors, but I will not discuss those processes as they are not universal.) The donor, in this case the DEA, could not have provided Alfred State with cash to buy equipment, but could easily justify providing the College with the equipment itself.

When seeking donor support for an entrepreneurship program, there are two likely types of donors: individual entrepreneurs and corporations. Although most people may not necessarily associate corporations with entrepreneurship programs, the fact is that corporations are often very, very willing to support entrepreneurship programs because corporations actually really want to attract entrepreneurial thinkers to their ranks. Corporations do not want people who just do the same task over and over – they are actually very interested in attracting leaders and employees who can work in teams and find innovative solutions to problems.

Individual entrepreneurs and corporations require quite different fundraising approaches, which is important because institutions also have to be able to identify individual entrepreneurs that for one reason or another behave as though they were corporations as it is important to be able to recognize which approach will best match the type of entrepreneur from which it is seeking support. In my experience, entrepreneurs tend to share some common characteristics and, at the risk

Risk and Reward

of generalizing, I have found that entrepreneurs tend to demonstrate the following (and while there are certainly exceptions to this all of these characteristics are actually quite complimentary!):

First, entrepreneurs tend to either be self-employed or employed by an organization founded with other like-minded people. Second, entrepreneurs tend to be more risk-tolerant than the average person. Third, entrepreneurs tend to be more emotional and passionate about their work – and this is a very distinctive feature of entrepreneurs – the tendency to be extremely passionate about projects and the work they are doing. Fourth, entrepreneurs really want to make a difference through their giving – while all donors who give in significant amounts want to make a difference, I find that entrepreneurs tend to be very focused on that aspect of giving.

Compared to salaried employees, individual entrepreneurs also approach philanthropy itself differently: first, because they are typically self-employed and so are often used to being decision-makers and second, because they are generally fairly risk-tolerant. As a result, individual entrepreneurs are often much more receptive to considering untested first-time ideas because they are more willing (and excited) to hear about projects that may be more "out there" and which might not excite other donors in the same way. Often an institution can approach these entrepreneurs, not with a half-baked idea, but with an idea that falls outside "the norm" and they are often more willing to hear and even to attempt to modify an idea, perhaps as a means of making it more successful, realistic, fundable, or generally feasible. Also, because entrepreneurs often desire to make a difference and have an extraordinary passion for their work, they actually have a strong inclination to be philanthropic – after all, there is often a strong overlap between passionate and philanthropic people. Finally, because entrepreneurs tend to have a more variable income, an institution has to be prepared for a "not this year but come back next year" answer. Because very often with entrepreneurs the response is not necessarily a definite "no" so much as it is a "not right now," it can be essential to both understand and be prepared for that response. Being able to accept that answer graciously will also help to maintain that positive relationship, allowing the institution to return the entrepreneur with the same idea (or perhaps even a different one) at a later date.

I should mention that occasionally entrepreneurs have partners who do not share an interest in a project proposed by an institution. As strange as it sounds, I recommend approaching business partners in much the same way as spouses because they have much of the same role in decision-making. When approaching an entrepreneur with an organization that operates as a partnership, it is important to engage both partners fully. If, ultimately, the proposed project does not resonate with one of the partners, the original entrepreneur will still have the opportunity to be personally involved separate and apart from his or her organization. In fact, this outcome is actually quite common when, for instance, an entrepreneur is an alumnus and thus has a personal stake in the mission of an institution, and so wants to be personally involved in a project but has a partner with no such relationship with the institution.

As previously mentioned, dealing with entrepreneurs is not like dealing with full-fledged corporations because corporations are typically very different. While corporations can absolutely be very supportive of philanthropic projects, they often require a solid business and/or financial rationale for providing that support. Often this rationale comes about in the form of some benefit – perhaps in the form of positive publicity or some form of tax advantage – that the corporation receives in exchange for its support. Generally speaking, the process of seeking financial support from corporations will be much more transactional than seeking out support from individual entrepreneurs. After all, for individual entrepreneurs, at least part of the benefit of providing support to an institution will almost always involve an emotional connection or personal satisfaction, whereas corporations are often going to require a more objective rationale for providing philanthropic support. As a result, an institution's relationship with corporate donors will often be very, very different.

Risk and Reward

If you, individually or as an institution, are not yet fully engaging the entrepreneurs in your community or within your alumni base, you are in for a real treat. Entrepreneurs are inquisitive and smart and have an independent mindset that can be incredibly refreshing. While this independent mindset can often cause entrepreneurs to be prescriptive, and might sometimes even lead them to provide advice that your institution might not feel ready to consider instead of simply supporting a project as originally envisioned, I recommend that you pause and listen, because entrepreneurs often see solutions that the rest of cannot see. After all, it is that unique perspective that makes them well-suited to entrepreneurial projects, and it is why they are successful. When seeking philanthropic support, taking the opportunity to sit down with someone that can see solutions to problems that you may not even be able to see, can provide an amazing opportunity for institutional growth. Embrace it, treasure it, enjoy it.

CHAPTER 5

Entrepreneurial Mindset Case Study: Last Chance U (When Your College Is Seen by Fifty Million People)

How This Strange Thing Happened

Never seen *Last Chance U*? No surprise there – the intended audience for this book is not among the intended demographic for that television series. Even so, the show is so popular among specific demographics that it has literally re-shaped television worldwide, which you can read about here. For those readers who have not seen the series, watching this trailer is a must before going ANY further! In addition, more information about the series is available on Wikipedia here. (Print version readers, these are easy to find.)

The exact viewership of *Last Chance U* is not known because Netflix does not publish that information, but our inside information suggests that about fifty million people per year will see the show about Independence Community College and, because the show will stay on Netflix's platform for years, the number of eventual viewers will likely ultimately reach the hundreds of millions.

One of the questions I am often asked is: how did this project actually start? In the early spring of 2017, some folks from *Last Chance U* reached out to members of the College's athletic staff to gauge interest. Because there was much interest on the part of our athletic staff, it became obvious pretty early on that higher-level institutional buy-in was

Risk and Reward

necessary to move forward. Consequently, I got looped in at a fairly early stage, and the athletics staff and I communicated with the producers, director, and logistics staff several times over a period of at least a month to figure out exactly what might be required of the College if it were selected to participate in a project with *Last Chance U*. From the very earliest conversations, the project seemed like a very good fit for everyone involved. The director, producers, and logistics people were good listeners, and they did their best to answer our questions. *Last Chance U* let us know exactly what they needed, and it was pretty simple, as they basically wanted very little from us except for access for filming. They agreed to pay the College $30,000 in exchange for granting them that access, which was intended as reimbursement for the additional work the project would create for the College's athletic and media staff. In addition, they made it clear that they required a short list of accommodations that were necessary for the actual physical production of the series:

- Physical access to film in dorms, classrooms, at all football practices and on all practice fields and at all games, including in the locker room, the coach's booth, the sidelines, the stands and the back of the end zones;
- The ability to mic up players and coaches for games;
- The ability to film one-on-one player and coach meetings;
- Cooperation from football players and staff to accommodate one-on-one interviews;
- Cooperation from the College's play-by-play crew to connect *Last Chance U's* audio into their mixing board during games;
- A room on-campus for the film crew to store gear and access to restroom facilities for the crew;
- A copy of all of the footage shot by the College's media team along with access to their archives;
- Van parking at home and away games;
- A sideline tent during games;

- Coordination with the College's media team for away games; and
- The ability to turn off the music at practices and games (it was Netflix's preference, for legal/licensing purposes, that the PA system not blast unlicensed pop music during the games – while it was fine if the band was playing, actual songs played from a computer or CD player presented a problem, so the producers simply provided discs of music to which Netflix had rights).

At a certain point, it became obvious to all of us having the discussion with Netflix that this was a project that could be taken to the next level, which meant a conversation with the College's Board of Trustees. When contacting the Board to describe the project, I wanted to capture both the upsides and the downsides, and also convey that no decision had been made – after all, the final decision would be the Board's. Here is the e-mail I sent describing the project to the Board:

> Dear Members of the Board,
>
> I'm writing to let you know about an intriguing possibility that Tammie, Jason Brown, and I are exploring. I had a phone meeting tonight with two producers from Netflix, who are interested in featuring ICC and Independence in their next season of "Last Chance U," which is one of Netflix's most popular original series.
>
> You can read a very brief summary of the show here: http://www.imdb.com/title/tt5863126/plotsummary
>
> There's no way that ICC could buy this kind of exposure – it would be worth millions. However, there's no free lunch – having a crew film on campus for an extended period would be quite intrusive. Tammie, Jason, and I are basically just talking with them to see what their expectations would be. We'll talk with them again on Wednesday.

Risk and Reward

Of course, we won't make any commitments. If they actually decide that they want to feature us, then the ball will be in our court, and we'll have a careful conversation about the pros and cons. I'll keep you fully informed. In the meantime, please keep this confidential.

Best,
Dan

The Board's reaction was cautious but positive. The chief concern raised was the portrayal of the East Mississippi Community College (the first college featured in the show, in seasons one and two) as disinterested in academics. I shared this concern and explained that the reason I was exploring the project with *Last Chance U* was because the producers described a desire to move in a different direction with the show – they liked the fact that our coaches were demanding academic success from our athletes.

Once I felt that the athletic team, Board, and I clearly understood what *Last Chance U* expected from the College to move forward with the project, I felt strongly that the next step should be to consult with all of the employees at the College. Even considering taking on a project like this was daunting, mainly because risk aversion was deeply engrained in the College's culture from bottom to top – so much so that during an accreditation conference I attended in my first semester as president, our employees themselves unanimously identified risk aversion as the primary managerial attribute of our school! I hosted a two-hour open forum with all employees to get input and feedback regarding *Last Chance U*. During the open forum, College faculty and staff identified the following positive incentives for taking on the project:

- The tremendous opportunity for the College and the community;
- The very positive implications for both football and general athletic recruiting;
- The opportunity to showcase the positive qualities of the College to a national audience; and

- The belief that people might "behave better" with cameras around (I had not anticipated that view).

The concerns raised by College employees included:

- Concerns that the title "Last Chance U" did not reflect the College's focus on academic quality;
- The lack of a clear benefit to the academic side of the College and concerns about educational resources being diverted to athletics;
- The College's lack of control over the final product;
- Logistical concerns including whether faculty could expect to receive advance notice if filming was proposed for their classrooms;
- Concerns about whether, if athletic recruiting was improved, that would have a negative impact on the level of academic ability of the average incoming student; and
- The realization that, by definition, telling entertaining stories about students would require some sort of protagonist (presumably the student) and if that was the case, concerns about who the antagonist might be?

Over the next few weeks, the College continued to gather information from the director and producers of *Last Chance U* and to solicit feedback from the campus and community. As local people became more accustomed to the idea, I noticed that the initial high-level opposition and fear reduced to some extent. At a certain point, it because clear that a final decision was needed, and because of the size and scope of the project, that decision belonged to the Board of Trustees. The Board held a public meeting that included a public comment agenda item. The meeting was fairly sparsely attended, and the concerns raised were fairly modest. At the end of the meeting, the Board voted unanimously to participate.

Why did the College engage in this project? There really was not a single reason, because I think each area of the College had its own motivations. However, the final decision belonged to the Trustees, and they were

Risk and Reward

quite clear about their motives, which were the same as mine: a belief that there was no better way to bring the lovely town of Independence, Kansas to tens of millions of people. The viewership of the show is enormous, and because episodes remain available on Netflix for years, the viewership will only grow over time. Independence is a fantastic place – a small, safe, charming town with a rich history and friendly people, but the same can be said about many towns, and yet most small towns never break out of the noise. *Last Chance U* seemed to offer a unique opportunity to do what the town's Chamber of Commerce simply did not have the budget to do – advertise the positive attributes of the town to a very large audience. While the College would presumably derive some benefits, those were much more difficult to predict, especially given the challenge in accurately predicting the net effect of the project on the College considering the potential negative publicity that could realistically be generated as a result of participating in the project with *Last Chance U*.

Was I personally afraid of what might happen – to the College and the community – as a result of the College's collaboration with *Last Chance U*? Yes, in the sense that I knew upfront that the College would have no creative control over the final product, which is never a completely comfortable feeling. In our employee open forum, one of the theater faculty pointed out that all stories need a villain, and asked me how I knew that the character cast as the villain would not be me? I felt strongly that this would not happen – the president of the college is a minor figure in the series, which is about the football players, not the college administration. My reply, however, was something more fundamental – that I trusted the director, Greg Whiteley, to tell the story accurately enough that no College employees would be portrayed as fundamentally different people than they actually were.

The Experience for the Campus

The filming, which lasted two years, was an experience unlike anything I had ever been involved in before.

There certainly were drawbacks to the project that had a significant negative effect on the College and the Independence community. It would be interesting to compare my list of drawbacks with a similar list compiled by others who participated in the project. However, I can only really consider the question from my point of view, and I think it is also very important to remember that even though filming has finished and the episodes at the College have been released, the College and community are actually still experiencing the earlier stages of a very long-term project. As I write this, the Independence seasons have only been out for about two years, and assuming that the series will be available on Netflix for years to come, I can only describe the effects up to this point, and I think that it would be premature to think that these comprise the totality of those effects.

The negative effects as of this writing seem pretty clear:

1. The attention the series focused on athletics increased the overall tension between athletics and other areas of the College, which not only impacted relationships within the College, but also impacted the relationship between those outside of the College who support athletics and those outside of the College who support other areas of the College's mission.

2. There were a considerable number of people, both locally and elsewhere, who, as part of their system of values or their religious beliefs, were offended by the profanity both in the series and as a reflection of the College. Many of them did not hesitate to express their feelings about this, both privately and publicly.

3. There were educators and community members who did not approve of the methods used by the head coach in the third and fourth seasons of the series, and they made these opinions known, some publicly, some privately.

Risk and Reward

4. The series made the College (and higher education in general) an easier target for critics and opportunists, many of whom seemed to understand that their criticism or commentary would reach a wider audience if they focused on *Last Chance U*. For example, members of the community who had always opposed athletics at the College now found a new reason to argue that athletics "mattered" too much. I heard this argument frequently, even though football did not "matter" enough to create significant shifts in resource allocation. (Our football program was rather modestly funded compared to its conference rivals, and over the period of the filming of season three and four of the series, the program's budget remained relatively constant.) During the College's accreditation review, concerns about the impact of football were raised repeatedly by employees and other locals, even though the final report by the accreditors found no basis for the complaints. As another example, a Kansas website devoted to transparency published an editorial about the series asking, *"Who is Paying for All of This?"*, with the underlying assumption that public resources were being wasted. I had to laugh at that one – the actual answer to the question was readily obtainable and already available in the public record. Whatever the purpose of the editorial, it was not to actually answer the question it purported to consider. I suspect even the author knew how lazy the piece seemed – it was the only editorial I have ever seen that particular periodical publish that was not attributed to an author! As another example, about four months after the first season of the series at the College aired, higher education's leading trade journal published a garden-variety hit piece about the College, focusing on an ordinary personnel matter. Personnel matters exist everywhere and would not usually be the

subject of a lead story in a national higher education publication, but the ambitious author of the story astutely recognized that if she could invent a connection between an employment issue regarding a tenured professor and a hit Netflix series about football, the story would be more widely read. So that is just what she did. The beauty of that particular approach was that, in the case of personnel matters, the College could not offer any information without liability, and thus could not dispute the account provided in the story. Basically, I would say that publicity from *Last Chance U* encouraged a sort of parasitic journalistic corruption, in both regional and national publications.

A distinctive and unique part of the experience was the presence of cameras everywhere. Due to the prevalence of cell phones, most people accept the idea that they can be filmed or photographed at any time, but that is quite a different experience than being filmed by an entire professional film crew, toting large cameras, holding boom microphones over people's heads, and placing hidden microphones under their clothing. The *Last Chance U* film crew did have full access, although that was a bit different in practice than in principle. In practice, they were very considerate, and if someone had a substantial objection to something being filmed, they did not film. Those types of objections certainly were not raised often – in two years of filming, I can only remember two occasions when I personally declined to be filmed doing anything. The first occurred when the College received correspondence from the NJCAA, which athletics staff and College leadership needed to discuss. The rules of the NJCAA did not allow the College to comment on the NJCAA itself publicly, so, I simply explained the prohibition against filming that type of conversation, and the film crew respectfully agreed to step out of the office for the duration of that conversation. The other time was when a community member mentioned to the director that I am a good shot with a handgun, under what circumstances I have no idea, and so they asked me to show them my personal gun collection.

Risk and Reward

Because I personally feel that guns are a hot-button issue and that it would be irresponsible to be photographed with a gun, I declined, and they readily accepted my explanation.

The major exception to the film crew's largely unrestricted access was in the classroom. Our agreement with the *Last Chance U* film crew was that recording a faculty member in the classroom required the express consent of both faculty and students. That worked out well – in the two seasons that the series was filmed at the College, I never received a complaint from a professor that their class was filmed inappropriately. In addition, any individual person, whether an employee or student, who was incidentally filmed and did not wish to appear in the series, could simply state that and his or her face was blurred in the final episode.

Finally, the campus experience in the filming of Season Four was utterly different from the filming of Season Three of *Last Chance U* for three main reasons: the football team had a losing season, the head coach, Jason Brown, resigned amidst an internationally-publicized scandal and the College built a turf practice field that generated a great deal of controversy in the community.

The Losing Season

Why did the Pirates do so badly in the fourth season of the series after winning the conference championship in the third season? I was not on the football team, and so not an insider on the football team, like a coach, and in that sense, I am much more like an outsider who simply went to watch the games like any spectator. Consequently, I can only provide my personal impression. However, it seems to me that there were two major factors that most significantly contributed to the Pirate's losing season. First, a team needs to have a healthy starting quarterback, without which the team will quickly start down the road to ruin. (The College's quarterback was injured early in the season.) Secondly, there needs to be a winning culture within a program to assist in creating team resiliency in the face of defeat, which was something that the Pirates simply did not have. After all, remember that the previous season was the

College's first real winning season. The season before that, the Pirates actually had a winning record, but they barely had a winning record, and certainly were not a traditional powerhouse. Season Three of *Last Chance U* was really the first season where the College was just starting to turn things around, and as such, the Pirates did not have the psychology of a team or an institution that has had long-term success in the sport. Once a team's season starts taking a downhill turn, a program really needs both the coaching staff and the players to have a psychological resiliency that allows them to say, "Hey, you know, we're Alabama (or whatever powerhouse team), we can suffer a loss or two, and it's okay," but the Independence Pirates did not have that mentality. As a result, it was really easy for the Pirates to get thrown from the saddle and start to doubt their ability to win because winning had not become a solid part of Pirate culture. So, in my opinion, the College's losing season was mainly the result of two things: losing a key player in a key position and lacking a sense of tradition or cohesion around being a Pirate sufficient to hold the team together during challenging games and in the face of losing games. In many ways, not having that powerhouse mentality actually made the fourth season of *Last Chance U* that much more fascinating because it was the first time the series had the opportunity to explore the dynamic of losing rather than winning and, for me at least, this dynamic was actually the most interesting part of the series. The consensus seems to be that having a losing season allowed the series to portray a unique perspective on the personalities in the series and personalities involved in football in general. Essentially, season four allowed the series to explore the process and emotions involved in coming to terms with losing more often than winning – allowing the series to explore a new and previously unexamined dimension in football and athletics.

Head Coach Jason Brown

In the first season of *Last Chance U*, I described Jason Brown as "a creature of pure testosterone." He was, at the very least, a dominant personality. During the College's search for a new head coach in 2015, Jason interviewed very well for the position, and the Athletic Director

Risk and Reward

selected him for the position with my full support. The College and community were tired of losing season after losing season and were hungry for a new approach. Jason was definitely that.

As anyone who has watched the series knows, Jason is from Compton, California, and that environment indelibly affected his personality and the lens through which he views the world. He played football from an early age, seeing success at both the high school level and in college. After attending and playing football at Compton Community College, he took a football scholarship to Fort Hays State University in Hays, Kansas, where he was a quarterback and graduated with a degree in Kinesiology. Upon graduation, Brown became an NFL free-agent and was picked up by the Kansas City Chiefs. After a short stint with the Chiefs, he moved on to play in the Arena Football League for the Bakersfield Blitz, Chicago Rush, and Los Angeles Avengers. When Brown's playing career ended, he moved to coaching, where he found considerable success both in recruiting students to his programs and in helping his players get recruited to Division I football programs. Ultimately, he came to the College when its longtime coach retired.

Jason met with considerably coaching success in his first season – it was our first winning season in a long time. The community was delighted; the games were more fun, and the athletic department worked hard to promote Jason's success both on the field and in the academic success of his students. *Last Chance U* arrived in Jason's second season, and the team's success multiplied. The Pirates won the Jayhawk Conference championship for the first time since the 1980s, and they did it in front of the nation on a hit television show. Jason, and indeed the whole College, found himself in the national spotlight in a way that was new and exciting.

Jason's third year (which was the fourth season of *Last Chance U*) was very different. The team lost most of its games, and ultimately Jason Brown resigned following an inappropriate text message exchange with a student. I do not typically comment on personnel matters out of respect for the privacy of employees or students. However, in this case, both the employee and the student involved discussed the matter publicly and in detail, were interviewed on multiple media outlets, providing an enormous amount of information in the public record through the news media about the incident. Jason even wrote a book that included a section about the incident. As usual, in personnel matters, I will confine myself to what is in the public record.

The way events unfolded was actually not very complicated, although people have certainly tried to make them complicated: First, there was a text from head coach Jason Brown to a student that appeared to make the national origin of that student an issue in his decision-making process. There are all kinds of opinions around how coaches do and should interact with students and what is and is not effective, but the fact was that College policy as well as state and federal law forbade discrimination on the basis of national origin. As a result, Jason Brown was immediately reprimanded (and deserved to be reprimanded) for his text exchange with the student. There was also the matter of the subsequent escalation of the conflict between Jason and the student. Listen carefully to the student's account of events on the last episode of season four of the series, as well as the information available in various news accounts, and notice that a couple of days after the original text incident, when the student was in an all-team football meeting, Jason Brown allegedly berated the student in front of the entire football team and coaching staff, which if true is hardly the actions of a person who understands the problem with his original actions and wants to be an active part of resolving and improving that situation.

There is no point in ignoring the context of the story at this point. It was an international story and received intense media coverage, all of which reflected poorly on the College. It was the kind of issue that could arise anytime an employee chooses to behave in a way that creates very bad publicity for a taxpayer-supported institution. After all, the Trustees of the College are elected by the same taxpayers that support the College, and those Trustees need to be able to explain decisions and actions by the College to those taxpayers when they meet them on Main Street or in

Risk and Reward

Walmart. I do not believe that Jason fully grasped or understood the extent to which his fate was in the hands of those six elected officials who endured a great deal of public criticism for his actions, especially when he showed no signs of wanting to make the situation better for them. So given that his text added a new element (possible unlawful discrimination) to his well-known abrasive style and that the situation continued to escalate after the original text, and that the escalation gave the Trustees no reason to believe Jason was willing to be an active part of the solution, I think that his departure from the College really was the only possible outcome. I do not think that Jason fully understood the political context of the situation, as evidenced by the comments he made in his book about my "failure" to prevent his termination. Ultimately, I served the College at the pleasure of its Board of Trustees, and the situation was such that I was not even in the room when Jason's fate at the College was discussed.

Occasionally, sports reporters have posed the following question to me: Would I let my son play football for Jason? I should say upfront that I probably would not let my son play football at all because of the possibility of injury, and that I will never have to make that decision because I do not have any sons and, at the time of this writing, college football remains nearly entirely an all-male sport. Even so, I understand the hypothetical question. I would say that on a day-to-day basis most football players are actually with the coaches that address their immediate positions, and those are the personalities that are actually mentoring them on a daily basis, talking to the coaches at four-year institutions about whether or not students should be recruited, and so forth. There is a tendency for fans to focus on the head coach, but when asked which coaches they were close to personally and which coaches kept them going, football players will rarely focus on the head coach. Instead, players typically mention the coaches that oversee their individual athletic position because that person is the coach that they work with on an hourly or daily basis. In effect, the head coach is not the only, or even the primary person, making a difference in the lives of individual students on a daily basis.

Some of the criticisms of Jason were unfair or poorly informed. For example, Jason received criticism that he portrayed community college as just a stepping stone for these students, something for student-athletes to finish before moving on to the next thing. I hear this criticism frequently, and I am not really sure that I fully understand it. Of course community college is a steppingstone for these students. After all, community college is a stepping stone for all of the people who attend institutions hoping to obtain a certificate, degree, or to transfer to another school. By definition, community colleges are an intermediate step toward further education or employment. Ultimately, I suspect most college students, whether they attend a community college or another type of higher education institution, see college as a stepping stone. There is no question that community colleges, in particular, are a stepping stone for most students, and many aspects of the *Last Chance U* series capture that reality. Whether it is student-athletes who want to transition to the next level athletically or students who aspire to start a new career (e.g., veterinary technicians hoping to transition into a career caring for animals), college by its very nature is a step on the road to something greater. I honestly feel like the success of *Last Chance U* stems from the way it captures the idea that everybody has goals, and that the college experience is really transitory for all students. Perhaps what troubles people is that *Last Chance U* shows these coaches telling students, "oh, come on, just get your work done, then you can keep going." In other words, coaches are emphasizing that community college is a means to some other end to motivate students whose life goals often did not include going to community college because their life goals involved something that they see as beyond that. These comments are coaches' way of trying to get students to re-focus on their larger goals and to use that motivation to be successful in the current situation. Unfortunately, when the coaches are speaking to that larger goal, some people misinterpret that as denigrating education when, in fact, it is often the coach recognizing the personal dreams of the students they are coaching. After all, many college students, athletes included, are not always going to love having to go to class or finishing assignments. Transforming students into lifelong learners is much, much better than just getting them through the degree process, and this is a project that everyone at an institution has to pitch in to do. From professors to advisors to staff, we in higher education are continually trying to reinforce the idea that students need to think beyond the next test, the next course, or even the next semester. Of course, this is made more difficult when students themselves see the educational process as just a hurdle to cross, and, in many cases, educators must actively fight these preconceptions about education. Repetition and consistency are key, and those of us in education have to remember that sometimes we as educators get through to students, but other times we just do not.

The Faculty

One of the nice outcomes of having *Last Chance U* on campus was one that I predicted in advance: our faculty shone. I am often asked whether teacher Heather Mydosh was as devoted to students as she appears on the series. I know that I was very pleased to see Heather featured on the series because I know what a good teacher she is, and I know how devoted she is to her students, but the truth is that she is even better than the series depicts. *Last Chance U* shows Heather dealing primarily with a specific student, but at Independence Community College, English professors have a heavy teaching load, typically at least five sections per semester, which means Heather was teaching over one hundred students per semester in an academic area that obviously requires a great deal of detailed grading work and personalized attention. Heather came to the College shortly after I did, nearly a decade ago, and during that time, I have seen firsthand all the ways that she goes out of her way to help her students. She helps them diligently, and she gives her time selflessly. I feel such a tremendous sense of respect and admiration for her and so many other teachers like her at the College because that level of devotion to students is exactly how the College brings real value to the students and community members that engage with it.

Some of the scenes with the faculty and staff are so powerful that people suspect the scenes are staged. I have been asked this many times, in many forms, and I can say without hesitation that no, it was not. The staging issue arose right away when, in the first episode of the first season, there was a scene where a cow got loose on the practice field and was shot with a tranquilizer gun, and some of the locals felt that scene might have been staged. When asked about this in an open forum, *Last Chance U* director, Greg Whiteley, said, "My friends, I don't have the budget to stage that kind of thing. We only have so much time; we only have so many takes; we only have so many camera people." The people on camera were not actors and trying to stage something with amateurs honestly would probably not be very convincing. The reason *Last Chance U* is successful is because of its authenticity – *because* it is not staged. After all, without the students' stories, which are so clearly authentic, it would really just be a documentary series about football games. The real story revolves around relationships that develop between the faculty and students who are struggling, and how the faculty help students get through those struggles. Those are the most gripping moments in the series. Writing about the faculty at the College is actually a bit difficult for me to do without feeling a little choked up, because, for example, Heather Mydosh is somebody who looks incredibly devoted to students in the series because she truly is all about helping students whether the students are featured on *Last Chance U* or not. Just imagine the amount of time people like that are putting into their jobs! These are people who are so passionate about what they do that there is nothing they will not do to see a student succeed, whether they are a student-athlete or not. It is incredibly inspiring to me.

I was pleased to see that the *Last Chance U* audience recognized the dedication of our faculty. I have read many social media posts since the final season at the College was released and while the majority of the posts focused on the head coach, Jason Brown, many also praised the faculty. A college exists primarily for the good of its students, and the people who work at colleges are primarily interested in the welfare of the students. It was not a devotion to Jason Brown that inspired the

Risk and Reward

College's dedicated English faculty Heather Mydosh and LaTonya Pinkard to spend hours working with students, including those documented in *Last Chance U*. Instead, it was a desire to help students achieve academic and life success. It was not a desire for television stardom that caused philosophy instructor Jared Wheeler to find creative and meaningful ways to reach all of his students – athlete and non-athlete alike. It was a love of the subject matter and his desire to influence students' lives for the better. Mydosh, Pinkard and Wheeler's efforts did not go unnoticed. I have read many nice comments online and received complimentary phone messages and e-mails from *Last Chance U* fans. So there are many ways to think about *Last Chance U*, but one of the ways I certainly think about it is that it showcases the faculty members who are right there, at a community college, producing successful students who studies show are better prepared to transfer to a four-year institution than any other community college in Kansas. The antics of the coach were, to me, a sort of sideshow whereas the success of the students and the skill of the teachers were the real events highlighted by the series.

My Own Experiences with *Last Chance U*

Concerns about the personal risks of being involved in the production of *Last Chance U* preoccupied many of us during the months leading up to the filming and throughout the filming of the series because as administrators of a higher education institution minimizing risk to the institution was a paramount concern for us. In my case, obviously, the series was not about the president, and it will never be about the president, because if anyone ever tried to make a similar series about college presidents it would be a dismal failure. After all, the series is aimed at a young demographic, and that audience definitely would not have much interest in the somewhat dull life of a middle-aged man. In the end, for me personally my involvement in *Last Chance U* was more headache than reward (although I really hate to use the word "reward" because, like most people in public education, very little of the work that I do is for the purpose of personal reward). That said, in a situation like this, the personal reward simply does not justify the risk. The entire process is very intrusive, and it is very risky. During filming, everything a person says and does is recorded, and believe me, if someone says something interesting enough, it is darn well going to make it into the final cut of an episode. There were definitely a few times when I had to just to shake my head, and wonder was exactly was I thinking when I said that? What exactly was the tone of the conversation at that exact moment? As an example, I remember last year, in one scene towards the end of the season, they showed me saying an absolutely foolish thing. I was talking about Jason, and I said something to the effect that maybe if you are from California, you cannot string two sentences together without swearing. I must have received hundreds of messages on social media and by email from people in California who said, "how dare you say something like that… I am from California, and I can absolutely string together a sentence or two sentences without swearing." Everything people say while being recorded in this type of situation absolutely can come back to haunt them…

People have asked me if I am recognized because of my role in the series. Yes, I am, and honestly, it never ceases to amaze me, and I personally find it hilarious. As someone that barely appears on the show, especially compared to the key players and the coaches or faculty, there is an expectation of near-anonymity that simply is not there. A perfect example occurred just a short time ago, when I was traveling to New York and was in an airport with my family, and immediately someone said, "I've seen you…where have I seen you? Where do I know you from?" and then they said, "oh, wait, aren't you that guy on television?" My two teenage daughters think it is absolutely hilarious that people want to stand there and take a picture with a person like me simply because of a Netflix series, but it just goes to show the power of the media to make a person seem more important than they are.

Some people have speculated that the show somehow led to my departure from the College – that is an easy claim to refute. I decided to resign before the second season of the series at the College was even released (and before anyone at the College had even seen an advance

Risk and Reward

copy), and obviously, I am a pretty minor figure in the series itself. In fact, I had been planning to leave the College for some time (later in this book, I describe my belief that presidents at small, rural institutions like Independence Community College should leave their institutions after about a decade of service). The Board, my family and I agreed that the time was right and that summertime, which is a relatively quiet period on a college campus compared to the regular academic year, was the best time for that transition to occur. I only continued with the College as long as I did because I wanted to see two specific situations at the college resolved: The first was an accreditation site visit that I wanted to see through to a good outcome, which I did. The second involved a complex legal case involving the termination of a faculty member for racially-disparate grading, and it was important to me to ensure the College was properly represented throughout that case. Knowing the College had reached a positive resolution with regards to both of these situations helped to ensure that my resignation from the College was both timely and amicable. In fact, I am very grateful to the Board for the complimentary comments they made about my tenure at the College at the time of my resignation.

Was It Worth It?

In my opinion, the experience with *Last Chance U* was ultimately "worth it" for the College. It is a difficult concept to explain because calculating the worth of something that has as many different facets as the project with *Last Chance U* is difficult. It is difficult to calculate the value of an institution becoming a household name versus being the unknown that it was before the project – after all, I am not really sure how to even start to quantify that change. Even so, in my opinion, it was worth it in terms of the value to the College itself, in terms of corporate support, and in terms of fan support. That said, there were also certainly downsides. For example, I will never ever disguise the fact that the project was terribly polarizing for the Independence community. There are clearly some members of the community that did not at all like the way the community was portrayed in *Last Chance U* and others in the community who had strong feelings about Jason Brown and did not want to be associated with him.

Everyone has to do their own calculation because the truth is, I would say no one will know if the *Last Chance U* experience was worth doing until two or three years from now when, one way or the other, all of the dust has settled. Because of that time lag, it is challenging to assess in the short term.

Knowing what I know now, would I do this all over again? Absolutely! 100%. I have never seen a single project worth doing that did not ruffle some feathers and did not require some tough calls. This project gave opportunities of a lifetime to students and employees alike, and it did bring the beautiful town of Independence to tens (and eventually hundreds) of millions of people. Did it provide a uniformly positive view of Independence? No. But as a result, the view it provided was more authentic than a glossy promotional piece. I would choose widely seen authenticity over barely-seen puff pieces any day – which brings me to my final point about my experience with *Last Chance U*.

What Fifty Million People Taught Me About Authenticity

Let me begin with a question. Do you think you have been seen by a million people in the past year? That is actually not terribly difficult if, for example, you have a channel on YouTube. When my daughter was five years old, she created a YouTube channel about Webkinz, which are little stuffed animals, and since then, she has had well over a million views on her channel. So, if you have appeared in any online video in the past year, it is actually possible that you might have been seen by a million people. But what about five or even ten million people? That is a little more difficult. Now how about fifty million views? I do not know about you, but it is challenging for me to even imagine fifty million as a number, let alone as fifty million *people*. Taking this one step further, imagine being seen by fifty million people – and having *no* control over how those fifty million people experience you?

Risk and Reward

A project like the filming of *Last Chance U* is very different from creating a YouTube video and subsequently retaining total editorial control. Those employees at Independence Community College who were featured on *Last Chance U* have been seen by somewhere between fifty and eighty million people and over the next few years will likely be seen by as many as a hundred million people, in a setting over which the College really had no control whatsoever. In this section of the book, I have described the impacts and experiences involved in participating in filming *Last Chance U*. Even so, one question that people often ask me relates to how one can be authentic and remain true to oneself in the face of on-going and intense scrutiny – being followed around by a film crew with large cameras while wearing a microphone. What follows is a brief description of my "lessons learned" from the experience of being seen by about fifty million people in a context in which I had little to no control over the way I was actually portrayed.

Those who have seen the series know that the series certainly does not focus on the President of the College, but rather its football team. That said, there was a fair amount of filming both of me personally and of the president's office. The film crew interviewed me in my office periodically, and those interviews were generally pretty lengthy. They also occasionally filmed me around campus and in more personal settings. For example, the camera crew came to my home several times to film me preparing and serving my family dinner and discussing the motorcycles that I have in my garage. The *Last Chance U* crew certainly filmed me during college events, and there were many, many cameras at Pirate football games as well. In short, there were plenty of opportunities for me to appear on camera and thus, depending on one's point of view, significant opportunity for things to go terribly awry and for my "mistakes" to be preserved forever in an episode of the series.

To fully appreciate the pressure of the situation, one must understand that as a college president, I enjoyed fewer of the normal freedoms that most Americans take for granted. A fellow president once told me that he was really looking forward to retirement so that he could get his First

Amendment rights back. When someone decides to serve in a public service role, such as a college president in a small rural community, that person loses more than just his or her right to free speech. People in these roles quickly discover that they have given up a certain amount of social autonomy: They can no longer wear whatever they want to Walmart. They have to think twice before deciding not to shave for the day. They are often restricted from driving certain types of vehicles – all because they are a public figure. In addition, they come to realize that everything they say is subject to scrutiny for hidden meanings (take it from me, there is almost never a hidden meaning). In my experience as a college president, it is nearly always the case that the president has simply said precisely what he or she meant, even if people then try to reinterpret those words in some other way. Regardless, college presidents, like many other public figures, have to choose their words very carefully because the goal is not merely to be understood but also to speak in ways that discourage misunderstandings, which happen easily and all too frequently, especially in those situations that lend themselves to misinterpretation and conflict.

The *Last Chance U* filming experience simply added to the traditional restraints inherent in work as a public figure through the weirdest phenomenon of all – the presence of cameras, sometimes right in my face, and in some cases a mere ten inches from my cheek. Unbelievably, that was often not even the weirdest part of the whole experience because the weirdest thing was when the film crew decided to leave the camera right in my face, sometimes for one minute and other times for up to ten minutes! For example, at every football game, the members of the film crew would film me watching the game. When that happened, they would just come over and stand right next to me, careful not to obstruct my view of the game, holding this giant camera, right up in my face, not because I was actually doing anything particularly interesting. No, they were filming me *just in case* I happened to do something interesting, which of course, most of the time, I did not. No pressure, right!?!

Risk and Reward

Ultimately, as I became accustomed to the presence of the camera, I came to understand that people in this situation really have three basic choices in how they will react:

First, people can choose to deliberately do something interesting, but guess what? If they do that, it is highly likely that their actions will not make it into the series because including something that happened merely as a show for the camera would betray the whole purpose of the series, which is documenting reality. I remember before filming had even begun, I had a meeting with the director in my office and I sort of offhandedly said, "oh, well, if you are going to interview me here in my office, I had better clean off my desk." He immediately said, "Oh, no, no, no! Don't clean off your desk." Ultimately, the film crew did not want people to do anything inauthentic simply because they were on camera, and so while someone could choose to act a certain way on purpose for the camera, ultimately doing so generally does not really accomplish anything.

Second, people can decide to do nothing because they are afraid of doing anything that might make them look stupid or cause people to criticize them. Based on my experience observing people being filmed, this is the reaction of most people (except maybe for some teenagers who enjoy hamming it up for the cameras) and, by the way, it was certainly my original reaction to being filmed.

Finally, people can choose authenticity. For myself, I realized that I could choose to do nothing, but the film crew was going to be filming me for a couple of years, which meant I would end up spending a couple of years of my life doing nothing, and who wants to do that? Not me.

As a result, I learned to be more authentic. I learned to be more comfortable in my own skin. I learned through sheer exposure, through sheer repetition, to ignore the cameras and to find ways to be a more authentic version of myself. Personally, I think that it was a pretty valuable personal lesson. In fact, towards the end of filming the fourth season, I remember sitting with the director in a theater while filming an event, and we were discussing just how difficult people find it to be authentic in front of all the cameras. During that conversation, I made the statement that it seemed like authenticity was a very rare and valuable commodity in his business and, at its core, was the reason for the success of the series. He agreed.

Some people's response to this experience might be, "well, I am never going to be in that position. I am not going to be the subject of a documentary series." But let me explain why authenticity is useful, and why I feel I am a better person because of the experience, and why authenticity is an overlooked and often underappreciated trait, no matter who you are. Surveys consistently show that the trait employees most admire in a supervisor is authenticity – a boss that walks the walk, and authentically connects with others in the workplace. Supervisors that lack that kind of authenticity are the ones that employees dislike the most because they are the bosses who are generally perceived as phony. Essentially, inauthentic bosses are perceived as liars, and conversely, the bosses who are seen as authentic are perceived as honest and not hiding anything. Yet, even though authenticity has a very real impact on a person's performance in the business world, it is not something that is really taught to or even encouraged or developed in college students. Perhaps training students in the value of authenticity should become a part of the college curriculum and not just for business students because, after all, supervisory skills are required in almost every discipline.

Although this book is primarily for administrative leaders in higher education, I really do not think that the higher education leaders engage in sufficient discussion about the role of authenticity in leadership, and the impact that the pressure to satisfy the requirements of some preconceived model of leadership pushes people in leadership to pretend to be something that is fundamentally different from themselves. College presidents are expected to be dignified – to present themselves in a certain way, to dress a certain way, to drive a certain type of vehicle – even if doing that means embracing a certain level of inauthenticity. These expectations conspire to create a public persona that can become so inauthentic as to cause genuine dismay in others when they discover that the public persona is fundamentally different from the private persona.

Unfortunately, social media encourages students to do just the opposite, to carefully craft an online persona that presents them as what they would like to be, and not necessarily as the people they actually are. My conversation about authenticity with the director of *Last Chance U* occurred because as we were watching students on a stage at a ceremony, it became very apparent from the students' stances and facial expressions that they were unsure of who to be solely because they were standing in front of a large group of people. And yet, the most successful communication instructors are successful because they convince students to be *more* like themselves, not less. There is an educational benefit to helping students understand the meaning and desirability of authenticity, and to help them understand that authenticity can yield rich dividends both in their careers and in their personal lives.

For myself, I began living a better, more fulfilling and enriched life when I learned to be a little more authentic in my daily life – even in those moments when the cameras were pointed in my direction – because I ultimately came to understand the importance of being myself as a means of developing personal connections with the people around me. After all, it is the connections we make with our students and colleagues that make the workplace a gratifying place to be.

So *Last Chance U* taught me something. It took time because it was not easy, but I learned that if I can be authentic with fifty million people watching, I can be authentic in any situation.

CHAPTER 6

What Limits the President's Ability to Innovate?

The higher education, leadership, and business literature are filled with material about innovation, and making genuine contributions to the subject difficult. However, there is an issue that lies at the nexus of college presidencies on the one hand and innovation on the other. While that issue is largely ignored, it is a crucial limitation on the ability of certain types of presidents to innovate. There is no point in talking about innovation and entrepreneurship as if the sky's the limit – because there is often a very practical limit in the gradual diminishment of the effectiveness of the president under certain circumstances.

A year or so ago, a reader of my blog contacted me and posed the following questions: What is the life cycle of a community college presidency? Why do some presidencies end quickly while other presidents serve for decades? Are there any lessons to be learned from the way college presidencies end? As someone who has recently experienced the entire lifecycle of a college presidency, I am in a unique position to discuss these challenges. Interestingly enough, a good friend of mine had urged me not to talk about this topic while I was a sitting president, because she felt that talking about the finite life of a college presidency seemed a little fatalistic and might be interpreted as a sort of resignation – and that it would not be helpful to the College to have people speculating about the end of my presidency. I ultimately agreed with her at the time, but now that I am no longer a college president, having resigned from that position with Independence Community College in 2019, I feel I can discuss this topic openly and with a little better perspective and most importantly without causing unintentional negative consequences for the College.

As I have mentioned previously, Independence Community College is a small rural community college in Kansas, and as its president, my experiences centered on the challenges facing colleges in rural communities with limited resources and relatively small student and community populations. Consequently, I am going to specifically limit my observations to the unique challenges of presidencies in those types of small rural colleges, mainly because the forces at work in large universities are so varied as to make it much harder to draw specific lessons. Likewise, the experiences at large universities are sufficiently different from my own experience as to make it difficult for me to speak knowledgeably about them.

The average length of a college presidency in the United States is about four years. However, that is a misleading figure for multiple reasons. First, this figure includes disastrously short college presidencies that implode quickly, thereby artificially shortening the average length of all presidencies. Most have either personally experienced or heard stories about presidencies that begin on a high note, full of promise, only to have that presidency implode, sometimes ending within the first six months of its tenure. While fascinating, they are also not all that common, and so I will not focus on those here.

There are other reasons why four years is a misleading figure. I think that the real average is shorter, in part because there are plenty of presidents who are not fired from their jobs and do not resign abruptly. Instead, they reach an agreement with a board that does not want them, in which they agree, for example, to ride out their existing contract or the current year of their contract. Often, they spend the rest of that time as not wholly, but mostly, absentee because the board understands that they are going to seek other employment, making the effective date at which they stopped doing a full-fledged job as president earlier than the official date when they leave.

I will not be considering presidencies that fail early, where the person is not a good fit for the institution in some way and departs relatively quickly. That said, I think it is worth considering the lifecycle of what I will refer to as a "normal" college presidency. In this case, the president is an acceptable fit for the college, has a good set of skills, and, as is often the case (especially with community colleges), the institution lies in a small community.

First, two relationship deteriorations occur for most presidents whose college sits in a relatively small community – and it is vital to understand the nature of each of those two deteriorations because while they are not necessarily inevitable, they are widespread. The first is well-known, and people discuss it all the time, but the second one is barely discussed, even though it is far more important because it is actually the one that better defines the lifecycle of a presidency.

Consider the one that is well-known: the honeymoon period. The honeymoon period begins when a president coasts into town on a wave of goodwill and optimism. In many ways, it is like a marriage, although unlike a marriage, it is a relationship involving many people, most of whom have entered into the relationship involuntarily. Even so, these people want the relationship to work because they want to be part of a successful organization. The president is treated generously, and his or her motives and decisions are viewed charitably.

As with all good things, the honeymoon period must come to an end, generally in one of three possible ways: It dies a natural death, it is murdered, or it dies as a result of suicide.

In the case of the natural death of the honeymoon period, the relationship between the president and an institution simply reaches a sort of equilibrium. The employees of the institution reach a point where they want to receive as much from the president as they are willing to give (or, as is sometimes the case, they want to receive more than they are willing to give). In either case, their willingness to give is lessened: they are not as willing to hold their collective tongue when angered, they are not as willing to withhold their opinion when they disagree, and they are not as willing to suspend judgment when a decision has been made with which they disagree. The natural death of the honeymoon period, when it occurs after an appropriate length of time, is not a bad thing because healthy relationships should eventually come to a sort of equilibrium.

However, sometimes the honeymoon period is murdered. Most commonly, the murderer is an external force that acts upon an institution and requires the president to make one or more wildly unpopular decisions: Maybe state funding is decreased and as a result, a department or program headed by someone beloved and longer serving than the president gets the ax. Maybe there are new athletic regulations that make the conference more competitive, and suddenly, a college's perennial winning team has a losing record and is no longer the same source of pride within the community. Maybe there is a tragedy on campus, perhaps a violent act to which the president reacts in ways that are later determined to be inadequate, insensitive, or otherwise less than responsive. The list of potential examples is endless since many outside forces act on campuses, but the result is the same: the president simply does not have enough political capital or goodwill to overcome the negative reaction to the situation and simply fails to react effectively to the external challenge. Presidents cannot escape the bell curve of performance any more than any other employee. After all, presidents are people and, like all people, they are flawed and sometimes make poor decisions, and if that decision is made around the wrong people or a little too publicly or creates enough negative consequences for an institution, no amount of political capital or goodwill can sustain the honeymoon period, and it will die.

Then there are the suicides – those honeymoon periods that die through the egregious missteps of a president who commits an ethical lapse or a crime, sends an inappropriate e-mail, harasses a colleague, diverts funds for the grandiose remodeling of offices, impulsively fires a beloved employee, or any of the multitude of other missteps that might show that the president's judgment is not merely flawed but fundamentally flawed. Those cases get the most ink in the newspapers, but they are the least interesting – in most cases, the president deservedly loses his or her job. The ending is abrupt and spectacular, but there is less to be learned from these cases than the others because it is typically obvious that a serious problem exists, and the president is at the root of that problem.

Most often, the honeymoon period ends not with a bang, but with a whimper. Presidents begin to notice that their cabinet members are slightly less deferential. Their faculty, always opinionated to begin with, express those opinions more forcefully and in less flattering ways. The local press begins to describe problems and, eventually, publishes a critical editorial or maybe a critical letter to the editor from the public appears in the local paper. Most presidents could not exactly pinpoint the moment when their honeymoon ends, but many can pinpoint when they realize that it had *already* ended.

When did I personally realize that my own honeymoon period at Independence Community College had ended? I can pinpoint that pretty specifically because it was due to an unforced error made by me. The College participated in a character-building program called Character First, and this character-building program required group meetings of the employees every month. Because the entire College was participating in the program and the College was paying quite a bit of money to participate in it, I required that all employees, including faculty, attend these monthly meetings. It was not part of the workload that was described in their contract, and the faculty were upset with me – legitimately upset with me. Even though the character building program that the College was participating in was expensive, and even though it had value for the institution, being respectful of the faculty contract was more important both as a legal contract and as a contract about something central to the mission of the College – education and the institution's relationship with its faculty. By placing the character-building program ahead of the teaching contract, I made a clear error in judgment (even though nobody directly challenged me on the decision – that is, nobody grieved my decision as being contrary to the terms of the contract). In response to the pushback I received about that decision, I remember thinking, first, I should not have done that, and second, my relationship with the campus has changed a bit, and this incident clearly illustrates that.

While there is no hard and fast rule about how long a presidential honeymoon will, or should, last, I have noted two trends. First, the larger the institution, the longer the honeymoon tends to be, probably because the president is personally more insulated from most of the constituents of the institution. Second, the unluckier that president is, or the more incompetent he or she is, the shorter the honeymoon period. So, except for those cases that are so rare they prove the rule, the ending of the honeymoon period is the first inevitability of a college presidency.

It is the second, and less well-known, inevitability that interests me more. Over time, presidents not only experience a loss of goodwill within their institution, but they also experience a progressive net loss of goodwill with the communities their institutions serve. As the old saying goes, "friends come and go, but enemies remain," a saying that is very apt when it comes to relationships between college presidents and the community members their colleges serve. College presidents are, in a sense, CEOs of large organizations and nowhere is this more apparent than in a small community (i.e. a community with anywhere from 2,000 to 20,000 citizens) or in a community where the institution is one of the area's largest employers.

One of the biggest threats to a college president's relationships in the community relates to employee turnover. On average, a college will have turnover in the range of five to ten percent of its employees every year, some of which will leave the institution voluntarily, and others involuntarily. In illustration, let's assume that a college employing two hundred faculty and staff members has employee turnover of about seven percent of its employees, half of which leave the college involuntarily, creating about seven involuntary dismissals for the institution each year. For the most part, those dismissed live and work nearby in the community, and for the most part, they are unhappy about being dismissed. In a small college in a small community, the president will get some, or even all, of the blame for those decisions and so each year the president permanently damages his or her relationship with those seven people.

One might ask whether and to what extent terminated employees actually blame the president? In my experience and the experience of my colleagues, the results are fairly uniform. When people are hurt by a college, whether they blame the president directly or simply blame the college in general, and the president by association, the relationship with the president is harmed. Even decisions with which the president had no direct connection are still a source of criticism because it is generally believed that the president could have intervened after the fact but chose not to do so. Occasionally, this happens in fairly vivid detail: A supervisor terminates one of their direct reports, that direct report comes to the president in the hopes that the decision will be overruled. When the president lets the decision stand, the employee blames the president, in addition to their supervisor, for the termination of their employment. I would be astonished if there was a president that has not experienced this firsthand.

Of course, it is not that simple because terminated employees have spouses, children, and friends within the community. If, for instance, each terminated employee represented a circle of anywhere from five to fifteen other community members who were just as upset at the president as the employee (or to simplify for purposes of the arithmetic, one assumes that each terminated employee represents ten angry community members), that equates to a total of seventy community members per year who are angry, and likely permanently angry, with the president of the college. Assuming the accuracy of those numbers, staff turnover alone would be responsible for destroying the president's relationships with seventy members of his or her community each year.

Risk and Reward

After just five years, involuntary dismissals of personnel would be responsible for creating 350 angry people, and, in a community with a population of 10,000, by year twelve a full ten percent of the entire population of the community would be angry at the president, based solely on relationships damaged through personnel disputes.

Factoring in any academic program cancellations, the disbanding of sports teams, perhaps the ending of some long-held tradition or the demolition of a beloved facility at the end of its life or any one of the multitudes of situations that could result in the collective anger of hundreds of people against the president in one fell swoop in any given year, the number of potentially unhappy community members is vast. As a personal example, I remember once merely proposing a change to modernize the seats in a theatre in one of our performing arts venues. To listen to the people who had been involved in the original construction of the facility, one would have thought that I had proposed closing the College. Years later, some people are still talking about it – even though the College never did change the seats.

So to finish the arithmetic, if one assumes that an average of just thirty community members per year are unhappy with the decisions that the college made, and for which the president was asked to take ultimate responsibility, in addition to the people who are upset over personnel matters, that amounts to a total of one hundred ruined relationships per year within a community of just 10,000 people. Is that sustainable? How could that possibly be sustainable? Put simply, it is not. It is not possible to build a hundred new relationships from scratch every year in a town of 10,000 people. Even in the unlikely event that someone could build that many new relationships, sooner or later that person would run out of people with whom to build new relationships – and it is cumulative – in a decade it amounts to about a tenth of the entire population, and an even greater percentage of the adult, voting, taxpaying population.

Some might object to the above reasoning, arguing that it is possible to make decisions that negatively affect people without losing their goodwill forever. While I agree with this completely, I would clarify two points.

First, most supervisors can make decisions that others do not like without ruining relationships, especially with regards to most of the controversial decisions that a leader makes. However, my focus is a specific subset of decisions: the ones that either cannot be done diplomatically, or that require diplomacy that is beyond the skill level of almost all administrators. A typical example of this at my institution was the process of contract renewal for faculty. In the state of Kansas, faculty are not afforded due process until they receive tenure, or put more precisely, receiving tenure means receiving the right to due process. This means that by definition, an employment decision about a faculty member prior to the guarantee of due process provides that faculty member with little or no recourse about the decision that has been made. In Kansas, very little can be shared with non-tenured faculty (or non-faculty staff) about the rationale behind non-renewal decisions, since that is thought to inadvertently create a sort of due process for that employee. The consequence of all of this is that a college is forced to make life-changing decisions for an employee but cannot offer a substantial context for that decision to the employee. This situation is a perfect recipe for hard feelings. Secondly, it is important to understand that it is not necessary to lose people's goodwill forever for my thesis to be correct. One need only lose that goodwill for the foreseeable future, that period in which the president hopes to drive positive change at the institution and needs some critical mass of goodwill and support to do that. I have personally seen ruined relationships heal after a couple of decades but by then the operational advantage of repairing the relationship may have been lost.

The deterioration of these relationships is particularly detrimental for presidents in small towns. For presidents who live in large metropolitan areas with a population of a couple of million people, angering a couple of hundred people a year probably feels like barely a ripple in public sentiment. There are exceptions, of course – perhaps in a small town or community that is thriving. In such cases, program cancellations or personnel cuts due to budget constraints may not be necessary, and the number of people negatively affected by the president's decisions would generally be much smaller. The president may also be a very effective leader with the ability to develop very strong relationships with key players in the community and with employees, thereby effectively creating a sort of floor of support that can offset general public sentiment. That said, it is extremely rare to create a true floor beyond which public support cannot fall without a number of external factors being in place, such as an economically thriving community or a growing population base that creates robust enrollment.

When I discussed this presidential lifecycle issue on my podcast, I thought it was interesting that not one current or previous president contacted me to disagree with me, despite normal optimism and the general can-do attitude of most presidents. If there was a single line in my podcast that resonated with other current and former presidents, it was the saying that I referred to that "friends come and go, but enemies accumulate." Most of the people who contacted me wanted to express their agreement with my observations and had their own stories to tell about the permanence of damaged relationships. These stories definitely reflect something worth remembering about engaging in conflict with someone – one may have to deal with the aftermath of that conflict for years and years and years to come. Many of the examples that people gave me are classic and familiar: an employee is fired but remains in the community and never forgives the institution and the president, or cost-cutting requires the cancellation of a program and the supporters of that program never recover from the loss. Even more interesting to read were the examples of absolutely petty reasons for the destruction of a relationship or grudges that were held, that prevented a relationship from developing or evolving positively. One president told me a story about how several employees reacted negatively when she upgraded the *doorknob* in her office to comply with fire codes, and those employees were still mentioning the doorknob change in her evaluations five years after she made the change!

That may sound amazing, but I have been there myself. I remember when I arrived at Independence Community College, there was a tradition to give the employees turkeys at Thanksgiving, and this tradition had been going on for several decades. Over that time, it had morphed into something very different than originally intended. By the time I arrived, it seemed to be primarily a source of conflict and resentment. Originally, the turkeys were given to the employees in the form of a gift certificate to a local store. However, some people had complained that they did not like patronizing that particular store. As a result, the practice had changed to include all of the local stores that carried turkeys, but then people complained that they did not like turkey or that they chose not to eat meat. Consequently, the practice was changed once again to simply be a gift certificate in the amount of the approximate cost of a turkey with the understanding that people could buy whatever they wanted. The gift certificate was, I believe, in the amount of fifteen dollars, and people began to complain that this was a pretty pathetically small gift to the employees for Thanksgiving.

It was at this point that I arrived at the College, and it seemed to me that the gift was simply making a lot of people unhappy, and the gift had been given for so long that it no longer felt like a gift to employees, but rather an entitlement. As a result, there was no corresponding group of grateful people to offset the unhappy people. So the College appeared to me to simply be spending a few thousand dollars a year on something that produced a net harm to morale on campus, so I decided to stop the practice entirely and instead devote the money to the funds allocated each year for our employee holiday party to upgrade the event a bit. *Seven years later*, that decision was still being described negatively by several employees on my evaluations. At the time I made the decision, I never would have guessed that people would still be upset about a fifteen dollar per person decision. Seven years later, I might have made a very different decision as a result of knowing that.

I expect that everyone who has been in this position has a similar story to tell. However, the driver of these kinds of conflicts is not mere pettiness. Very often, the source of the conflict is embedded directly in an institutional procedure or even a state statute. Take an example from my own state of Kansas. As in other states without centralized governance of community colleges, it is very easy for faculty unions in Kansas to see the president of an institution as the personification of animus toward workers because there is no statewide organization that negotiates on behalf of faculty at individual community college campuses. Each individual campus has its own faculty association, which negotiates only on behalf of the faculty at that campus. As a result, on the faculty side of the negotiating table, there are the individual faculty members with whom the president may work daily and on the institution's side of the negotiating table is typically either the president or a group of administrators with the president actively participating. This creates a dynamic in which the very people the president works with every day are asking for something, and very often in negotiations, the president has to say no, to some if not all of those requests. While the faculty might get some assistance from the statewide union, at least in my case, the faculty were always present at the negotiating table.

What are the interpersonal repercussions of this system of negotiation – not just for the president but for the college? It is not hard to guess – the primary topic of discussion at negotiations involves something that the faculty want, and not just any old thing – the topic is their livelihood and the total compensation they will receive for the work they do for the institution. Not only does that compensation amount to a form of validation of every faculty member's work at the institution, but it also provides faculty with financial security – it ensures their cable bill gets paid, it puts a roof over their heads, food on the table for their families, etc. From the perspective of the faculty negotiation team, the president basically sits on the other side of the negotiation table and argues that faculty are not worth nearly as much as they think they are. Presidents nationwide like to privately feel sorry for themselves for some aspects of their work, but since most do not have to personally represent their Board of Trustees in faculty negotiations, I think most of them have it pretty darn easy. Everyone should have to sit at the negotiating table, look a representative group of outstanding faculty in the eye, and attempt to put a dollar figure on what those faculty and their peers are worth – it is a difficult, often awkward, often vilifying, and sometimes traumatizing experience. Technically, in a state like Kansas, the Board of Trustees has the power – in the end, they could impose a contract – but for various technical and legal reasons, this capability is not nearly as powerful as some people think. More importantly, although the board has the power, the faculty have influence. While there is often not much sympathy for education administrators in our society, there sure is a lot of sympathy for teachers and faculty (and yes, much of that sympathy is deserved).

However, this sympathy also results in a pretty amazing double standard. While I am sure that at some places, some vilification of faculty has occurred during negotiations, I can say that neither I nor to my knowledge any of my college president peers have engaged in that. As college presidents, we have a job to do, and we do it. We are not negotiating for personal gain, but obviously, the faculty are absolutely negotiating for personal gain. (To be clear, that is not a criticism – the system is structured and intended to achieve that.) However, the personal incentive embedded within this type of faculty negotiation structure, combined with sympathy for teachers in general, leads to some very lamentable outcomes. Faculty unions are now comfortable with the idea that administrators can be criticized personally for the institution's position in negotiations. In fact, they are so comfortable with it that much of the personal criticism that occurs seems almost unremarkable or goes unnoticed by individual faculty. However, if administrators were to behave in a similar way, faculty would become very upset. I will give an example to illustrate the double standard: In 2018, the president of a community college in Kansas was subjected to strong criticism by the faculty at his institution. I am sure that some of the concerns were warranted; the school was on probation from its accreditors and was experiencing other regulatory problems as well. After some discussion, the Board of Trustees decided to terminate the president's contract. When this decision was announced, the faculty present at the board meeting stood up and applauded. When I read the news accounts of this, I could not help but wonder what would happen in a meeting of the Board of Trustees at Independence Community College if, when a low-performing faculty member was terminated, the administration all stood up and applauded. Actually, all of us in academia know what would happen, regardless of the institution. The faculty would be (rightfully) appalled – and I do not mean appalled in the sense that they would be upset about it for a few minutes and then the moment would pass, I mean that the episode would become the stuff of faculty lore. Letters to the editor would be written, complaints would be filed, references to the incident would be included in the evaluations of those administrators, and so on.

So, in the case of contract negotiations, there is a system that periodically bleeds goodwill from the president, by making him or her the de facto agent negotiating for the needs of the entire institution, even when those may conflict with the interests of the institution's faculty. While this may be moderated in times of plenty or at institutions with more resources and when negotiations are easy because there are enough resources to go around, for a small school in a socio-economically depressed area of a state that insufficiently funds higher education, the norm is a relationship-straining disagreement about how resources should be allocated.

Ultimately, this is not about being a good president or a skillful president or having the president sit down and honestly evaluate him or herself (although that last one is of course important). It is actually about understanding the context within which college presidents work, and understanding that the context, especially in socio-economically depressed, rural colleges, produces an almost mathematical inevitability that erodes the effectiveness of presidencies in smaller communities.

Although I probably am using the word "mathematical" in a way that would make a mathematician cringe, I am not sure how else to characterize the sentiment correctly. I would say that in a small community during a lengthy period of scarce resources, where the leadership of a college is forced to make difficult decisions about priorities in those circumstances, over time a president will alienate more people than he or she could possibly gain as friends. I am not sure that is a mathematical certainty, but I have never seen an exception to that. I would remind the reader of what I said earlier, where I described the question of blame in largely mathematical terms: The difficult decisions that a president makes will alienate a certain number of people. One can arbitrarily make an educated guess regarding how large that number will be, but the fact is that each year the number of people that a president alienates will be greater than the number of new relationships that he or she can reasonably create locally in a small community because there simply are not enough local people with whom to create new relationships. So, I freely admit that while it is not necessarily "mathematical" in the way a mathematician would use that term, it is as a practical matter very predictable and once explained, it does create a sense of mathematical inevitability in that the one number is simply greater than the other under certain circumstances.

What does this ultimately mean for the effective lifecycle of a president's ability to innovate? Well, I would say that every new president, even if they are familiar with an institution, will need to take some time to learn the way around parts of the job and to learn about the people involved with the institution. Even new presidents who were promoted internally have to learn about the parts of the institution that they did not have access to before becoming the president. All of which means there is a (steep) learning curve and a time investment required during which a president needs to familiarize him- or herself with the institution and its culture. In most cases, even if the president is coming to the institution from the outside, that learning period actually roughly corresponds to the honeymoon period. The next thing that happens is that the president presumably is going to use what he or she learned during that initial phase to make changes, ideally to innovate in different ways. Some of those changes will succeed, and some will fail. But the ones that fail will, of course, jeopardize relationships because there is a very low tolerance for failure in general in our culture, and because some of the failures may harm people. Even so, there is a critical window, from approximately year two to year six, in which presidents can get a lot done. They can innovate; they can do new things because a critical mass of opposition has not yet formed.

In an educational setting, a critical mass of opposition really just consists of a bunch of different individuals and groups with their own agendas and issues. At a certain point, these individuals and small groups coalesce into a collective group, at which point their collective influence becomes far greater. A critical mass of opposition can create a force that acts against what the president wants to accomplish at an institution, and that force will often grow over time. At a certain point, it becomes increasingly difficult for a college president to innovate. When opportunities present themselves, there is the desirability of the opportunity on the one hand, and the opposition and its effectiveness on the other. At some point, these forces sort of cancel each other out, and it becomes much more difficult for a president to be effective as an innovator at that institution.

When does that happen? In my experience, a president's effectiveness begins to decline typically around year ten of a presidency. While there are obviously exceptions to this, in most cases, particularly in smaller towns, a president that has been at an institution ten or more years will likely not be as effective as an innovator as he or she was earlier in the presidency, not for lack of new ideas, but because the forces acting against innovation are simply greater. Once that becomes the case, it is probably time for a president to consider moving on to a new institution. By the way, it is not necessary to guess whether or not this shift has occurred. Most good colleges are going to be collecting data about employee and public sentiment, and that data should reveal a generic level of support for the president and for his or her new initiatives. My prediction is that while that level of support will vary slightly depending on when individual data points are collected, the institution will find an overall erosion of the support for the president in the second five years of a normal presidency.

Now, all of this probably sounds pretty depressing, particularly for someone that is, or wants to be, a college president, but it really is not depressing for several reasons. First, there are lots of inescapable forces that act on college presidencies and this is just one of them. These forces are just a context, and there is not anything wrong with a president understanding that, within the context I have described, he or she may have a limited lifespan in which to do their best work. In fact, knowing that may motivate some people to act. Second, understanding that this process is happening can be helpful. A president who understands the mathematical nature of the erosion of public support will be less distressed by that erosion when they understand that in certain circumstances it may be inevitable. Third, and for me this is the most important, is an awareness that the college does not exist for the president. The president works for the college, not the other way around. The fact is that if for any reason the president has become less effective than whomever their generic replacement might be, then that president needs to do what is best for the college and move on. After all, what is best for the college is what is best for the students which is presumably the reason the college exists in the first place – for the students' welfare, not the president's. Presidents need to see themselves as perhaps temporary caretakers of the institution, not in the sense that the president must maintain the status quo, but with an awareness that the president's role at the institution is smaller than the institution – a college is bigger than its president and presidents honestly tend to forget that at times.

Speaking of inescapable context, I have received a fair amount of what I can only describe as anti-faculty comments, comments in which the general message is that faculty have too much autonomy and so they can make things too difficult for a president, and that it is this autonomy that is the real problem. *I could not disagree more.* The autonomy of faculty is one of the reasons that the American higher education system is one of the best in the world and is often the envy of the world. Faculty are highly educated employees, who in many cases have been at their respective institutions for a long time. As long-standing members of the institution, they often care very deeply about the institution. When these faculty disagree with the president or another administrator, most often their concerns and the underlying disagreement have real merit.

Risk and Reward

Administrators ignore the opinion of faculty at their peril and at the peril of the institution. Of course, autonomy, or more generally speaking, freedom, has the potential to be abused, and that is something we have all seen. However, it is important to remember that administrators also have a fair amount of freedom in virtue of their authority status, which can also be abused, and as such, I do not believe faculty is the issue. Having worked in organizations outside of academia, I have experienced similar phenomena in non-educational institutions – employees that believe they have been mistreated, remember those slights, real or imagined, against them, and act on them perhaps for years to come. Although I do not think this is particularly unique to education, I do believe it is more pronounced in education. Regardless, these issues are absolutely not a function of the way the American educational system treats faculty because in my opinion, the American educational system does not give the faculty *enough* autonomy. After all, in the vast majority of cases, when faculty are given autonomy and responsibility, they rise to the occasion and do an excellent job of meeting that responsibility. In my career, I have repeatedly encountered faculty who are very entrepreneurial in their thinking, especially when they are given the freedom to experiment.

Some people are uncomfortable with my recommendation that a president should move on to a different institution after a certain amount of time, specifically under the specific circumstances described – in a small community, at a small college, etc. Often these people point to presidents who have excelled in their role as president for far longer than ten years. Although I have no doubt there are such people, if you examine those presidents and their tenures closely, there are usually one of two recurring themes: 1) the president possesses much more interpersonal and leadership skill than the norm or 2) the college has simply not had to make the kind of difficult decisions about resource prioritization that strain community and employee relationships. It may be that presidents who survive and even thrive in their presidencies longer than ten years have simply not had significant outside forces acting negatively on them. So although there are presidents who remain for a long time at their institutions, it is important to carefully consider the external forces acting on their institutions or whether they are presidents of small community colleges in small communities that are having to deal with very difficult resource decisions or very significant external forces.

Personally, I do not think that what I am describing is any more depressing than gravity is depressing. Presidents need to understand that they exist as part of a larger context and need to recognize that and understand their roles and the role of other external factors that act on his or her presidency. A college president needs to appreciate and accept the extent to which he or she is contributing to the various complexities that are impacting the college and the extent to which factors beyond his or her control are contributing to it. Only by understanding this can a president know whether he or she has done everything that can be done, and ultimately recognize when the lifecycle of his or her presidency has run its course. If and when that happens, a president needs to recognize and understand it and then take the initiative to step aside and make way for the next person who can innovate more effectively because that is what a president owes his institution.

When I have discussed the issue of the presidential lifecycle before, a recurring theme in the comments I have received has been that I am correct that presidents need to move on. In fact, many people who commented to me suggested that I am underestimating the need for presidents to move on. That is, they commented that I only identified one circumstance under which they should be moving on, when there are in fact several circumstances. One of the recurring themes in those comments was that different circumstances require different leaders with different skillsets. An institution's needs are going to ebb and flow. At one time, an institution may need a very dynamic leader; at another time, they may need a sort of Steady Eddie. As the needs of an institution and the community within which it exists change, the president needs to recognize that his or her skillset (even though they are skills, even though he or she may be very good at what he or she does) are not necessarily what the institution needs *at that time*. The president needs to recognize that and, if the time is right, move to an institution where his or her skillset meets the unique needs and challenges facing that new institution and allow a new president with different skills to address the changing needs of the president's home institution.

Section 3

Responding to a Crisis

Introduction

What is an organizational crisis? I find the most helpful conception of a crisis to be the one adopted by the <u>Institute for Public Relations</u>, which characterizes a crisis as a significant threat to operations that can have negative consequences if not handled properly. The elements in this definition are important: the crisis is a threat to *operations* (as opposed to a strictly personal crisis) which *can* have negative consequences (not all crises must have a negative outcome) if not handled *properly* (the actions the institutions take in response can worsen or improve the situation).

Most administrators are not trained in public relations, and many of our normal human responses to stressful, high-stakes, crisis situations actually tend to make these situations worse, not better. I am going to spend very little time talking about what to actually do in a crisis, primarily because each crisis has unique aspects, and in most cases, the response to an individual crisis has to be tailored to the specific elements of the situation involved. Although the majority of this chapter will focus on what *not* to do in a crisis, I will briefly make two points about crisis management that do not get discussed often enough in academia, even though they are actually fairly well-known in general crisis management circles.

First, many things that may at first appear to be a crisis simply are not. How many times have you read an email, felt a strong reaction, and then an hour or even a day later, realized that the problem was not as critical or widespread as you thought, or it had aspects that you did not know about that mitigate what otherwise seemed like a crisis? If you have been a leader for any length of time, you have probably had this experience – probably often. Second, what appears to others to be a crisis may not be either. How many times has somebody walked in your office or your phone rang, and somebody is at the other end who perceives a crisis? You listen carefully to them; they are typically very upset, even agitated? Often this person will simply be too close to the situation and may be having trouble getting a little perspective, and they think that the situation is more of a crisis than it actually is. I would say that at least once a week, I am approached by someone who believes that something is a crisis. I sort of slow walk it a little bit, let them get a little perspective, and usually either by the end of that day or by the next day, the person will come to realize that although the situation may be important, it is not even remotely a crisis. People can overreact to a situation and demand heedless, thoughtless action without full consideration of all the elements at issue – and a good leader cannot give in to hysteria or jump to meet their demands. However, it is important to take the matter seriously and to commit sufficient time and thought to the situation – do not dismiss the complaints of those around you too quickly, perhaps as mere emotionality, but instead listen carefully.

Crisis management for any CEO occurs within three spheres of influence. A person or group's first sphere of influence is the constituency that is closest to that person or group. For the leadership of an institution, that first sphere of influence will generally include one's institution (including its students, employees, and most loyal donors and friends), and perhaps the immediate geographic surroundings of the institution, such as the town (or for a more urban institution, maybe a geographical region within its city) within which the institution lies. Depending upon the size and relative influence of the institution, that sphere might extend to a slightly larger region, but for the most part, the first sphere of influence generally lies with the institution, its students, employees, alumni and friends, and its immediate geographical area.

An institution's second sphere of influence extends just beyond the bounds of the first, and often includes the state and perhaps even the region of the country within which the institution lies. Once again, the size and influence of the institution, and the size of the region within which it lies, will have an impact on the reach of its second sphere of influence. For example, at Independence Community College, the second sphere of the College's influence included the state of Kansas, but there was some geographical overlap because it was located in the southeastern corner of the state. As a result, its second sphere of influence geographically encompassed a portion of Missouri and Oklahoma as well. An institution's second sphere of influence is geographically larger and includes people and organizations that have much less direct interaction with the institution, which necessarily means that the institution will have much less impact on the people and organizations within its second sphere of influence. Thus, when an institution acts to impact those within its second sphere of influence, it is going to have much less of an impact because the people in that sphere are often much, much farther from, and have much more sporadic contact with, the institution and its values, mission and general activities. Finally, there is the third sphere of influence, which includes an institution's national and international audience. I would argue that the ability to influence that sphere is limited to an institution's willingness to screw up and embarrass itself by saying and doing the wrong things (ask me how I know). The idea that it is possible for most institutions to positively influence this sphere in any meaningful way, or to actually make a national or even international audience respond to an institution in a certain way, is a total fallacy, especially for small and relatively uninfluential institutions. Obviously, the way that an institution's leadership interacts with its primary sphere of influence, its employees, students, and community partners, will be quite different than the way it interacts with other spheres. As a rule, most institutions can do very little to affect their third sphere influence at all, except to avoid making situations worse.

Clearly, institutions spend most of their time impacting their immediate surroundings, by interacting with employees, students, donors, and other stakeholders and staying engaged in a way that keeps people as informed as possible in as constructive a way as possible. Although this will clearly depend a great deal on the specifics of each individual crisis, I recommend pausing and asking a simple question: who are the people or groups that would want to be engaged in this issue? This simple question can offer rich dividends, and I have found that many of my mistakes in dealing with crisis situations came about because I failed to engage all of the relevant constituencies. The next question is to consider is how best to engage those relevant constituencies – and this will vary widely.

For example, at Independence Community College following a widely publicized and highly inappropriate text exchange with a student, our football coach, Jason Brown, resigned his position at the College. This generated both national and international news coverage because of his starring role in the Netflix documentary *Last Chance U*. As one of the most impacted and significant constituencies affected by the situation, I decided to hold an open forum for employees immediately. During that open forum, I did not tell employees that there was no problem, and I did not tell them how to think or act. Instead, I tried just to listen as employees expressed anger and frustration and dismay, and I openly told them that I felt the same way. When they asked me questions about specific facts that I was legally allowed to answer, I answered them. When they asked questions that for whatever reason I could not answer, I told tell them that, and explained the reasons why I could not answer – although there really were not very many of those. One employee said that she did not know how to feel proud of the College knowing that this thing had happened, and that gave me a chance to share with the group how I refocus my own perspective in the face of overwhelming negativity. Often in these situations, I find that it is really easy to get fixated on one specific thing or event. However, the fact is a college is a large and complex organization, and at any given time there is a lot to be proud of within an organization. As a result, I try to remind myself of all the wonderful things going on around me. Focusing on what I am proud of, and the positive things my colleagues are doing, helps me feel better and reminds me that I am working in a very special place, with very special people. During that open forum, I shared this technique with the group, not to encourage them to ignore the negativity or to forget the way current events might negatively affect the College, but to urge them to see the entire situation within the larger context of the reality that even

Risk and Reward

in the face of a truly negative series of events, the work they do exists with the context of the larger organization, some parts of which are truly positive, inspiring and life-changing for the students and others around them.

The second sphere, which includes the larger local (and certainly the regional and statewide) media as well an institution's own social media presence, is the sphere in which leadership's actions are going to touch the largest number of people, and it is for that reason that an institution's communications within this sphere of influence must be specific, focused and brief. The approach to communicating with this sphere is, in many ways, a complete reversal of the approach to interaction with the first sphere – except in unusual cases, interaction with this larger sphere should be succinct to ensure accurate reporting. For example, when the news initially broke about the text message exchange between our football coach and a student, the College released a very brief statement:

"The Independence Community College Board of Trustees has met to discuss the situation and offer their input regarding the recent controversy regarding a football coach's texts to a student. There are a number of elements the college must consider in this case, and we expect resolution within a few days. Until that time, the college has no further comment on this personnel matter."

In essence, the College was informing the media that it was aware of the situation and its significance, but it still needed to complete its investigation. It was a polite and succinct way of telling the community that there was no additional information to share at that time. Of course, providing the media a very generic statement like this will not satisfy them – there will be many follow-up questions, but leadership cannot give in to the demands for additional information that it may not yet have.

Once we had additional information for the media, we issued another statement, and this one offered very specific new information, presented succinctly:

Message from Independence Community College President Daniel Barwick:

> Independence football coach Jason Brown has submitted his resignation to the college, effective immediately. Athletic director Tammy Geldenhuys has appointed the current offensive coordinator, Kiyoshi Harris, as interim head coach. This has been a painful episode for the entire campus and community, and its conclusion allows us to fully focus on the students we serve as a college. We should be defined by the outstanding educational quality and value we create for our students, and we believe that we can move past this incident together with our community, faculty, staff, and student body. The college has no further comment on this matter.

Of course, the purpose behind this type of press release is to offer specific information about the resolution of the situation, in this case, that the coach had resigned, and to inform the public of next steps as a result of that resolution, in this case, the continuation of the football program through the appointing of an interim head coach. In this case, the press release acknowledged the painful episode and clearly articulated a conclusion of the situation while also spring-boarding into a reminder that the College would continue to focus on educational quality and the value it creates for students. The press release essentially invited the College's faculty, staff, and students to move forward together as a community, and made it clear that the College would have nothing else to communicate about the situation.

There are some very real reasons not to communicate with the media beyond this point. First of all, the press release itself conveyed all the elements that the College needed to convey to its constituents: an update and resolution of the situation, information about the future of the relevant program, and a reminder about the positive aspects of the institution. However, there is also another reason not to communicate any additional information to the media: providing any additional information, such as conjecture about future projects, additional information about the situation, or answers to any questions submitted by the media are very likely going to get the institution into trouble. Remember, most college administrators are not trained to talk to the media and engaging with the media increases the likelihood of providing unauthorized information or saying something that will anger a constituency or otherwise upset someone or result in engaging in a conversation about something that is fundamentally negative.

For these same reasons, it is generally pointless to attempt to engage that larger third sphere of influence in the hopes of changing the wider national and international conversation, in any way that goes beyond the same press release provided to local media. (The national media is going to quote from the same press release provided to the local media. If the national media contacts an institution directly, the institution should simply restate the information, position, or policy contained in the press release.) Beyond that, I do not believe in doing anything to engage that third sphere of influence because it is largely impossible to affect the national conversation in anything other than a negative way that merely perpetuates the discussion. For instance, any attempt to affect that third sphere of influence on behalf of Independence Community College in the above-mentioned example would have to be based on the premise that the reaction of the worldwide media is somehow within the control of a small community college in a corner of Kansas, which is simply not the case, and would involve wasting resources that could be used much more productively in other ways. Still worse, there is a good chance that engaging with the national media will result in making the institution come across in an even more negative light and/or perpetuate a story best laid to rest. That said, expect pushback from peers and colleagues, and to be surrounded by people who are acutely aware that a national conversation is happening, that that national conversation does not reflect well on the institution, including some of those same people, whether they be other administrators at the college or trustees. Many of these people will want the institution to avail itself of the opportunity to engage with that wider sphere of influence in the hopes of somehow changing the tone of a very negative conversation, but the idea that a small college can do that successfully or reliably is simply false.

While obviously being in the national spotlight in a negative context can be frustrating, sometimes it is important to simply accept that something bad has happened, and that situation is going to dominate the national conversation for some amount of time (and may become part of campus lore). It will be unpleasant while it happens, but that time will probably be short. After all, as Thomas Hobbes once said, life is "nasty, brutish, and short," and thankfully so is the news cycle. That does not mean completely ignoring the national media – after all, the situation necessarily requires an awareness that the institution is being portrayed negatively in the news, which will necessarily encourage people to view the incident through a negative lens. Contradicting that view and fighting against that narrative can be exceptionally difficult because complex issues do not lend themselves well to explanation. In most cases, it is better to focus on consistency of message than attempting to re-shape a national dialogue.

The local media present more grounds for optimism for two reasons: 1) the local media care about the entire institution, not just that single incident, and at some point, other important news from the institution will generate a new narrative. Of course, most institutions do not have that opportunity at the national level because the national news is not interested in minor achievements, especially at small institutions. 2) The local media is likely to provide more detail about a specific incident, allowing a college to offer additional information that may reflect well on it.

In summary, there are three basic rules to handling a media crisis: 1) understand that there are different spheres of influence and some of them are simply outside an institution's ability to influence substantially; 2) engage with influencers in the second and third spheres (at the state, national or even international level) in a very, very concise manner (detail is the enemy) and never say anything off-the-cuff to the state or national media; and 3) focus attention on the first sphere of influence – the institution's employees, students, local community, local media, alumni, donors – because these are the people who have invested the most in the institution, care most about the institution and are owed the most by the institution. After all, these are the people that, when the noise of the current crisis has died down, will still be involved in new educational programs and activities. They are also the people who are most likely to continue to be friends of the institution in the long term. At a Board meeting shortly after the above mentioned events occurred, I was sitting in my seat waiting for the meeting to start and as I was sitting there, one of our longest, most prominent supporters came up to me, and she knew that had been a rough couple of weeks at the College. She hugged me and said, "I will always be a Pirate." I cannot adequately express how that felt except perhaps to say that I felt like at that moment, I could get through anything with the help of our team of dedicated people and that the College <u>would</u> get through the situation because we were all in it together.

CHAPTER 1

Case Study: The Turf Field Controversy

Featured prominently in the fourth season of *Last Chance U* was the local controversy over the construction of a multi-use artificial turf practice field. The decision to build this field created immediate debate locally and created a public relations crisis that damaged the College's reputation in the community. The College was never able to effectively address this issue, which is why the controversy was featured on *Last Chance U*, and which is why it is presented as a case study here.

Why was the turf field such a controversy for the Independence, Kansas community? Perhaps the best place to start is to review the events that led up to the building of the field. As an aside, this is not just my version of events – this summary largely mirrors the summary of events created by a team of employees for the College's accreditors and was not contested by either the campus or the accreditors.

The decision to build a multi-use turf practice field was part of a long-range institutional plan. That long-range plan was: 1) developed by the Board of Trustees as part of a campus-wide collaborative process; 2) driven by a need to improve facilities over time; 3) supported by data identifying the need from both a continuous improvement standpoint and a student safety standpoint and 4) included an analysis of resources needed and possible funding. Although the College's facilities plan identified the project as planned for construction within the next five years, projects were not prioritized within the plan itself as it was recognized that varying levels of public funding versus private

Risk and Reward

philanthropy could make some projects more feasible than others at any given time. It was assumed that the multi-use practice field project would be explored sometime between 2019 and 2021, likely as part of the initial stage of a capital campaign.

However, in Spring 2018, an unexpected event occurred: the landlord of the turf field the College used for football practice (local Independence school district USD 446), citing concerns about wear and tear of its field, exercised its option to cancel the lease. They offered a new lease which allowed the use of the field only for competition, leaving the College with no turf practice facility (and, in fact, no full-sized practice facility at all, because its secondary practice facility was a small grass field on campus, which was both smaller than regulation size and in poor shape). Before the cancellation of the lease, the College had already established that student safety would be significantly negatively affected if no artificial turf field was available, due to a higher rate of injury on the grass field. Luckily for the College, previous planning had also already created the groundwork for addressing the problem. Public College documents show that as early as 2011, the College had begun planning for the possibility of building a turf practice field, as evidenced by the collection of information and data necessary to produce a plan for the renovation of a football field. The entire project, including the unplanned lease cancellation by the landlord, unfolded as follows:

From 2008 to 2011, minor repairs to the College's existing, but inadequate, grass practice field were made; however, none of these repairs resulted in resolving the field's underlying problems. Athletic staff had multiple meetings with contractors and experts, all of which came to the same conclusion: the entire natural turf needed to be rebuilt and replaced, and at the same time, the field needed to be enlarged.

In Fall 2011, as a direct response to the large number of student knee injuries related to practicing on the grass practice field, the athletic department began conversations with artificial turf companies regarding the cost, time frame for construction, and varying levels of quality available for a new grass or artificial turf practice field. Since the local school district was also talking to turf companies for the 2013-2014 renovation of their stadium, the College was able to acquire cost estimates that confirmed that replacing the practice field with artificial turf was too costly for the College at that time. As a result, the College elected to negotiate with the local school district to use their newly renovated artificial turf stadium. Through negotiation, the College was granted access to the local school district's stadium for three practices per week during the fall and spring semesters for ten years, limiting the need to practice on the College's existing grass field to two practices per week. As a result of this arrangement, which continued until 2018, the College elected to de-prioritize the construction of the multi-use turf practice field in its facilities plan.

In December 2017, the local school district notified the College that it intended to cancel the College's lease and restrict the College's access to use the stadium for football practice. As a result, the athletic department reached out to an artificial turf company to assist in the construction, resource planning, and funding of a practice field renovation project. Also, the College reached out to three or four other turf companies for cost estimates to create a proposal for the renovation of the College's existing grass field with artificial turf along with a fundraising plan targeted for 2020-2021 completion. From January through June 2018, the College constructed funding models and contacted outside donors, obtaining several sizable commitments, which the athletic department and I eventually assembled and presented to the Board of Trustees in June 2018.

In May 2018, the College's Board chose to accept the replacement contract with the local school district, which did not allow football practice at the stadium. (They had little choice – the few other options, like practicing in another community, all came with either logistical nightmares, high costs, or both.) The loss of the stadium, with its artificial turf practice field, created two immediate concerns: the first was the safety of student-athletes practicing on a poor condition grass field six days a week, and the second was the potential liability to the College associated with forcing student-athletes to practice on a poor condition grass surface of a different type than they would compete on each Saturday. (There have been a surprising number of successful lawsuits against schools regarding this very issue.) The cancelation of the contract also created an urgency for the College's football program as the cancellation occurred a mere six weeks before the beginning of the football season.

Fortunately, due to the College's prior consultation with artificial turf contractors, the College was able to locate several companies that could complete the project within eight weeks, and the school district agreed to allow the College's football team to practice on its field two days per week during the eight-week period required for construction. The College also determined that additional practices could be held using its former soccer field during those eight weeks.

Up to this point, the College was able to address an urgent, unplanned construction expense effectively. The crisis of having a nationally ranked football team with nowhere to practice had been replaced by a cost-effective plan to improve campus facilities to address the problem. The crisis appeared to have been averted... but then the real crisis emerged: Following multiple meetings with donors and the Independence Community College Foundation, a special Board Meeting was held on Saturday, June 23, 2018, to discuss and ultimately vote to approve the construction of a multi-use artificial turf practice field to serve multiple athletic and non-athletic groups (football, stunt/cheer, softball, band, physical education/activity classes, and local youth sporting groups) in support of the mission of the College. The Board approved expenditures of up to $572,000 for the field, and the College's Foundation agreed to match up to $200,000 of that from new donor funds. In addition, the Board approved the decision to assess a new athletic facilities fee to student-athletes to help pay for the College's portion of the project over the length of the loan payment. With that funding, along with already budgeted funds allocated for use in the maintenance of the existing field, we projected that no additional taxpayer funds would be needed to either build or maintain the field. With funding, construction plans, and cooperation with the foundation in place, I felt a sense of accomplishment and believed that the problem had been effectively addressed. I was a fool. Although the project was approved, the Board meeting was held unusually early in the morning and on a Saturday, and with shorter than normal notice – the announcement was sent out at 4:40 PM the day before, which to make matters worse happened to also be a day when the College was closed – as it was during the summer months when the College traditionally closed on Fridays. (The Board had no choice – Saturday morning was the only time that the Board members were available because two Board members were leaving immediately for extended trips without any departure flexibility.) The weekend meeting and early start time of the meeting gave ammunition to those who felt that the project was rushed and that the process was not transparent. There was a significant outcry from the community, including the local press, and on social media. I felt blindsided: I had forgotten that most members of the public did not know as much as the College did about the project, I underestimated the need to inform them, and I underestimated both the negative response to a last-minute notification of the meeting and to the early-morning meeting itself.

The project was completed under budget, and as of this writing, eighty-five percent of the project has been privately funded. Because the College's facilities plan was part of many planning documents at the College and because it had been prepared several years prior, and most of the planning and research for the multi-use artificial turf practice field was done quietly as preparation for a 2020-2021 project, many College employees and members of the public only became aware of the issue of the turf field when the lease was canceled by the local school board, an event that received significant local press coverage. This resulted in the perception that the construction of the field was undertaken from the planning stages to commitment during a very short window of time following the lease cancellation, and to many, the project and discussion about its necessity seemed rushed. While the construction was certainly rushed so that a practice field would be available for students, and

Risk and Reward

engagement with donors was certainly rushed to meet financing needs, the overall research and planning for the project was not rushed, but was simply on-schedule to meet a projected 2020 or 2021 completion deadline, had the local school district not canceled the College's lease.

There was a wide gap between public perception and reality as it relates to the amount of research and planning that went into the process and funding for the construction of the multi-use turf practice field. Given that Independence Community College is a public institution, it was important for the College to better inform the public that tax dollars did not fund the construction of the practice field and that inf fact the field was funded largely by private donors, primarily local supporters who were long time supporters of the College and who had funded many other endeavors at the College. Despite common perception to the contrary, I believe the practice turf field probably would have been funded in exactly the same way and to the same extent, regardless of the involvement of *Last Chance U* and Netflix in athletics at the College.

The building of the multi-use practice turf field at the College was divisive within the community for two interesting reasons. First, there was this idea that somehow the public was paying for the field, which, as I have illustrated, was simply not true, and the second idea, equally naive or misinformed, was that donors could just as easily have been convinced to donate funds for a different project, even though that is just not the way fundraising works. When people donate, they donate to causes they are interested in, not just any project someone requests money to fund. I think that the people who financed the multi-use turf practice field did so because that was the Indy Pirate project they wanted to support. Although the presence of Netflix and the filming of *Last Chance U* provided an interesting wrinkle or focal point for the construction of the turf practice field, the show primarily portrayed the existing public perception about the research, planning, and funding of the field. It is obvious from many of the public comments that many people were simply unaware of the facts. While many people knew that the College built a $600,000 practice field, there was very little recognition that individual private supporters provided funding and that they funded the construction of the project because that was the specific project that they wanted to fund for the College. Often people will comment and say, "well, that money could have been used for other things," but the truth is people with experience raising money for specific causes know that when people donate money toward a cause, especially large sums of money, they are very rarely going to allow that funding to go toward a completely different project. These donors agree to donate funds for a designated project because that is the project into which they want to invest. In this case, these donors, these wonderful people and organizations that gave the money necessary to build the practice turf field at Independence Community College, did so because they specifically wanted to support Pirate athletics. Were they ever going to use the funds they donated to the practice turf project to support other areas of the College? Very unlikely, in my opinion.

So while the show does capture the division within the community, those close to the situation understand that the division in the community was largely based on those two mistaken understandings of the situation – the general belief that somehow because the College is a public college, tax money was used to pay for the field, and the idea that somehow the donors funding the field could just as easily have been convinced to fund something else, even though that is really not true because that is just not the way philanthropic donations work.

In my estimation, the problems created by factors beyond our control (the need to complete the project quickly) and factors within our control (the College's failure to understand the consequences of the need to act quickly and to compensate for those) persisted for nearly two years. Once I became aware of the mistakes that had alienated a large portion of our community, College leadership worked hard to engage affronted constituencies and to inform them of the nuanced realities of the project. For instance, I gave an update on fundraising for the athletic field at every Board meeting to reinforce to the public how much of the field was privately funded, and I met with many individual people over the first year. Nevertheless, the damage was done – there was a substantial opportunity cost, and some relationships were permanently severed. Furthermore, College leadership could not comfort itself by saying that those who were upset were already opponents of the College – in at least two cases, it was a defining moment for long-time College supporters.

For me, the entire episode was an exercise in crisis management, and provided three significant lessons in crisis management as it relates to community expectations and communications when engaging in large-scale institutional projects:

1. College leadership, myself in particular, should have spent more time considering who might be upset by the decision to invest in a large, athletics focused construction project so the College could proactively reach out to them. Without that contact, these constituencies were forced to form their opinions based on incomplete news reports and histrionic social media posts.

2. Once community opinion reached a critical mass, there was no quick fix – we could engage those who were willing, but also had to wait for tempers to cool even to begin to consider engaging with many others in the community.

3. Most importantly, the underlying reasons for the crisis were avoidable: The school district made a decision that caused the College great hardship in a compressed time. Both the athletic department and upper administration (myself included) at the College should have had a better relationship with the school district, a relationship that would have precluded such an abrupt decision without any forewarning. Although we had a good working relationship with the district administration, it was obvious that a better relationship with the school board itself, which had the final say in such matters, might have benefitted the College.

CHAPTER 2

Termination and Due Process

With the possible exception of the years-long accreditation related improvements made at Independence Community College (detailed in the next chapter of this book), the most instructive situation I encountered at the College was the termination of a tenured professor. Its instructive opportunities were rivaled only by how disturbing and destructive it was to the institution. Besides *Last Chance U*, it is the episode at the College that I am most often asked to discuss. On the surface, the case seemed straightforward: a faculty member was alleged to have been issuing racially disparate grades and was terminated for that. However, the case was extremely complex, involving race relations, liability for the College, the most complex statistical analysis I ever had to consider, national, local media and social media attention (all of it negative), high costs, and precedent setting legal issues. The professor had been at the College several years longer than I had and was ultimately terminated from her tenured teaching position for what the Board of Trustees described as "racial discrimination involving disparate grading of Afro-American students." There are varied and important lessons about crisis management to be drawn from the case.

It is difficult for me to write this chapter because it was a sad chapter in the history of the College, involving the termination of an employee. An explanation of what happened requires a restatement of the facts of the case, although I have no wish to unnecessarily reinforce what is in the public record about an employee whom I am sure would like very much to leave the entire situation behind her.

Most attempts (by some estimates ninety-five percent) to terminate tenured teachers are settled quietly, or at least without the case going through an expensive and time-consuming hearing process, which tenured professors in Kansas have the legal right to request. In this case, the professor took the case all the way through the administrative process, which was unusual, but she also made several other unusual choices that dramatically impacted the experience of everyone involved. First, she immediately took her case to social media, as did her friends, significantly expanding the number of people who became aware of the allegations against her. Second, although she had the option of requesting that the due process hearing be conducted in a closed session, she elected to make the sessions public, which meant that colleagues, community members, and the press could attend and hear the allegations and evidence against her, as well as her rebuttals (and attend they did – the newspaper coverage was extensive). Finally, she cooperated with national media who were interested in the case. The result is that except for executive session discussions among the Board of Trustees, everything about the case, from the decision to seek termination, to all of the supporting documents (minus protected documentation identifying student information), to the testimony of all witnesses, to the decision of the independent Hearing Officer, is all a matter of public record. Thousands of pages were created in the case, all of which are available for public review. As such, no information in this account breaks any new ground in terms of available information; it simply presents that information in a more accessible summary format. It is the lessons to be drawn from the episode that are important.

During the second half of my presidency at Independence Community College, I began to hear more and more informal complaints about the professor from both her coworkers and students, some of which were race-related. The majority of the complaints reviewed and considered during the termination process were submitted through the College's

Maxient feedback system, or to the concern log system, which was the feedback system that preceded the College's purchase of Maxient. In addition to student complaints, one of the professor's African-American colleagues reported that the professor had made inappropriate comments to her on two separate occasions (the professor's comments were also witnessed by other employees of the College). After the second incident, she decided to file a complaint with the College's Human Resources department, which issued a step one warning (verbal but documented discipline) to the professor as a result of the complaint. Even after she received the warning, other employees continued to complain, primarily about her treatment of African-American students, and students complained as well.

The turning point was when I was visited by two faculty members who were concerned not so much about the professor but about the fact that the College had little firm ground to stand on in disciplining her. Up to that point, we just had stories – some were secondhand, and others could not be verified. We had only one that was beyond dispute, and we had issued a warning in that case, but the complaints had not abated. These two faculty members stated that the students who complained about unfair grading were nearly always African-American, and they argued that if, in fact, she was behaving in any biased way toward her African-American students, then that bias should be measurable in her grades. (This conversation also ultimately became part of the public testimony at the professor's due process hearing.) I visited with our Vice President of Academic Affairs and asked her to coordinate with our Institutional Researcher to initiate some sort of grading analysis.

The Institutional Researcher, and later an outside professional statistician, performed an analysis of the professor's grades against a relevant comparison group (the two other full-time professors in the same discipline at the College, both of whom had been employed during the entire six-semester period of the analysis), and additionally against all other professors at the College who had also issued grades to the African-American students in the professor's class. This analysis was done using six semesters of grades for all students (approximately 1,120 duplicated students maximum, approximately sixty-four class sections maximum, depending on the specific test performed). Thirty-eight different analyses were performed. *All* showed either a) that there was a statistically significant disparity between the professor and other teachers, or b) that the disparity was specifically related to race. Specific findings, which were ultimately included in the College's report regarding the matter, included:

1. The African-American students in the professor's class had significantly lower overall grades than the African-American students in the comparison group.

2. There was a statistically significant difference between the median grades from the professor and the comparison group, both for all students and African-American students. In other words, using generally accepted statistical procedures, it was determined that the difference could not have been the result of random selection.

3. The negative gap between the professor's African-American students' grades and the professor's *overall* students' grades was significantly larger than the gap between the same gap for the comparison group. The negative gap between the professor's African-American students' grades and the professor's Caucasian students' grades was significantly larger than the gap between the same gap for the comparison group. In other words, African-American students did worse compared to other groups of students in the professor's class than they did in the classes of the teachers in the comparison group.

4. The professor's African-American students received F's at nearly twice the rate of the average of the comparison group. Additionally, the professor did, with statistical significance, assign F grades in higher proportions to African-Americans as

compared to non-African-Americans, and compared to the comparison professors.

5. When the performance of students in the online environment (where racial identity may be less obvious to the instructor) was compared to the performance of students in the hybrid and on-ground environment (where racial identity may be more obvious to the instructor), the professor's African-American on-ground students performed worse than her African-American online students. The relationship was the opposite for the comparison group. In addition, the result for the professor was unique to her African-American students.

6. The professor's African-American students did worse in her class when compared to all of the other classes they took, whether from teachers in the comparison group or not.

7. When developmental students, who are the weakest students from an academic preparation standpoint, were removed from all samples, the racial imbalance persisted, with the professor's non-remedial on-ground African-American students earning average grades of less than half of the comparison group.

I presented some initial information to the Human Resources Director. Based on that conversation, we decided that the professor should be removed from the classroom to avoid additional liability. The Human Resources Director and I decided to remove the professor from her classes at the start of spring break, to provide time for a transition of course load to new instructors, and to prepare for the very real possibility that her employment with the College would need to be terminated. We continued to run additional tests, all of which yielded the same results as the previous tests. Our Institutional Researcher was conscientious – she agreed to run any test that was practically feasible and kept thinking of new tests that could be run that might show an alternative explanation.

We spent a great deal of time discussing the possibility of discipline coupled with professional development rather than termination. That would have been my first choice in most cases. But after much discussion with the leadership team and the Board, it seemed clear that on a strictly practical level, a constructive disciplinary process would be difficult or impossible. Of what would the disciplinary process consist? In what ways would the College need to restrict contact with students during a period of retraining? How would success be determined? Regardless of what process was used in evaluating success, would that process require jeopardizing students? In such a situation, should students have the right to opt-out of whatever part of an instructor's retraining involved students? How would one retrain a professor in this situation? Nearly all of an instructor's duties at a teaching college, from teaching to advising to committee work to working with student clubs, involve contact with students. It appeared that a professor would have to be removed from the immediate college environment during, at the very least, some part of the training. However, that would be very unusual, and at a small college, it is very likely that the reasons for it could not be kept entirely confidential. Would this not just create the stigma that we had hoped to avoid by choosing the discipline route rather than termination? Likewise, given these obvious problems, why would a professor agree to any of this, since there seemed to be a likelihood that he or she would regard all of the College's actions as unwarranted? Finally, the cost to the College would be considerable – the training itself would undoubtedly cost money and would be in addition to the cost incurred by the College to essentially hire another full-time instructor to perform the professor's duties for an indefinite period while the training progressed. How exactly would College leadership defend those lines in the budget to the campus and the public during a public budget development process, while ensuring confidentiality? For these reasons, discipline was not seen as a viable alternative to termination.

Based on all of the analyses we performed, our discussions, and the informal and formal complaints we had received, I decided to recommend termination to the Board. (Our contract with the faculty treated discipline and termination as separate, meaning that if a faculty member's conduct met the state standard for termination, discipline was not a prerequisite.) Before making this decision, the leadership team and I asked ourselves devil's-advocate-style questions, many of which I ultimately shared with the Board of Trustees in our report, entitled "Report on Race-Related Statistical Analysis and Review of Race-Related Complaints against [the professor], ICC Instructor (all of which was also provided in both written form and testimony as part of the hearing process). Some examples:

> ***1. To what extent should we be concerned about the sample size and time limitations of the statistical analysis? Is limiting our analysis to six semesters, approximately 1,120 (duplicated) students, approximately 64 class sections, and only three instructors cause for statistical concerns? Would it be preferable to invest in a larger, and more inclusive, analysis of grading patterns, especially outside of the professor's discipline/department?***

Answer: A more sophisticated analysis would always be desirable. However, there are four issues to consider:

First, if the data is sufficiently compelling that we believe African-American students' federal rights are being violated, then we have an obligation to take steps to protect their rights. We have enough data to act responsibly to protect the rights of a specific group of students before making a wider or longer-term study of general grading patterns. Discrimination may exist elsewhere, and the institution has an obligation to search for that discrimination, but that is an ongoing search that will never be fully complete as new instructors and new curricula come on board. The College is not paralyzed while those long-term projects are addressed.

Second, there are many types of grade studies, and expanding the data sets would not necessarily enhance the accuracy of the study type we have performed. That is because we have chosen to focus on a comparison group of faculty who are similar to the professor in what we consider to be relevant aspects: discipline type, sections taught, full-time status, common institution, common master syllabus, and course objectives, common textbook, common research and citation standards, common entry and exit diagnostics, common assessment rubrics, etc. Expanding the comparison group, or adding new comparison groups, would reduce the number of similarities, advantaging it in some ways and disadvantaging it in other ways. Due to the size of the college, it is simply a fact that all internal studies of grading done at ICC will involve relatively small sample sizes.

Third, our analysis specifically extends beyond the original comparison group, and compared the outcomes of the professor's African-American students to dozens of other faculty.

Fourth, it would not be realistic for the College to perform a larger-scale analysis in the timeframe necessary to address complaints. We can perform large-scale analysis as part of our regular quality comparison efforts, but as a practical matter, addressing specific complaints will always require a narrower focus to address primarily those involved in/affected by the complaint. Ideally, as part of its ongoing institutional research efforts, more baseline data will be available to be used when a complaint arises. It should also be pointed out that this is the most comprehensive analysis the College has ever performed in response to a discrimination complaint.

2. Is it possible that there is no discrimination, but rather an anomaly that makes it appear that the professor (or even perhaps the comparison group) is unfairly singling out students, when in fact, the composition of both classes just happened to favor finding that African-American students did better in classes taught by the comparison group and fared worse in the professor's class, even though no racial discrimination had occurred?

Answer: It is always possible that anomalies are present in the data. However, we have attempted to mitigate that by using data from over sixty different class sections, from six different semesters, from three different teachers, and using classes that are required, to minimize self-selection. In addition, we considered several sources of anomalous findings, some of which are specifically addressed in our analysis, and took steps to confirm those sources. That is the purpose of performing a wide variety of analyses. We were unable to find evidence offering an alternative explanation for the data. Finally, a crucial point remains: a professional examination of the distribution of final grades for African-American students indicated that there is only a 0.02% chance the outcome could have been the result of a random selection of students and grades. Thus, there is a statistically significant difference between the median grades for the instructors, effectively eliminating the possibility that there is *no particular* reason for the difference; i.e. that it occurred randomly. The average grade, and the median grade, for the professor is nearly a full grade lower than those for Instructors A and B, when only considering African-American students. Once randomness has been eliminated as an underlying cause, we believe that the qualitative and quantitative evidence overwhelmingly shows that the underlying cause is racial discrimination.

3. Even if we can show that discrimination in grading does exist, is it relevant that this does not conclusively show that the discrimination is purposeful or even avoidable, as it could be a bias that is inherently (and unintentionally) built into the professor's curriculum or the expectations of her course?

Answer: First, no attempt has been made to measure the professor's motivations or attitudes. Our only purpose is to discover whether her African-American students' rights are being violated. Although our analysis does appear to show that the professor is the source of the outcomes, the College takes no position at this point on whether the outcomes are intentional. We do believe (as does legal counsel), that the professor's work with students must stop to preserve the rights of, and prevent harm to, African-American students.

Second, there is significant similarity between courses across faculty, because of discipline type, sections taught, full-time status, common institution, common master syllabus, and course objectives, common textbook, common research and citation standards, common entry and exit diagnostics, common assessment rubrics, and required teacher credentialing. This is not to say that bias does not occur; rather, this analysis simply demonstrates that the outcomes are statistically distinctive in the professor's case.

Third, the issue is not whether bias or discrimination occurs at all, or whether it may also be occurring at all in the courses of other teachers, or whether there are variations in courses. The issues are whether any specific students are harmed as an outcome, and whether that harm is disproportionately occurring, in a statistically significant way, in the classes of a specific teacher.

4. Is it possible that the "discrimination" is not actually present in the professor's curriculum/class, or perhaps not solely in the professor's curriculum/class, but rather is present in both the professor's (in favor of non-African-American students) and the comparison group's (in favor of African-American students) curriculum/class? Is it also possible that the discrimination is a result of discriminatory grading and curriculum by the comparison group and not the professor?

Answer: There are two responses to this:

First, the issue is not whether variations occur – they do. Variations in which outcomes for specific students are good (compared to other instructors) without accompanying harm to other specific students (compared to other instructors) do not necessarily suggest discrimination – it may suggest, for example, that the teacher has found particularly effective methods for reaching certain students. Grading, unless a curve is strictly enforced, is not a zero-sum game in which, if some students do well, others must necessarily do poorly. So evidence of better outcomes for African-Americans in the comparison group does not necessarily imply that discrimination is producing bad outcomes for other students.

Second, this argument is one that may be raised in response to a specific measurement, but this argument cannot be applied to all of the different analyses made, both qualitative and quantitative. It would not explain, for example, why there is such comparative breadth and depth to the complaints against the professor, while there are fewer or no complaints against members of the comparison group. It would also not explain why the average performance of the professor's African-American students is markedly better in classes other than hers.

Third, as shown in the analysis, if there is discriminatory grading by the comparison group, the results fall outside the boundaries of statistical significance.

5. *Even if it is not possible to do this analysis for every professor every semester, would it be desirable to have a periodic analysis of grading?*

Answer: Yes. The President has requested that the Academic Affairs Office conduct a grading review to coincide with, but not be part of, each program's cumulative program review, beginning in the 2018-2019 academic year.

Engaging the Professor

On a Friday in March, the College's Human Resources Director, Vice President of Academic Affairs, and I met with the professor, along with another faculty member who was present on behalf of the professor and the faculty association. The meeting was short. Using a prepared text, I explained to the professor that based primarily on a statistical analysis of her grading compared to the grading of other faculty in her department, the College had found that her grading may have violated the federal rights of African-American students, and may have carried significant liability for the College and for her professionally and personally. At the close of the meeting, I gave her a summary of the individual complaints and the statistical findings. In light of the strong evidence, I told her that I would be recommending to the Board that her employment at the College be terminated. I explained to her that because of the nature of the complaints and the results of the analysis, as well as the potential for her own liability, she might prefer to resign her position rather than be publicly terminated for cause. I gave her until the close of business the next Tuesday to choose to resign, and I urged her to consider resignation. I explained that we were prepared to pay her through the end of her contract year (about fifteen weeks of pay and benefits) if she chose resignation prior to Board action. I explained that as of the meeting, she was suspended from the College with pay and instructed her not to have any contact with any African-American students or employees while she remained an employee on administrative leave.

I was very conflicted about offering her the opportunity to resign. Many hospitals, for example, have policies in which they do not allow doctors who have committed harm to patients to simply move to another institution. Even though it might be best for the hospital to settle the matter quietly, concern for future patients is understood to outweigh the interests of the hospital. Although the professor was entitled to a hearing, and the matter was not yet resolved, the data that we had gathered regarding the outcomes for the professor's African-American students was troubling. What was our responsibility to each affected party in this case including future students? Understandably, however, the Board of the College had no interest in a protracted public fight with a faculty member who had strong local support, and there was no appetite for an all-or-nothing approach.

Her response was pretty much as I expected: she was shocked and dismayed. She speculated that we had not done sufficient research and insisted that she was not racist. The faculty association representative asked a question about how the analysis was done, and I simply replied that examination of the statistical analysis was best suited for a due process hearing, but that the materials I had given her contained a great deal of detail about methodology. The meeting ended, and of course, the professor was visibly upset, as I suspect anyone would be in that situation.

Risk and Reward

The Vice President of Academic Affairs met with the professor's department faculty to inform them (as much as we were able) and to distribute her teaching load among them. This was done with no issues.

The professor chose not to resign, which meant that the Board had to adopt a resolution declaring its intent to terminate. The College's attorney prepared the proper documents, and a special meeting was held. The Resolution passed by the Board was simple and designed primarily to comport with state statutes and read as follows:

> Be It Resolved by the Board of Trustees of Independence Community College:
>
> WHEREAS, [The professor] was initially employed by Independence Community College, Independence, Kansas on the _____ day of _____, 20__ as a teacher;
>
> AND WHEREAS, [The professor] is currently employed as a teacher by Independence Community College;
>
> AND WHEREAS, [The professor] is entitled to due process protection and Independence Community College, Independence, Kansas, pursuant to KSA 72-5436, et seq;
>
> AND WHEREAS, the Board of Trustees of Independence Community College, Independence, Kansas finds that the contract of [the professor] should be terminated effective _____ for the reasons hereinafter set forth.
>
> NOW THEREFORE, Be it Resolved by the Board of Trustees of Independence Community College:
>
> <u>Section 1</u>: It is hereby declared the intent of the Board of Trustees of Independence Community College, Independence, Kansas, to terminate the employment

contract of [the professor] as a teacher effective _____, 2018.

Section 2: The Clerk of the Board of Trustees is hereby authorized and directed to give written notice promptly to [the professor] of the Board's intent to terminate her contract.

Section 3: The notice shall contain the following reasons for the Board's intent to terminate the contract: racial discrimination involving disparate grading of Afro-American students.

Section 4: The notice shall state that the teacher is entitled to a hearing before a hearing officer with regard to the Board's action, provided that she file written notice of a request for such a hearing with the Clerk of the Board of Trustees within fifteen (15) days from the date of the notice.

Section 5: The action of the administration to suspend the professor with pay pending termination, until further action of the Board of Trustees, is hereby ratified and the suspension with pay shall continue pending further action by the Board of Trustees.

Because the resolution was issued at a special meeting of the Board, the media was quite interested, and immediately reported the outcome. A former student and housemate of the professor's immediately started an online petition. Because the student did not understand the process (and of course was quite upset), the petition was full of factual errors. For example, the petition stated that "[A] professor at Independence Community College was fired" (the professor had not yet been fired and remained a paid employee of the College). He also wrote that "The ideal professor, however, [the professor] was unfairly fired from her job. She was accused of being a racist." (College leadership was actually quite careful, whether in the resolution, our report, or our internal correspondence, never to state that the professor was a racist, in part because we had no evidence at all that the grading disparities were the result of an intent to create harm or were motivated by conscious racism. Instead, we focused exclusively on the fact that the grades were racially disparate, and *never* made any claims about the professor's motivations or beliefs.) He further wrote of the College: "Not only did they label her this without giving her a chance to prove them wrong, but they published it in the local paper to make things worse." (The College has never published anything related to this matter in any newspaper or other media, and of course, when asked to comment by the press, we declined. I think that the student may have been referring to the fact that all Board meetings are open to the public, and the local news media typically attends and reports on the meetings. However, it is important to understand that Board meetings are not meetings with the public, they are meetings that take place in public.)

In addition to those acting on her behalf, the professor herself took a very public stance on social media. While I understood that she saw this as a justifiable defense of herself and her reputation, I also understood that her public stance was going to hurt the College for several reasons. First, because the College would not comment on personnel matters, one hundred percent of the information that the public was getting was negative towards the College. Second, regardless of any blame the public might assign, we certainly did not want people associating the College with racially disparate grading. Third, I knew how these things worked – anyone who already did not like the College for any other reason would adopt this new issue as a cause and trumpet their support for the professor, magnifying the public effect – and that is exactly what happened.

As I mentioned earlier, we used an outside statistician to review our findings. He pointed out that he could not determine whether any of our findings were "statistically significant," because we had not calculated the odds that all of our observations could have happened as a result of chance. He was willing to calculate that for us (he certainly thought it very unlikely, as our work to this point had been very thorough). He performed two separate tests for randomness, with one finding only a 0.01% chance the outcome could have been the result of a random selection of students and grades, and the other 0.02% (the chance can never be zero). He also made observations about each finding, suggesting ways that the charts or narrative could be clarified. He suggested a few new charts, which we then made.

The professor then made a formal request for a due process hearing, which she was entitled to have if she chose to have one. Was our evidence strong enough to hold up in a due process hearing? All of us understood that there were no guarantees. Even if we had a strong case, there was no telling what a hearing officer might do or say. But with regard to strengths on the side of the College, at that point we could say the following:

1. Our Institutional Researcher felt that the analysis was very thorough – she specifically said that she could not even think of additional tests to run unless we simply began to examine *all* faculty for their own biases, which would also yield some additional comparative data regarding the professor.

2. Based on conversations with the College attorney and a specialist attorney, we felt that the College's case was strong.

3. The Human Resources Director was in full agreement that termination was appropriate.

4. Our only alternative had been discipline, and it is difficult to determine as a practical matter how that would have worked in this case.

5. We planned to retain the services of an outside statistical consultant to examine and confirm the methodology we had used internally.

6. It is important to understand that the real source of liability was not what we had done, but the possible conduct of the professor. We concluded that we had acted responsibly with the information that we had, and the information we had left us with very few options.

In the aftermath of the termination, several faculty members asked whether College leadership had investigated other instructors to ensure that disparate grading was not more widespread. We did not have the manpower to examine every instructor at one time, nor did we have a complaint basis for doing so. After all, if there was howling when we did it following complaints, imagine what it would be like if we did it without prior complaints. However, our analysis of the professor's grading did produce a fair amount of data about other faculty, most of it reassuring. As an example, we compared the professor's African-American students' grades in her class against their grades in ALL of their other classes, which meant comparing her grades in that respect to the grades of at least twenty other faculty members. The average grade for other faculty members was considerably higher. Since we had no evidence of widespread grade inflation by the rest of the faculty, that was encouraging. Although it did not rule out individual instances of discrimination, it did suggest that many (most?) of our faculty did not show systematic bias.

We received a rebuttal to the statistical analysis from an expert hired by the professor, and I sent it to our statistician and our institutional researcher for their opinion. I am not a statistician, of course, but it did not appear from the analysis that the author addressed some of the stronger points in the College's analysis.

First, the rebuttal did not seem to resolve the issue of the differences in online grading, which suggested that the professor's African-American students did worse in person with her than they did in her online classes. In our analysis, when the performance of students in an exclusively online environment (where racial identity can often be less obvious to the instructor) was compared to the performance of students in the on-ground or hybrid environment (where racial identity is often more obvious to the instructor), the professor's African-American on-ground students performed worse than her African-American online students. The relationship was the *opposite* for the comparison group. We always regarded that analysis as significant, in the sense that the relationship between grades and students' race was particularly evident. Our purpose was not to show that the disparate grading was purposeful – only that the disparity existed, and that disparity required the College to take action.

Second, every exhibit in the rebuttal only compared the professor to two faculty members. Why? One of our most interesting analyses dealt with all teachers, not just the comparison group. That analysis found that the professor's African-American students did worse in her class when compared to all of the other classes they took, whether from teachers in the comparison group or not. We compared the academic performance of the professor's African-American students in her class to the performance of the *same* students in *all* of their *other* classes during the *same* most recent three-semester period. In other words, rather than compare the African-American students to other students, we compared them to themselves: the average of their performance in the professor's class versus the average of their performance everywhere else. That analysis showed that the professor's African-American students were receiving much lower average grades (more than eighty percent of a full letter grade) in the professor's class than they were receiving from *all* their other teachers, regardless of the subject. Once again, we always regarded that analysis as significant, in the sense that the relationship between grades and students' race was particularly evident. Our purpose was not to show that the disparate grading was purposeful – only that the disparity existed, and that disparity required the College to take action, and I thought it was a sign of the weakness of the rebuttal that it did not address two particularly strong analyses.

Although the author of the rebuttal was an economics professor, he appeared to be unaware (or was choosing to be unaware) of the significance of F's and why we would focus on them. An F means that a student receives no credit for the course, and thus must either retake the course at some cost, or will be prevented from graduating for lack of adequate credits, or will graduate with fewer credits and thus will need to pay for more credits at a transfer institution. Our report pointed this out, and I think that the rebuttal focused on an analysis of all grades because it diluted the apparent harm.

Our statistician wrote a rebuttal of the professor's statistician's report. In essence, he believed that a) the rebuttal did not represent very good statistical work, b) the work it contained actually supported our case, and c) most of what it contained was not statistics but guesses about human behavior and motivations.

The Hearing

The hearing was scheduled for a Thursday and a Friday in February 2019. It ended up taking up the full time, and then some. Only twenty-five percent of the hearing involved the professor's witnesses, who testified on Friday afternoon. The rest of the two-day hearing focused on the College's witnesses. The first faculty member to testify gave an emotional account of how the professor had told her twice that she was only hired because she was black. There was very little cross-examination of her. Another faculty member testified that a) she had observed the professor's ill-treatment of her African-American students until finally she asked to have her office moved, and b) the events that led her to urge me to undertake an examination of the professor's grades. Although there was substantial cross-examination of her, it did not seem to amount to much. My notes show that most of the substantive questions centered around what possible role football coach Jason Brown played in that faculty member's recommendation to examine the professor's grades, and whether I was close to that faculty member.

Another faculty member then testified, but it appeared that most of her brief testimony was to corroborate. She received similar, although briefer, cross-examination. The testimony then moved to administrators. Our Compliance Officer testified first, primarily about two issues – our legal obligation to protect the students and the process of producing the professor's report. The Compliance Officer provided what seemed to me to be the only real meat for the professor's side at that point, namely that she was the only administrator who was not convinced that we had met the burden of evidence until she read our expert statistician's report, which was *after* the Board voted to terminate. The cross-examination focused on something that would become a recurring theme: did she contribute, and in what ways, to the final report about the professor? They appeared to want to show that although the report showed many contributors, I was, in fact, the only real author. The Compliance Officer rebutted that view, describing her extensive role.

Our Vice President of Academic Affairs testified next about complaints she had received about the professor and her role in creating the final report about the professor. She testified that she believed strongly that the burden of proof had been met, and that she believed the professor needed to be removed from the classroom and could not return to the classroom under any circumstances. On cross-examination, once again, it appeared that they wanted to show that the Vice President of Academic Affairs had no role in creating the report, and seemed disappointed to find out that the she, like the Compliance Officer, had contributed substantially to the report and the overall process.

Our Institutional Researcher testified next. Her testimony was lengthy. Our attorney took her methodically through all of the research and analysis she had done. Much of it was highly technical in nature. On cross-examination, the Institutional Researcher was thorough and composed – she was unfazed by the lengthy questions and was very prepared. She dashed their hopes that she did not understand the data or that her role had been minimal, and explained what she had contributed to the report, how she had double-checked the final report to be sure of its accuracy, and like the Vice President of Academic Affairs, expressed her conclusions about the professor forcefully and clearly.

Our statistical expert testified next. He was perhaps the weakest witness – although his report was forcefully written, on the stand, he was rather hesitant. Mostly, the issue seemed to be that he was uncomfortable answering any questions that he thought represented an oversimplified version of his findings or his approach.

I testified next, and frankly, it was a bit anti-climactic. We had assumed that they would go after me hard, as I was the final witness from our side. I believed that they would essentially advance the narrative that either: a) I had fabricated the whole thing myself to get back at the professor for something, or b) I had fabricated the whole thing at the request of Jason Brown. Neither of those things happened, most likely because up to this point, there was no evidence of either. In the end, I thought my questioning seemed rather uneventful. The puzzle was that, with our witnesses now finished, they had not established any motive for us to rush to judgment or fabricate the charges against the professor.

Their expert witness went next. He was very polished, expressing himself very confidently and responding well to questions. I had the feeling he had testified many times. I thought he was strong, and so did others, but our Institutional Researcher thought his testimony was irrelevant.

After that, there was a short series of character witnesses for the professor: a former student, two current faculty members, and a former faculty member. They all reported never seeing anything that gave them concern about the professor. There was little cross-examination, as the real issue was whether the College followed the correct process per statute, not whether her colleagues thought well of her. At this point, it was 4:50 on Friday, and the professor was the only remaining witness. Her attorneys claimed that her testimony would take about 2.5 hours, and so they requested to put it off. We agreed to finish the hearing at a later date. They requested that the hearing take place in Topeka (nearly three hours away) in a month. The College agreed because I believed that she would never have made that request if they thought it was going well.

When the hearing finally resumed a month later, the professor was on the stand for about five hours, including our cross-examination of her. It appeared that the primary reason she was on the stand so long was to humanize her to the Hearing Officer – she went through many details of her life and career. She was fairly composed. Her testimony on direct broke no new ground as far as I could see, although she did offer some ordinary explanations for some of the complaints against her. On cross-examination, she maintained that the College had not justified its decision to terminate, and that the analysis of her grading had been inadequate, not only statistically but because we had not examined individual assignments. Her cross-examination was lengthy, so I cannot reproduce it in detail here, but it became clearer what her team's strategy was.

When asked whether preventing racial disparity in the grading of African-American students is something that the College should be concerned about, she replied, "Yes, very concerned."

When asked if she had ever been provided with any other reason for the recommendation of termination besides disparate grading, she replied, "Nothing other than what would be, what I would consider, I don't know, subjective." When asked if she was referring to mere speculation, she replied: "Yeah, speculation…"

When asked if racial discrimination involving disparate grading of African American students is a valid reason to terminate the employment contract as an instructor at the College, she replied: "Yes, I would agree that if you're grading a student differently and not based on what they earned, then yes, that would be a valid reason." (Although it is important to remember here that she denied any discrimination, and maintained that her grading was accurate.)

She was adamant that she had no intent to discriminate (which made sense, since she also maintained that she had not discriminated in the first place, whether intentional or otherwise). Although she agreed that the College prohibits discrimination based upon race against African-American students, and agreed that includes both intentional and unintentional acts of discrimination, when asked to confirm that regardless of what the data says, she was not intentionally grading African-American students lower than your other students in her class, she responded: "Yeah. I believe that there is an anomaly and I fall in that."

I felt that although her testimony was lengthy, it did not particularly strengthen her case. She had agreed multiple times that the College and the Board should be deeply concerned about the possibility of discrimination, agreed that discrimination was a reason for termination, was never able to present any evidence supporting an alternate theory of why the College would fabricate data or even want to terminate her, and her primary argument was that the College's analysis was faulty. By the end of her testimony and closing briefs, it appeared to me that they were hanging their hats on the following strategy: making the legal claim that it was the College's obligation to show that she had *the intent* to discriminate, in addition to showing that disparity had occurred. Her closing brief argued: "ICC did not show any intent by [the professor] to discriminate against any students. Without any evidence of discriminatory intent by [the professor], ICC does not have substantial evidence..." The College's position was that intent was not relevant - its closing brief argued: "The law prohibits both discrimination based on disparate treatment - that is the intentional treatment of individuals differently on the basis of their race - and disparate impact - that is the unintentional treatment of individuals differently on the basis of their race. As such, the disparate impact analysis focuses on the consequences of a facially race-neutral policy or practice, rather than the underlying intent of the decision-maker. Discriminatory intent or purpose is simply not required or even an element in a disparate impact analysis."

Several months later, we received the Hearing Officer's decision. The termination decision was upheld. The hearing officer wrote: "The closer and more difficult question is whether [the College] met its burden of proving that its termination of [the professor's] contract for 'racial discrimination involving disparate grading of Afro-American students' was supported by substantial evidence. The Hearing Officer finds that [the College] met its burden in that regard." With the termination decision upheld, the professor was terminated.

Because there was a thirty-day window for an appeal, I cautioned our team to remember that in the original case, the professor did not settle with us. Therefore, we should not act in ways that might encourage an appeal – no public celebrations or gloating. As such, our public position was simply that the Hearing Officer's report spoke for itself.

Lessons Learned

Race is an issue in a class by itself. Personnel issues involving race require high levels of detail and sensitivity. I thought that it was instructive how many facets that race brought to the table. At its core, the issue was the College's position that African-American students had been harmed by the actions of a particular faculty member, and we knew that people would be deeply affected by issues of race.

It sounds quite naïve to say this, but as the case went public, I was shocked by two things:

First, it was painfully obvious that there were people who did not like the College for other reasons, who had never had any specific interest in race issues before but had decided to attempt to whip the public into a frenzy on social media. I strongly doubt that these people were oblivious to the harm that they could cause, but it was obvious that they found a new means of criticizing the College irresistible, and people made all kinds of irresponsible and baseless claims, like that this professor's pattern of grading was typical among all professors at the College (our data clearly showed that it was not), that our recent accreditation review had found that faculty members were ordered to give athletes preferential treatment (the accreditors had specifically explored this possibility based on complaints and found nothing), and others.

Second, I was also incredibly dismayed at the obvious racist undertones of the comments online by some of those who supported the professor (over ninety percent of the College's out-of-state students were African-American). One person wrote: "When one race is allowed privileges they have not earned, like a passing grade they don't deserve, it is bound to cause bad feelings." Another: "More lazy actions and crying in the corner, all held up under the guise of racism. Do the work, get the grades, and stop whining, when you're too lazy or arrogant to put in the effort!!!!" Another: "Everyone knows they are entitled. Hell we are supporting them from cradle to grave with our taxes." Another from a *law enforcement officer*: "Those dirtbags from out of the area were always slackers on my time. I arrested a fair number of them too."

There were, sadly, many others. None of these people appeared to appreciate the irony of their posts or that they actually made the professor seem worse by making her seem as if her friends and supporters held racist views. I was dismayed at the sheer number of people who engaged in obviously racially tinged online, public conversations without much thought to what they were really saying, and of course, I was further dismayed to find that many of these people were members of my own community. I was not alone in my concern – people who would read the comments online would frequently comment to me that these supporters were doing a disservice to the professor, and there was some speculation that a few of the comments could surface in a due process hearing and be used against her in some way. The fact that it was not difficult to find local people with racist views was immediately capitalized upon by the media – for example, when a prominent education newspaper published an article about our football program, the entire final third of the article was an exposé of the supposed racist attitudes in southeast Kansas, and I believe that some of the sources for the story were the people the paper was able to identify through their thoughtless online comments about the professor's termination. Of course, the majority of the professor's supporters were not racist – they were good, well-meaning people who were trying to right a perceived wrong – and so I thought it was sad to see them get lumped together with people whose views her more tolerant supporters certainly did not share.

Third, it was obvious that the racial element caused the professor to feel obligated to move forward to clear her name, once the situation had reached the point of making the name-clearing itself necessary. The conflict, the press coverage, and the permanent public record all seemed so unnecessary to me. We gave the professor, at every turn, an opportunity to avoid making the situation worse. When we initially confronted her with the evidence, we gave her both the opportunity to resign, and time to think about it. I reached out repeatedly, stating that the College had no desire to perpetuate the matter publicly and that we would be amenable to an agreement about her voluntary departure. Although several people took the case to the media and some also actively defended her on social media (apparently with her support – she stated online that people should share their concerns in their own online postings), we never responded to press inquiries, and the College never mentioned the case on any of its social media outlets. If the professor asked for delays in her hearing, we always agreed, in the hopes that more time would allow her to consider a voluntary agreement. When she opted to have her hearing in public, we argued against that, making the case that we felt that was a bad idea, not primarily from the College's perspective, but from hers. When the College prevailed in the case, we made no statement at all to the media, and no general statement to all employees.

I do not mean to minimize the personal turmoil that the professor was experiencing, nor her desire to clear her name. I suspect that at the time, she felt she had very few choices. I also suspect that she was advised from the outset primarily by people who were as upset as she was. The whole reason we gave her nearly a week to consider her options was so that she would not response rashly, but she appeared to take the case public within just a few hours of our meeting.

Issues of race are unpleasant or fear-inducing, and therefore supervisors avoid them. The professor's due process hearing could perhaps have been avoided if supervisors had been willing to take on race issues more fully when they began to be reported. In fact, I think that College leadership should have better recognized years earlier that race relations at the College were not good. Although steps had been taken, there was no institution-wide strategy. Early in my time as president, a faculty member was disciplined (and ultimately resigned) because, in part, he used explicit racial slurs. Amazingly, he saw nothing wrong with his language, and vigorously defended himself during the disciplinary process. I found a comparable level of obliviousness to race relations in other faculty members – in one case, several students complained that a faculty member was racist, and was disciplined. She appealed her case, and as part of that process, I interviewed her. I found her comments during the conversation deeply unsettling. The faculty member began the conversation by stating, "I don't see color" and "I don't care about race." However, during the entire conversation, every single student, adult, and group of students she referred to were described in explicitly racial terms. During the discussion, she divided her class into two groups, the "brown-skinned students" and the "light-skinned students." When she would discuss any individual student, she identified the race of that student. She described her own race and her husband's race. Whether her specific verbiage represented a simple language issue (she was not a native English speaker although she was completely fluent), or more serious issues is difficult to say, but I could say with certainty that if she was expressing herself outside of my office similarly to how she expressed herself inside my office, then I would guess that she was conveying to nearly everyone that she was, despite her initial assertion that she "didn't see color," deeply preoccupied with race, and that she expressed herself in ways that some people would find racially insensitive. I certainly did.

Incidents like this should have created the impetus needed for a more systematic discussion about race. If we had put initiatives in place to address these issues the first two times we removed employees for discrimination, could we have possibly avoided the professor's situation? Could the institution – through those conversations and awareness of implicit bias and other issues that may have contributed to any professor's grading disparities – have changed the course of the professor and other instructors' behavior without the end result of a termination and the extreme result of a due process hearing?

To what extent does an institution – and college leadership including the president – have a responsibility to ensure that someone is reviewing cultural issues (like the faculty issues that occurred before the complaints about the professor), thus ensuring that the college is responding to cultural or systemic discriminatory tendencies to improve the quality of life for students and staff at the institution? I think that there is a general avoidance of race issues, even though in retrospect, the College may have had a more systemic problem.

In all cases that might reasonably lead to termination, the college attorney should be the first stop. That way, subsequent research will be a legal work product and will be easier to manage later in the process. I have seen administrators (the more experienced, the worse it can be) take the position that the issue is something familiar and so the attorney is not needed. The college attorney needs to be a part of the conversation about training, handling these types of complaints, and creating new policies that can limit the potential for future complaints. Also, any time a college believes they might be engaging in potential litigation, they should work with their litigation counsel. In this case, I consulted two attorneys – our local attorney who assisted the college in general matters, and then switched to a specialist who had extensive experience conducting due process hearings. At each step of the process, counsel was involved – they provided input when we considered doing a quantitative analysis, following the analysis, when we met with the Board, when we discussed how to talk to the professor, when the Board needed to prepare its termination resolution, and of course, during all phases leading to the hearing. Most larger colleges have in-house counsel, so this will be much easier for them. This is one of the challenges that go along with being small – colleges without in-house counsel are using their attorney on an as-needed basis, and so using that attorney creates cost.

Disciplinary action which relies on statistical analysis requires that the analysis be perfect, and no effort or expense should be spared in that regard. Statistical analysis is not a toy. It is a technical field that should be approached by professionals. In the professor's case, I frequently encountered the belief that we had simply fabricated the data or the analysis or both. I found that this view, when held, is primarily held by statistical amateurs; all of the professionals we encountered seemed to fully understand that if a bunch of non-statisticians fabricated either data or analysis, the professionals would ferret that out in short order. True fraud would be exposed rather easily, and the consequences for the institution and for the individuals who perpetrated the fraud would be significant. So, I think that ordinary fabrication is probably uncommon. However, the statistical analysis itself, and the data upon which the analysis is performed, is a) critical to get right, and b) for non-professionals, nearly guaranteed to be done incorrectly. Reliable statistical work is neither simple nor intuitive, and should not be done hastily, with an agenda, or by well-meaning amateurs. Even if the well-meaning amateur gets it all right, the institution is still susceptible to the criticism that the accuracy was luck and that the avoidance of a trained professional implies indifference at best and malice at worst, none of which plays well either in a court of law or in the court of public opinion.

Everything that was presented in the due process hearing, which the professor chose to have publicly, could have been presented more privately by placing the professor on administrative leave during an extended period *prior* to making the decision about termination, and proceeding through the regular disciplinary process. This way, the professor would not have been shocked by the termination decision (if it eventually happened), and the College would have heard and addressed any objections to its evidence prior to the due process hearing. If I had the opportunity to go back and do this all over again, I would place the professor on administrative leave for at least six months while we continuing to develop the case and engaging in on-going discussions with her team.

Serious cases like this should be conducted by an impeccably-credentialed outside investigator, to remove the possibility that personal likes or dislikes might come into play, or to avoid the appearance bias. In a small college, with people all working closely together, with potential conflicts of interest, and with various biases and preconceptions, there are simply too many ways for an investigation to be influenced or compromised. Seeking outside help comes with a myriad of benefits, from maintaining the integrity of an investigation, to creating a respectable impression of fairness and equitability to public and internal constituencies, to removing a line of criticism should the process move to a more formal stage.

The College should have created a more sophisticated public relations response to the social media blitz the professor and her surrogates conducted. Ordinarily, the College's response in personnel matters is simply to say nothing, but I think it would have been possible to craft an effective "no comment" that contained elements that would have helped fill in some basic principles amid the information vacuum, like "our first priority is the protection of our students," "the professor will receive the full due process that she is guaranteed as a teaching professional," "this matter is complex and will not be resolved quickly – the College will not rush to judgment and neither should the public," etc.

This problem was exacerbated by a phenomenon that I have observed repeatedly among employees who are legally entitled to due process: people want due process for themselves, until they discover that due process takes time. People who want to be exonerated want to be exonerated immediately, and that exoneration quickly becomes more important than the process (although the process was more important to them right up until the time they were accused of something). Except for College spokespeople, I am not sure I have ever heard someone say, "there is a process for resolving this disagreement, and that process was the result of a legislative commitment to the fair treatment of teachers. Let's await the results of that process and then abide by those results."

The College should have found an effective way to disseminate the results after the verdict. I left the College almost immediately after the verdict, but the College should have conducted a low-key campaign to at least ensure that interested parties were debriefed as to the result, including local African-American leaders. When the Board passed its resolution regarding the termination of the professor early in the process, I identified various key constituencies to inform as much as I was able, and those parties appreciated that I reached out during a time of tumult, and those relationships were strengthened as a result. To my knowledge, no such outreach occurred after the verdict, and I did meet people months later who asked me what became of the case.

Final Thoughts

Do not underestimate the personal toll episodes like this take on college leadership. In general, this toll takes three forms: First, situations like this are time-consuming, and like any important issue, psychologically consuming as well. But its importance means that the time and the attention are, for the most part, well-spent. Second, these situations take a heavy toll on the professional reputation of leadership, both by the small group of people who personally support the faculty member being dismissed, and by the much larger group of people who are simply using the matter to achieve other ends. For example, I mentioned earlier that an article in a prominent education newspaper, taking advantage of the College's relationship with *Last Chance U* in the interest of collecting page views, linked the professor's case to the success of the football program. Even though the due process hearing, which came long after the article, upheld the College's decision to terminate, and the findings contained nothing about any connection to the football program, the damage to my professional reputation was permanent: the article portraying me as a vindictive tool of the football program will remain forever available, and the newspaper never retracted or amended any part of its story. Third, and most significant, is the toll of watching a colleague's reputation and career damaged. Even though nearly all of that damage was the professor's choice (she required the Board to act publicly, spoke publicly on social media, gave interviews to the media, and opted to have her due process hearing in public, creating a fairly substantial permanent, public record), the most painful part of the process for me was seeing the pain she experienced. I related earlier that some people who did not like the College for other reasons but had never had any interest in race issues before, attempted to whip the public into a frenzy about this situation on social media. It may be that at the time the professor thought that it was in her interest to seem as if she had an army of supporters, but the secondary effect was that it created a substantial social media record of the charges against her, which I always felt was not in her long-term best interest.

CHAPTER 3

Case Study: Accreditation Opportunities

Last Chance U was a complex time for the College and the Independence community. Football season is a busy time anywhere, but continued taping into the spring, media attention, release of the show itself, increased donor activity, the return of the show for a second season, change in the College's practice venue and construction of a new practice facility, and the abrupt departure of the head coach – all contributed to a sense of continuous activity. However, it may interest the reader to know that *Last Chance U* was not the primary focus of the College administration's attention and efforts. The primary focus was on accreditation, and that focus resulted in one of the greatest accomplishments completed by our team during my tenure at the College. The College faced a crisis that weakened its credibility in the community and its credibility as an educational institution: we were sanctioned by our accreditors. Overcoming this crisis was our top priority, and our efforts in the area of accreditation brought about significant institutional improvements under tremendous time constraints, with complex logistical pressures, and during a period of resource scarcity. Understanding how this happened is instructive for others who face the same challenges.

As most readers know, the regional accreditation process is a flawed but valuable one. External accreditation plays a constructive role in making colleges better educational institutions, analogous to the way peer-reviewed journal articles and studies help maintain the quality of publications and research. A strong, constructive partnership with accreditors helps position colleges both educationally and competitively in a future of scarce resources and strong competition. Although accreditation is a complex process and thus suffers many of the same flaws as all complex processes, it is vastly better than no external review of institutions. There are many cases in which external review revealed fundamental institutional problems of which colleges were unaware or ignoring, and in many of those cases, the early intervention by accreditors saved the college.

In my opinion, the process favors larger and wealthier institutions, as one of the fundamental questions of accreditation is whether an institution has the resources to deliver on its mission. Small, rural colleges like Independence Community College do the best they can with what they have, but a result is that they often squeak by on some of the criteria.

Independence Community College had never received stellar accreditation reviews although it had typically met accreditation criteria. It typically did well in some areas and merely adequately in others. The problem we faced is a common one: if a college is struggling to meet a criterion, and that criterion is then made even more rigorous, the college may finally reach a point where the accreditors demand substantive change. Such was the case at Independence Community College with outcomes assessment, which has grown generally in higher education in terms of its scope, rigor, and resource requirements. When I had been at the College for about two years, it became clear to me that the College was struggling to create a genuine culture of outcomes assessment. As we sought approval from the Higher Learning Commission, our regional accreditor, to offer entire programs online, assessment arose as a significant sticking point. The accreditor identified the primary weakness of the online program as an inadequate outcomes assessment program, and further identified an important factor in that deficiency – a faculty contract that inadequately clarified suitable levels of faculty participation in academic outcomes assessment.

Risk and Reward

Specifically, the accreditor admonished the College as follows:

> In its 2012-2017 Strategic Plan, Independence Community College committed to expanding online coursework and developing an entirely online degree by 2017. To prepare for this change, ICC committed key resources in finances and personnel. A full-time Director of Online Education was hired to review new online courses and provide support for existing online courses. An Online Committee was established to develop a template for all online courses, as well as to recommend policies and for course design and faculty-student engagement. All faculty, full-time and adjunct, teaching online were invited to participate in this committee, and the current makeup of the committee is primarily faculty . . . While there is evidence that some faculty members have worked in small groups to formalize assessment processes, such as the pre-test, post-test, and common writing assignment currently being used in the English Department, most faculty spoke of assessment as individual efforts to determine course quality without an overriding institutional procedure to ensure the validity of measures, consistency in the application of assessment measures, or evidence that the measures were used to reexamine curricular decisions. . . . [I]t is apparent from conversations with faculty that they have been reluctant to use course evaluations and assessment data systemically and collaboratively to document and improve student learning outcomes in the past. . . . The employment contract of Independence Community College faculty is scheduled to be renegotiated in the coming months and the administration plans on using the outcome of the distance education change request to accelerate the negotiation and place greater emphasis on outcomes assessment directly into the contract verbiage.

> The team felt that a renegotiated contract would be helpful.

The accreditor correctly identified that our contract lacked clarity on the issue of assessment, and that we would be negotiating our next multi-year contract during the upcoming academic year. Personally, I was grateful for their admonition, as up to that point the negotiating stance of the faculty union had been that assessment was not in the contract and thus not part of their job, and if we wanted to make it part of the faculty role then the College would have to negotiate that and increase faculty compensation. Unfortunately, the problem was not limited to the faculty contract. Staff had also resisted systematic assessment, and co-curricular assessment was uneven and largely no better than academic assessment. Frequent turnover in academic administration prevented continuity, and administrators, having found that the accreditors would accept a combination of half-hearted attempts in the past and promises for the future, were reluctant to die on that hill when other more pressing issues seemed more immediate.

As part of our regular accreditation cycle, the campus had its accreditation site visitation in April 2017. Like all colleges, we prepared thoroughly for the visit, but it did not go well. We did not know it at the time, but the visitation team left campus with a significant amount of data that was inaccurate. The report the team wrote reflected this inaccuracy and concluded that the College had severe and pervasive problems. Fortunately, that report is only the early part of a review process with opportunities to correct such errors and correct them we did. It took time – we first had to identify why the erroneous data had been created, why it has been passed along unnoticed, and then we had to produce the correct information, and persuade the accreditors that both the data was flawed and their interpretation of that data was lacking. This was not as easy as it sounds – even though the new information we presented to them was clear, the review system is set up in such a way so that accreditors who participate late in the process are reluctant to overrule their peers who participated in the evaluation earlier in the process. In our case, however, the evidence was overwhelming, and the accreditor ultimately agreed both that the original information they had received was not accurate, and that the state of affairs at the College was far better than the accreditation site visitation team had concluded.

Despite this, no easy solution presented itself. The accreditors certainly realized that their original assessment had been erroneous. A second examination of the College by a committee separate from the original site visitors reversed over eighty percent of the findings of the original site visitors. But two things were still true: 1) The College did have legitimate operational problems (over eighty percent of institutions that are reviewed receive some type of constructive criticism from accreditors as part of the review process). Just the fact that we had given them erroneous data during the visit indicated severe issues related to data collection and review. Providing the accreditor with inaccurate data during the initial site visit had obscured, at least to some extent, the nature and extent of these issues, and without an additional visit, the accreditors did not feel confident rendering judgment about the true state of College accreditation measures. However, an additional visit would be costly and time-consuming. 2) There was one issue beyond dispute – at the time of the site visit, the College had fallen behind in its schedule for academic program review. A failure to properly conduct program review alone could be grounds for probation. That said, it was our position that probation on the grounds of prior academic program review failures would be extreme, given that the College had been engaged in program review when the site visit occurred, had continued to engage in program review at an accelerated pace since that time, and that by the time the evaluation process concluded, the College would have remedied its delinquency in program review completely. (Further complicating the issue, but supporting our view, was that the accreditor's early assessments about our prospects for completing future program review on schedule were based on an error about the number of programs on the books at the College. They had miscounted the number of programs we had, overstating the number of academic programs by more than seventy percent.) The problem at this point was simple: while probation was truly not warranted, neither was a clean bill of health (especially in the absence of a second site visit).

In a letter to the Board of Directors of our regional accreditors, I presented a solution to the problem: simply place the College "on-notice," which is a designation that means that an institution complies with accreditation criteria, but is engaging in specific practices which may cause it to fall out of compliance if those practices continue. Because I knew that the accreditors had some legitimate concerns, I suggested that the accreditors create a list of improvements they wanted to see, and then return to the College for a second site visit to confirm that the College had made the necessary improvements. The accreditor agreed, putting the College on-notice, assigning the College a list of nine required improvements, beginning with program review and expanding to related issues including data collection, process development, and strategic planning.

Obviously, no president ever wants his or her college to receive any sanction from its accreditors but putting the College on-notice seemed to be a solution that both the College and the accreditor could accept and would prevent lengthening an energy-sapping process for both the College and its accreditors. It also allowed for the College to begin a new process – one that was far more positive, forward-looking, and beneficial for the College. A project like this is comforting to me: there is a defined list of objectives, a known timeframe in which to complete them, and an obvious incentive for the team to get the job done. Best of all, each of the nine areas of improvement provided the College with a way to not just reach some minimally acceptable standard, but also use the project as the impetus for massive institutional improvements that would go far beyond what was expected in ways that would serve the institution well for years to come.

As a result, the College fully embraced the accreditor's requirements and worked to improve in each of the areas specified. Process improvements and policy changes focused on this effort and significant resources were devoted to this effort. The results were substantial and effective and allowed the College to bring about significant, culture-changing, accreditation-driven improvements. During the one-and-a-half-year period between being placed on-notice by the accreditor and the subsequent accreditation site visit:

1. We created a comprehensive process for collecting, analyzing and addressing complaints from any constituency. Prior to being placed on-notice, the College had no centralized system for feedback, whether positive or negative, and thus no way to identify or address trends in complaint data.

2. We created a new compliance officer position and initiated an institution-wide focus on Title IX training and compliance, including a systematic review of College policies to ensure compliance with current Title IX guidelines and other relevant federal, state and local laws and regulations. The person we placed in that role was ideal in a number of important ways: as a licensed attorney, she was well-prepared to navigate the issues of compliance and liability and her demeanor was one that encouraged people to seek her out and express their concerns. She was also a careful and sophisticated writer, which vastly improved the clarity and effectiveness of the multitude of new College policies we created.

3. We expanded the institution's technology plan to permit long-term financial planning and to ensure greater network and cyber-security. Although the institution already had a comprehensive technology plan, we made it more robust from a cybersecurity perspective, and made the process ties to the College's budget more explicit.

4. We developed a long-term facilities plan that permitted long-term planning for deferred maintenance, safety, and ADA compliance. During the time it was on-notice, the College underwent a federally mandated, state-regulated civil rights audit that specifically focused on ADA compliance. Although the campus

was surprisingly ADA compliant for a fifty-year-old physical facility, the audit helped the College create a clear set of priorities for future facilities upgrades.

5. We completely overhauled the program review process, creating up-to-date annual and cumulative reviews for all programs and providing a data-driven basis for improvements at the course, program, and institutional levels. Previously, the program review process had been directed by the Chief Academic Officer, and turnover in that office had created intermittent progress in the area of program review. The new program review process placed regulation of the program review process under the control of a permanent committee, guided by policies and procedures created by that committee.

6. We enrolled the College in the accreditor's assessment academy as a means of reducing the insulation that employees experienced working in a small community college in a rural corner of Kansas. By rotating attendance at the academy, the College helped to ensure that an understanding of best practices in assessment would be widespread among College employees. In addition, the College implemented its new assessment plan, including quarterly assessment reviews by all areas of the College, as part of its operational plan process.

7. We changed the focus and process around institutional operational plan reviews and strategic plan reviews, emphasizing the use of hard data and mandating that only quantitative data be used in the evaluation process.

8. We identified appropriate comparison benchmarks and institutional targets for persistence, completion, retention, and graduation in all programs, which was incorporated into operational plans and the College's Strategic Plan.

9. Working together with students, we reinvigorated the College's student government association, which placed the president of

the student government in a permanent role on the President's Cabinet.

10. We formed a Faculty Senate, with the president of that organization representing faculty as a standing member of the President's Cabinet. When I came to Independence, I was surprised that there was no Faculty Senate. There was a faculty union, but membership was not required, and sometimes less than half of the faculty purchased a membership. As a result, no organization represented the entire faculty in matters that did not involve union contract issues. I had come to Independence from Alfred State College, which has a robust and well-functioning Faculty Senate and where, as a faculty member, I had actively participated in its leadership. Aware of the benefit of creating a genuine voice for faculty, I was determined to develop a similar organization for the faculty at Independence Community College. Prior to the College being placed on-notice, I had initiated conversations before to start a Faculty Senate, but faculty interest had been low. (This was not surprising to me – relatively few faculty at the College had worked at a college with a Senate, and so I think that they were not fully aware of the advantages.) Luckily, as they had done in the case of outcomes assessment, the accreditors provided the push we needed – they had criticized the lack of faculty governance, and so a commitment to satisfying them meant everyone had to take the idea of a Faculty Senate seriously. Following a brief negotiation about the division of labor between the faculty union and the Senate, a new Faculty Senate was formed, and their first meeting was one of my proudest days at the College. The new Faculty Senate played critical roles in the collaborative accreditation work that followed, and so the value of a Faculty Senate was immediately evident.

11. We re-formulated the annual strategic plan review process and stipulated that questions of strategic planning be considered by

administration and the Board prior to making institutional or departmental budgetary decisions.

12. We initiated a comprehensive strategic planning process that was broadly inclusive, was led by an external coordinator, and used the most comprehensive data gathering process the College had ever used for strategic planning. In all, over six hundred employees, students, alumni, and community members participated in the strategic planning process, helping ensure strong buy-in upon completion.

In terms of resources, the College made this effort a priority. Although Independence Community College is the smallest community college in Kansas, it made significant resource allocations to ensure that it did not merely meet the expectations of its accreditor but exceeded them. For example, the College purchased and implemented of proprietary complaint data collection software, created a new Compliance Officer/Title IX Coordinator position, which it staffed with an attorney licensed in the state of Kansas (it should be noted that at the time the College was the only community college in the state of Kansas employing a full-time compliance officer responsible for all areas of compliance), enrolled employees in the Higher Learning Commission's Assessment Academy, and made significant upgrades to academic spaces and other student-use spaces to improve facilities and promote fire safety and ADA-compliance improvements.

The entire College focused on the requirements of the accreditors, and accreditation-driven improvements became embedded in the culture of Independence Community College. For example, the College adopted a system of departmental and institutional Operational Plans. Through the development of this bottom-up planning process, areas of the College were able to tie the goals and activities of their individual departments to the College's overall strategic plan, and they were able to measure the progress on their own goals and measures, measured with quantitative data every quarter. The newly formed Faculty Senate had multiple discussions regarding accreditation-related topics and recommendations in just its first year of operation. I created a detailed, cumulative monthly report of accreditation progress, which was distributed to all employees, the Board of Trustees, the local media, and to our Higher Learning Commission staff liaison. Additionally, I hosted an open forum each month in which employees could discuss the accreditation progress report or any other accreditation issues. We altered the agenda of meetings of the Board of Trustees to always include an accreditation report from the President, and specific reports on items of particular accreditation related efforts or results in that month. Likewise, the agenda of weekly Cabinet meetings typically had a standing agenda item devoted to accreditation, in which progress was reviewed, or new initiatives were discussed. Each employee in-service had a specific section or sections devoted to accreditation issues. These are just a few examples, but the goal was simple – keep accreditation present in people's minds, at all levels of the organization.

More importantly, the actions we took, the sense of urgency, and the new cultural focus brought the College together to work toward a common goal. Initially, both before we made the results public, and when we disclosed publicly that the College had been placed on-notice, uncertainty about the College's status and future clouded the conversation. Some people, both inside and outside of the college, used our evaluation process with the accreditors and the subsequent on-notice designation to advance their personal or professional agendas. Some lazily conflated "probation" (a much more serious sanction) with on-notice, and some did it apparently deliberately to mislead. One news publication printed the earlier findings that were later found to be without merit, and never published an update or correction. I focused on the first sphere of influence – the immediate College community, creating a timeline, a set of tasks and responsibilities, and devoted myself to repairing relationships that had been strained by the episode. A college is a big ship that is slow to turn but turn it we did.

By the time of the accreditor's site visit, the College was able to show that it had successfully:

- Developed a significantly more sophisticated, data-driven system for receiving, processing, and analyzing complaints from any constituency;
- Created long-term technology and facilities plans;
- Overhauled the program review process;
- Created a means for systematically gathering and using assessment data to improve both curricular and co-curricular programs;
- Identified appropriate comparison benchmarks and institutional targets for persistence, completion, retention, and graduation in all programs and at the overall institutional level;
- Began to define decision-making responsibilities for departments across campus more clearly; and
- Developed a systematic process of regular collection and review of institutional data.

In April 2019, the accreditors visited the College to verify our claims of progress and their report following the visit was clear: we received the highest possible score in every area of evaluation. With regards to program review and assessment, they congratulated the College by stating that:

> The team applauds the progress made on the program review process and encourages the Program Review Committee to continue to refine and share their review process with the committee … [Independence Community College] demonstrated it has a culture of using data from student learning in curricular and co-curricular programs, as evidenced by the use of data for improvement of programs from program assessment processes and data… ICC demonstrates a commitment to educational achievement and improvement through

> ongoing assessment of student learning by collecting detailed identification of course outcomes, data collection and creating a clear alignment between strategic and budget planning and assessment.

With regards to our new data gathering and reporting processes, they noted that:

> ICC has made great strides to address the requirement of developing and implementing a plan for the systematic review of data connected with institutional complaints, especially student complaints.... The team applauds the work done on appropriate comparison benchmarks and institutional targets for persistence, completion, retention, and graduation in all programs and at the overall institutional level.

Our new planning and budgeting processes were equally lauded:

> The team applauds ICCs development and implementation to develop a technology plan that aligns with strategic objectives and budgetary plan . . . The team applauds the progress made on the development of a long-range institutional plan addressing deferred maintenance of facilities, and policies and procedures to assure that issues directly connected to impacts on student learning and safety are prioritized. . .. ICC is conducting planning at a multitude of levels. . ... The College has worked diligently to comply with the requests of this report by developing an integrated planning system that revolves around the strategic plan. The integration lies with the operational planning mechanism; operational plans by their nature are intimately connected to the strategic plan. . ... ICC has a multitude of plans (e.g., program review, academic assessment, student complaint, and survey data, and operational plans) to intentionally

collect data that is used for decision making. ICC faculty, staff, and Board members are using this data to inform decision making, including budgetary decisions, at the College . . . the Team is convinced that the Program Review process is fully integrated into the planning system of the College and has sufficient personnel to sustain the process . . . The Team is satisfied with the current progress that the College has toward using relevant data to consistently and systematically inform short- and long-term planning efforts.

But the outcome was even better than the accreditors realized. Not only did we come together to significantly exceed the standards of the accreditors, but we also did it under very challenging circumstances: a negative public relations environment, the need for cultural change at the College, the glare of the national spotlight while being featured in a hit Netflix series, a continual statewide decline in enrollment, and stagnant state fiscal support. We faced the challenges, focused on what we could influence, and broke a big job down into smaller, manageable tasks. It was neither easy nor fun. But I felt closer to my colleagues than ever, and all of us felt a sense of accomplishment that when the project was finished, the College was a better place.

Conclusion

I had not planned to include a conclusion for this book. Originally, I thought that the individual sections spoke for themselves, and a conclusion would not add value. But in the closing weeks of my work on this book, the world itself has added something of tremendous importance to all of us in the form of a worldwide pandemic. This pandemic has fundamentally altered all of our lives, and higher education has been affected radically as well.

As I sit writing this, the functions of educational institutions have been pared down considerably, with no certainty about when normal functions can be restored. Across the country, residential campuses are no longer residential. Classes are now held online. Dining halls and student unions are silent, empty places. Staff who can work from home do so. With no students and very few on-site employees, campuses have the same abandoned, ghostly feel as shopping malls. The marketplace of ideas sits empty.

The intellectual community that was higher education has not ground entirely to a halt, but it is barely limping along. The various annual or quarterly national and regional gatherings of academics to explore their peers' work in specific disciplines? Canceled. The monthly meetings of fiscal officers, academic leaders, and IT professionals have met the same fate. The book discussion groups, the graduate students presenting their work to their peers for feedback, the student clubs, the chats between faculty across the hallway – if these exist, are entirely online.

Ironically, the very element that made much of higher education possible, direct human interaction, is now the thing that is forbidden. Can great teachers reach students without being in the same room? For some, yes, but for some, no. Can a student whose home life is chaotic or even dangerous fully engage in the intellectual process when deprived of the structure of on-campus life? In many cases, no. Can school fundraisers raise resources without the opportunity to request support in person? For large gifts, this is, in many cases, not just difficult but impossible. Can schools create a strong community identity without sporting events, convocations, graduations, and the like? It seems much more difficult.

All of us hope, of course, that this situation is temporary, and that at some point we will be able to return to normal. But until that happens, colleges and students alike will have to make difficult choices. The longer the situation persists, the more schools will have to shift from endurance mode to survival mode. Some may not even survive.

My belief in the usefulness of this book is strengthened by the way the relevance of the content has been increased by the new reality we face. For example, in the first section of the book, "Fundamental Challenges," I made a number of recommendations for increased enrollment – a more sophisticated online presence for colleges, increased workforce development, cost control, student return on investment, and the development of new student markets. These are unaffected by the current pandemic we face in 2020, and in fact, are made even more relevant. In that same section, I questioned the practice of ever-escalating on-campus facilities and argued that the day of reckoning for those expenditures was coming. Perhaps that day will now come sooner. In other places in that section, I argued for the increased professional development of employees, for greater use of electronic donor acknowledgment, and the need to be respectful during negotiations over resources. Suddenly we find ourselves in an environment where teachers and other employees must learn new skills very quickly, where interactions with donors are now primarily electronic, and where we face tremendous resource scarcity. In the section of the book regarding public relations, I urged greater engagement and greater transparency with the constituencies closest to the institution, something that has taken on even greater importance during this time of crisis. In that same section, I explained how such aggressive engagement creates greater support for large, possibly unpopular decisions an institution may make.

In the introduction to this book, I outlined a series of principles that govern my professional life and tried to persuade the reader of their merit. I urge the reader to consider how that list has become even more relevant to our new reality:

I urged that people act with absolute integrity and mentioned my own philosophy to not do anything that I am not prepared to see discussed in the next day's newspaper headline. This new reality of hasty decisions, perhaps with less oversight or collaboration, invites irresponsibility.

I described a team outlook fostered by compelling communication and consensus-building. My goal has always been to grow my team through trust, recognition, and an appreciation of (and ability to articulate) the virtues and cultures of the individual units under my direction and the overall value of what we provide to our students – a college education. I believe that administrators tend to think too much in terms of "leadership" and not enough in terms of "team member." How you see your colleagues and how you see your relationship to them is crucial to how they see you. If we did not feel that we were all in it together before this, what foundation are we resting on as we face these new challenges?

I explained the importance of passion. I have stayed in education because I believe that the highest calling of a state institution is to prepare students to lead productive lives, which requires both workforce preparation and the skill of lifelong learning. To the extent that higher education is meeting the current challenge, it is doing so because college employees care about education and their students.

I advocated for visibility and accessibility. Successful leadership is about forging productive relationships with a wide range of constituencies. People enter into strong relationships when both parties are available, personally accessible, and mindful of the needs of each other. More challenging now, but no less important – and perhaps even more important.

I explained that I do not micromanage. I hire the best people that I can find and then I treat them like the professionals that they are and let them do their jobs. This does not mean that people are not held accountable for performance, but it does mean that I do not substitute my judgment for theirs. If micromanagement was a sort of sand in the gears before, imagine what it would be like now to be micromanaged by a remote boss! I cannot imagine. Much preferable would be a team of people who know what their jobs are and can be depended upon to do them independently.

I promoted a focus on systems, not goals. If there was ever a situation that illustrates the wisdom of that approach, this is it. I described that creating good ongoing *systems* should be the true objects of institutions, and that large, singular goals are not the best way to operate. The very first reason I offered for this view is that most large goals take time to achieve, and there is no way to know if a large goal developed in the present will still be an appropriate goal in the future. Over the next year, most colleges will either discard their goals or substantially revise them. The colleges that flourish in this environment will be the ones who had robust underlying operational systems that can immediately apply those systems to the revised goals.

I advocated for the creation of a safe, supportive, diverse environment. This is essential for student learning and for creating successful academic and employee retention. I explained that diversity is a goal for me, first, because I am an educator, and the data is clear that a more diverse educational environment is a better educational environment. Second, I believe in equality of opportunity, and part of creating that equality requires making an active, conscious effort to recruit, welcome, and foster diverse students and employees. Third, I am a team leader in the workplace, and the best teams are those which can generate a diversity of ideas that spring from diverse backgrounds and perspectives. Finally, I believe in institutional compliance, and in many cases a demonstrated commitment to diversity is a matter of institutional policy or law. Think for a moment about this list of reasons – if we cannot commit to these during a transformative time, will the community of ideas that is the hallmark of higher education survive?

Higher education is an industry, but it is an industry of people who serve people. Remembering that it is an industry keeps it responsible. Remembering that it is an industry of people keeps it humane. Remembering that we serve people keeps it noble. Whatever challenges lie ahead, higher education will flourish if we remember these things.

Summary

Small colleges face increasingly complex and difficult challenges, while struggling to remain competitive and relevant amid concerns about dwindling student enrollment, reduced funding, public relations issues, and ever-increasing federal regulatory and accreditation requirements and… the list goes on. For rural community colleges, the situation is often even worse: staffing shortages, recruiting concerns and fundraising challenges – the demographics and economic realities for rural institutions are often dismal. Do you wish you had an instruction manual to help you navigate these difficult situations? Now you do! Long-time community college president Dr. Daniel Barwick draws on national trends, the latest research, and his own unique experiences as the President of Independence Community College of Netflix's *Last Chance U* fame to provide timely lessons from which all college administrators can learn.

About the Author

Daniel W. Barwick is a higher education administrator, author, educational consultant, podcaster, blogger, and fundraiser. He was the President of Independence Community College (Kansas) and the Director of Institutional Advancement at Alfred State College and Executive Director of the Alfred State College Development Fund (New York). He hosts the world's most popular higher education podcast, The Mortar Board, and writes a blog of the same name. He lives in Independence, Kansas, with his wife and two daughters.

Published by ABJames, LLC
Delaware, USA